cket-tailed
mmingbird,
ru

Cape pigeon, Antarctic

Standard-wing
nightjar,
Africa

Ross's
gull
Arctic

Queen Victoria
crowned pigeon,
New Guinea

Great bird
of paradise,
New Guinea

Crimson-winged
parakeet,
Australasia

Red-crested cardinal,
S. America

Iden
k-of-the-rock
America

Bluethroat,
Eurasia

Lady Amherst
pheasant,
S.E. Asia

Wood duck,
N. America

Long-crested hornbill, S.E. Asia

Collared
forest
falcon,
C. & S. Americ

Long-tailed
broadbill,
S.E. Asia

Azure tit,
Eurasia

Painted
redstar
N. & C.
America

Chestnut-eared
acari, S. America

African wood ibis

Crowned crane,
Africa

White-faced ibis
Americas

Pondicherry
vulture,
Asia

Lapwing, Eurasia

Key to Endpapers

BIRDS
An Introduction to General Ornithology

R T Peterson—

BIRDS

An Introduction to General Ornithology

James Fisher and Roger Tory Peterson

Bird Paintings by Roger Tory Peterson

Aldus Books

SBN 490002161

Editor: Maurice Chandler
Designer: Susan Tibbles

New revised edition 1971 Reprinted 1972
Editorial arrangement and design © Aldus Books Limited, London 1971
Text: James Fisher © 1964
New and revised text: James Fisher © Exors. of the late James Fisher († SEP 1970)
Illustrations other than photographs: © Roger Tory Peterson, 1964

Printed and bound in Hong Kong by Leefung-Asco Printers Limited

Contents

Introduction 7

1 The Variety of Birds 15

2 How Birds Live 41

3 Birds of the Past 73

4 Birds on the Tree of Life 85

5 The Distribution of Birds 99

6 Bird Society 133

7 Bird Watching 161

The Regiment of Birds 168

Bibliography 184

Index 186

Introduction

Our world has suddenly become aware of its mortality; pollution and deterioration of the environment are on everyone's mind. Conservation has taken on a sense of urgency and is now an issue that cuts across all political lines. For a generation bird watchers have been sounding the warning but only lately have they been taken seriously by the populace at large; and even more recently the word *ecology* has slipped into everyman's vocabulary.

But why has the bird watcher so often filled the role of prophet? To put it simply, birds are far more than robins, thrushes, and finches to brighten the suburban garden, or ducks and grouse to fill the sportsman's bag, or rare waders and warblers to be ticked off on the bird watcher's check-list. They are indicators of the environment—a sort of environmental litmus-paper. Because of their high rate of metabolism, their furious pace of living, birds often reflect subtle and not so subtle changes in the countryside before other living things do. Therefore it follows that the observant bird watcher becomes a watchdog of the environment, often aware before anyone else when things are slipping out of balance. This book is not essentially about conservation but about its winged messengers, the birds: their history, their variety, their place in the ecosystem, and what makes them tick.

As Neil Armstrong, the first man to set foot on the moon, reflected when he looked back upon our "small blue planet," it is really the only home we've got and we had better take good care of it.

James Fisher   *Roger Tory Peterson*

James Fisher, my co-author and close friend, died tragically in a motor accident just after correcting proofs of this book, and it falls to me to be the sole signer of this introduction.

James Fisher enjoyed a life in which, for about half a century, his major preoccupation was with birds. Son of one distinguished amateur ornithologist, Kenneth Fisher, and nephew of another, Arnold Boyd, he remembered Howard Sanders's edition of Yarrell's *British Birds* as his first picture book. At the age of two he could identify all the birds in it from their pictures, so that visitors to the house fondly imagined he could read.

As for myself, while still a schoolboy I combined an urge to draw and paint with a deep interest in birds. Encouraged by a teacher who formed a Junior Audubon Club, I developed an obsession for depicting the subjects of my interest, and from that obsession I have never freed myself.

For close on 30 years each of us pursued and widened his interest in ornithology—in its literature and its art (to which we made our individual contributions) and, above all, in the field. Then in 1950, when both of us were delegates to an international ornithological congress in Sweden, we met for the first time on the Baltic island of Gotland. A friendship sprang up at once, and in the next four years we explored various parts of Europe together—France, the Netherlands, Scandinavia, and Germany, as well as Britain—always looking for birds.

8

Social sea birds: Murre colony on Funk Island, Newfoundland. (Photograph by James Fisher)

Our first essay in joint authorship began in 1953 when, at the invitation of Houghton Mifflin of Boston, Massachusetts, we toured North America, traveling from Newfoundland to Alaska by way of México, in preparation for writing *Wild America.* The book became a best-seller in the United States and at the time of James Fisher's death plans were in hand to produce a series of short films based on it.

The idea for a second joint work, *The World of Birds,* was put up to us in 1960 by Doubleday of New York and Rathbone Books of London (of which James Fisher was then Editorial Director). In the course of producing this book we each crossed the Atlantic several times, staying in each other's homes to work in close association. Fisher's work lay mainly with the multifarious learned literature of birds. His interest in fossil birds, rare birds, and extinct birds grew enormously as his research proceeded. I used the great museums of New York, · Yale, Harvard, and London, as well as the zoos of New York and London, to research my illustrations and ensure their accuracy.

It is not out of place to say more about that book since this present volume is based on it. In the original we wrote for our fellow ornithologists and bird watchers who shared our enthusiasm for the subject and who, for the most part, already had a fair knowledge of it.

The first part of the book (which was originally subtitled *A Comprehensive Guide to General Ornithology*) consisted of six chapters, each devoted to a single broad aspect of birds: their variety, their structure and adaptation, their fossil past, their evolutionary present, their distribution, and their behavior. The second part was made up of a chapter on bird watching, a family-by-family census of the world's birds with maps showing the distribution of each family, and a final chapter on birds and men, discussing the problems and possibilities of their continued coexistence.

In 1969, five years after the original book first appeared, we were asked to produce another volume, based on it but adapted to the needs of a rather different reader—one whose knowledge of ornithology was not yet, perhaps, as deep as that of our original audience, and who therefore needed an *introduction* to the subject, not a comprehensive guide. At first we hesitated, for while the new volume would clearly have to cover much of the same ground as its predecessor, both in text and illustrations, it would have to be somewhat simpler and shorter.

Social land birds: Relatively small flock of starlings making ready to join other flocks in vast English roost. Some European and North American roosts house several million birds. (Photograph by John Tarlton)

How to simplify and shorten at one and the same time was a hard nut to crack, since simplification almost invariably calls for expansion. Fortunately, there was one very lengthy section of the original book which, while of real value in a comprehensive guide to ornithology, was less essential to an introduction—the set of some 200 maps showing the distribution of bird families.

Having made this and other deletions we found that our new and slimmer volume gave us space to expand our original first six chapters by about one third. The rewriting also gave us the opportunity to up-date facts and figures. Finally, we decided that we could, with no great loss, abridge what was formerly a long and detailed chapter on bird watching, adapting it to the less exacting requirements of the reader who has not yet reached the stage where his hobby calls for elaborate equipment and sophisticated know-how.

The census of birds by orders and families (sometimes even by subfamilies) we decided to leave substantially as it appeared in the larger book, except for up-dating it in line with recent scientific findings. This decision was taken to help all readers who like to bring order and orderliness into their hobbies at an early stage.

Those who want to carry their studies further can, and we hope will, consult the original book. But there are countless other books they will also want to read as their interest in ornithology grows. On pages 184-5 we have listed about 100 bird books that will be of most general use to the English-speaking audience; it is a shorter and more arbitrarily selective list than the bibliography in the bigger book.

While joint authorship involves close cooperation it cannot turn two individuals into one; work must be divided and shared. In this book, as in that on which it is based, the text was first drafted by James Fisher; the paintings are all by myself. Each of us felt free to criticize and comment on the work of the other and to suggest amendments. And because we did not always share precisely identical opinions on every aspect of the subject, it proved necessary here and there to distinguish between us. When individual opinions differ they are clearly stated as being those of James Fisher (JF) or Roger Tory Peterson (RTP).

Roger Tory Peterson

King vultures

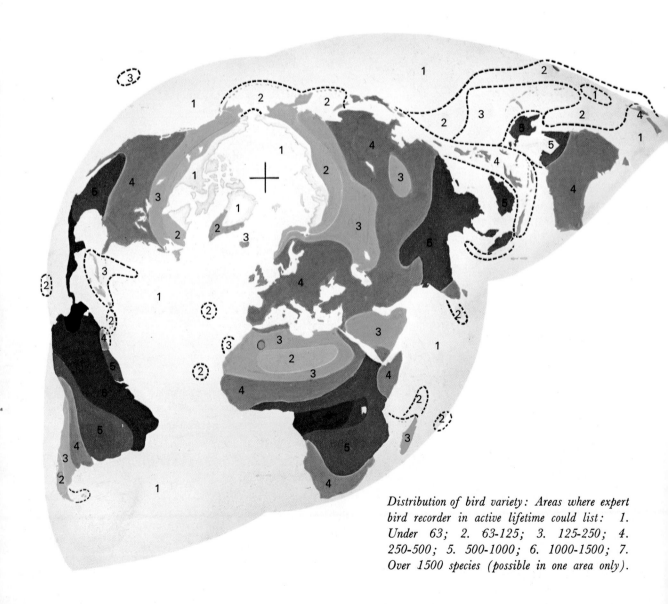

Distribution of bird variety: Areas where expert bird recorder in active lifetime could list: 1. Under 63; 2. 63-125; 3. 125-250; 4. 250-500; 5. 500-1000; 6. 1000-1500; 7. Over 1500 species (possible in one area only).

I The Variety of Birds

Distribution of Bird Variety

There is no square mile of the surface of our planet, wet or dry, that has not been crossed by the shadow of a bird—except, perhaps, parts of the Antarctic continent. The landmass of the Antarctic is so much of an ice system, through which only rare bits of land poke here and there, that it has no important flora at all. There is thus virtually no land-produced food for animals, with the result that all the vertebrates of the Antarctic are sea mammals or sea birds that depend basically on marine food.

Though at least four species of birds have been seen at or near the North Pole, only one (a skua) has visited the South Pole. But two petrels breed on mountains jutting through the ice cap, miles inland; and some penguin colonies are out of sight of its shore. Altogether, 16 species, all sea birds, nest on the Antarctic continent or on islands within sight of it. If we bring in the antarctic and subantarctic islands, we cannot raise our list to much over 50.

All the areas with similarly poor, or almost as poor, avifaunas (1 on the map) are polar or oceanic. The reason for the limited variety of land birds on remote oceanic islands is that in the course of evolution few land birds have ever found them; and even among ocean-ranging sea birds not many species have discovered them and used them as breeding places. Going east across the Pacific's scattered archipelagos we find a progressive diminution in the number of native land birds: about 127 in the Solomons, 77 in New Caledonia, 54 in Fiji, 33 in Samoa, 17 in the Society Islands, 11 in the Marquesas, 4 on distant Henderson Island, and none on Easter Island, the most isolated of all (although a pigeon, a tinamou, and an Icterid have been introduced there).

When a species has become adapted to an impoverished area it normally faces less competition than it would encounter elsewhere. So the birds that inhabit the poor areas tend to be specialized, and often very successful, with enormous populations. This is especially important in the Antarctic. Those birds that have managed to come to terms with its harsh climate, and live on its marine life, have broken through what must have been a very difficult evolution barrier, and their success is reflected in their high numbers. In the opinion of many ornithologists, the antarctic Wilson's storm petrel may be the world's most numerous sea bird. Some polar and subpolar auk and penguin islands have over a million birds in a single rookery.

Areas with an impoverished (2) or low (3) avifauna include important

Not many birds have learned to dwell near the poles, but those that have face little competition. So the few species in polar regions are usually well-adapted and abundant. Great flocks of king eiders arrive in May in high arctic North Greenland, where in some districts they are the commonest water birds.

archipelagos that have been more or less difficult for birds to colonize because of their remoteness, and most of the deserts, both hot and cold. Large areas of the northern world within the tree line—the taiga zone in Eurasia, the conifer zone in Canada and Alaska—have lists of under 250 species.

Medium-sized avifaunas of under 500 species (4) are found mainly in temperate savannah countries; also in some semidesert tropics and in the central East Indies. These are the faunas most of us know best. Typical lists, from recent countings, are Tasmania 255, New Zealand 256, Serbia 288, Hong Kong 289, Portugal 315, Alberta 317, Macedonia 319, Finland 327, Norway 333, Greece 339, Afghanistan 341, Maine 350, Ussuriland 353, Iraq 354, Ceylon 379, Israel nearly 400, Japan 425, Western Australia 436, Great Britain and Ireland—and the Philippines—about 450, Senegal and Sierra Leone 485, Eastern Nigeria 488.

If it seems strange that some semidesert tropics have avifaunas comparable with those of temperate savannah areas, one must remember that in the tropics as a whole there are more bird species per square mile than anywhere else, so that there is always a cadre of invading species available for any semidesert area. Furthermore, semideserts, with rainfalls of up to 10 inches or so a year, commonly have quite a lot of vegetation, though of a very specialized kind, and offer a sufficiently wide variety of habitat to encourage a large number of species.

Large avifaunas of under 1000 species (5) are found in the oriental tropics (e.g. Borneo 554, Malaya 575, Burma 953), New Guinea (650) and neighboring tropical Australia, the tropical savannahs and forest-edge of

Africa (e.g. Eritrea 551, Ghana 627, Cameroons 670, N. Rhodesia 674, Sudan 871, Africa S. of Angola and the Zambesi 875), N. and C. America (Texas 545, México 967), and S. America (Surinam 567).

In tropical forests species swarm, though few have the vast populations typical of some of the temperate and many of the polar species; and these numerous species make up three communities, each living at a different level of the forest (p. 112). Yet really huge bird lists (6) are few. The only country in Africa with a list of over a thousand is the basin of the River Congo, the most densely forested part of equatorial Africa: Congo (Kinshasa), Rwanda, and Burundi combined have 1040. But for Central America from southern México to Panamá about 1190 species are listed, for Venezuela 1282, for Ecuador 1357, for Brazil about 1440, mostly contributed by the great Amazon belt and other tropical forest zones.

The variety of birds in tropical South America is half as great again as in tropical Africa. The main reason is that South America, with its high Andean mountain system, its vast lowland plains, and its great northern and eastern highlands, has a far wider range of geological scenery than mainly plateau Africa, and a far greater range of altitudinally zoned habitats. It is no coincidence that the only country with a bird list of over 1500 (7) is Colombia, which, for its area, also has the greatest variety of habitat. At the last count its species totaled over 1700—twice as many as those of continental USA and Canada combined (775). It is the heartland of ornithological variety on our planet.

Winter in temperate eastern USA, which has a medium-sized avifauna. Three black-capped chickadees; two slate-colored juncos; two blue jays; cardinal and white-breasted nuthatch at feeder; cowbird flying; hairy woodpecker on post; and white-throated sparrow on ground.

Tropics support much bird variety. First met by us one day in C. México: l. to r., above: mountain trogon, masked tityra, emerald toucanet, red-legged honeycreeper; below: rufescent tinamou, white-fronted dove.

Long-tailed skua

Racing pig[eon]

Red-tailed
tropic bird

Laysan albatross

White ibis

Greenland
white-fronted
goose

Wings and Flight

Within their limits of speed and height, birds are more efficient aircraft
than man has yet been able to design. Boundary layer control, which reduces
drag by drawing air through the wing from top to bottom, was probably
solved by Archaeopteryx. Human engineers are still only at the experimental
stage with this principle. Dynamic soaring is known to man in theory only.
Yet albatrosses and the larger petrels have for millions of years exploited
the fact that in a windy sea there is (owing to friction) a steep descending
gradient of wind speed downward to the surface of the sea. This layer-cake of
different wind velocities enables big long-winged birds to glide in a complex
way in any direction within a segment of much more than 180 degrees.
They tack and zigzag if their objective is in the wind's eye; and use their
"engines" mainly for maneuver.

Figured above are some typical examples of wing adaptation. The Laysan
albatross has a wing of the highest aspect ratio (span high in proportion to

Broad-winged
hawk

Peregrine

Great
horned owl

Brown-throated
spine-tailed swift

House martin

Ruffed grouse

Pectoral sandpiper

Corncrake

fore-aft wing breadth, or chord), which gives the greatest lift for its dynamic style of flight. A bird that needs to accelerate fast, such as a ruffed grouse, has a low aspect ratio.

The wing-loading of birds (weight per square foot of wing area) varies from about a tenth of a pound to $2\frac{1}{2}$ pounds. The most agile flyers—which range from frigate birds, tropic birds, and the long-tailed skua, to some fly-catchers, wood swallows, and hummers—tend to have low wing-loadings and rather high aspect ratios: the red-tailed tropic bird is perhaps the biggest bird that has been seen to fly momentarily backward when checking in maneuver. Birds of prey that are long-distance migrants, such as the broad-winged hawk, make much ground by soaring, taking advantage of rising columns of air, and tend to have a lowish aspect ratio and low or medium wing-loading. A typical broad general-purpose wing is that of the white ibis, which makes longish regular flights and also soars. Owls such as the

In hovering, male ruby-throated hummingbird beats wings 55 times to the second.

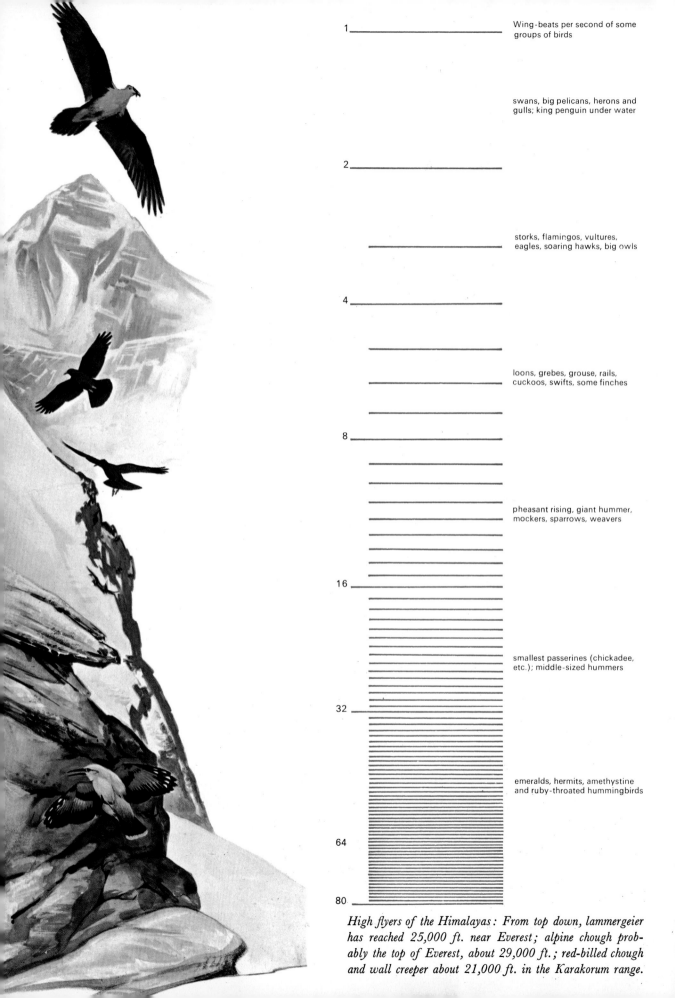

1 ——————————— Wing-beats per second of some groups of birds

swans, big pelicans, herons and gulls; king penguin under water

2 ———————————

storks, flamingos, vultures, eagles, soaring hawks, big owls

4 ———————————

loons, grebes, grouse, rails, cuckoos, swifts, some finches

8 ———————————

pheasant rising, giant hummer, mockers, sparrows, weavers

16 ———————————

smallest passerines (chickadee, etc.); middle-sized hummers

32 ———————————

emeralds, hermits, amethystine and ruby-throated hummingbirds

64 ———————————

80 ———————————

High flyers of the Himalayas: From top down, lammergeier has reached 25,000 ft. near Everest; alpine chough probably the top of Everest, about 29,000 ft.; red-billed chough and wall creeper about 21,000 ft. in the Karakorum range.

great horned owl have a rather similar wing formula, with feather adaptations (including downy filaments at feather bases) for silent flight.

Some birds with fairly high wing-loadings are capable of long migratory journeys: thus the white-fronted goose crosses about 2000 Atlantic miles from Greenland to Ireland, and the weak-looking corncrake reaches Iceland from Europe. Birds that use their wings under water—such as auks, diving petrels, and some ducks—have high wing-loadings that enable them to "fly" in the denser medium.

Many observations have been made on the speeds of birds, by timing them over measured distances, pacing them from cars and aircraft, tracking them by radar or rangefinder. Half the world's birds probably never exceed 40 mph. High speeds are not easy to measure; and speeds of over 60 are proved without reasonable doubt for only the loon, some birds of prey, waterfowl, the racing pigeon, and swifts. The brown-throated spine-tailed swift of Asia has been alleged to reach 200 mph, but the measurement was unreliable, and most ornithologists would put the maximum speed of the swift family around 68. The fastest birds admitted without reservation are lammergeier 79.5, loon 90, racing pigeon 94.3. The highest well-proven recorded speeds are stop-watch and airspeed indicator observations of peregrines at 165-180, in stoops.

Fast birds put pronounced sweep-back on their wings, which reduces drag and gives stability. Most waders, exemplified (p. 19) by the pectoral sandpiper, migrate at between 50 and 62. The swallow family can reach 46 (house martin); this is fast for a small bird, though faster are horned lark 54, European starling 55, and ruby-throated hummingbird up to 60.

The Peruvian diving petrel (left) and the black guillemot both swim with the full wing. The velvet (white-winged) scoter swims with half-folded wing, with the alula (see pages 22 and 23) projecting.

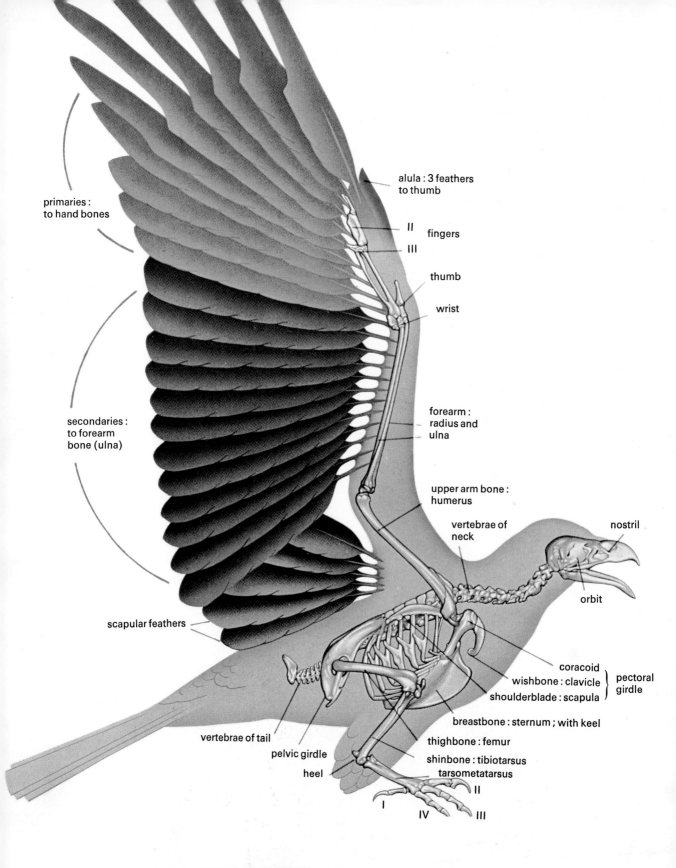

primaries :
to hand bones

alula : 3 feathers
to thumb

II
III
fingers

thumb

wrist

secondaries :
to forearm
bone (ulna)

forearm :
radius and
ulna

upper arm bone :
humerus

vertebrae of
neck

nostril

orbit

scapular feathers

coracoid
wishbone : clavicle
shoulderblade : scapula
} pectoral
girdle

vertebrae of tail

pelvic girdle

heel

breastbone : sternum ; with keel

thighbone : femur

shinbone : tibiotarsus
tarsometatarsus

II

I
IV
III

*Skeleton of caracara (a member of the falcon
family) showing arrangement and connections of
main bones and flight feathers. Left side removed.*

22

Anatomy

The central framework of a bird is a column of from about 37 to over 60 articulating vertebrae, the "backbone," culminating in a strong light skull to which its jaws are attached. Few skull-bones are more than plates and struts. A bird's huge orbits leave only a very thin partition between its eyes; its brain is restricted to the broadened back of its skull.

The vertebrae of the neck vary in number from 16 to 25. Below them comes a box, the thorax, based on 4 to 6 back vertebrae and connected by ribs to a breastbone or sternum, keeled in flying birds. To the front part of this bone is firmly attached a pair of coracoids. These bones are braced together across the front by the paired clavicles or collar bones (which in most birds fuse below to form a wishbone); and to their upper ends are attached the scapulae or shoulder blades, which run back along the ribs and back vertebrae. These three pairs are the pectoral girdle, bound to the thorax by strong ligaments.

The upper arm-bone's head articulates with the coracoid-scapula joint. This bone, the humerus, is a very strong rod, to the outer end of which are joined the forearm bones—radius and ulna. To them are joined several wrist bones, thumb and second and third fingers.

To these hand bones the great primary flight (and steering) feathers are strongly attached. The thumb carries a group of three feathers, the alula, which acts as an aeronautical slot. The secondary flight feathers originate from the ulna, the lower and thicker forearm bone. Sometimes tertiary flight feathers are attached to the humerus. No normal flying bird has less than nine primaries; secondaries vary in number and can reach 32 on albatrosses. The primitive Andean condor probably has more flight feathers than any other bird, with 11 primaries, 25 secondaries, and 13 tertiaries.

Right: Bone structure and wing system of the three classes of vertebrates that have attained true flight. Below: Typical flight feather; part of vane enlarged.

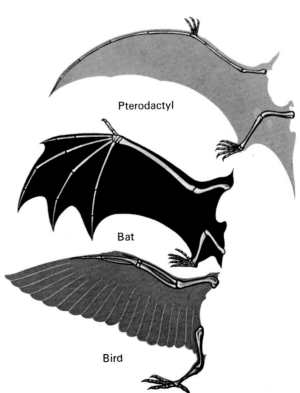

Pterodactyl

Bat

Bird

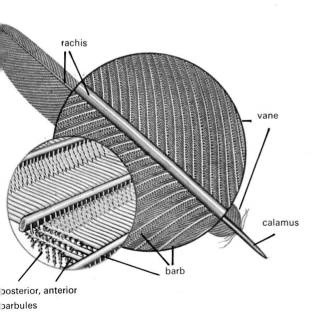

rachis

vane

calamus

barb

posterior, anterior barbules

The only truly flying vertebrates besides birds are the extinct pterosaurs and the living bats. The first depended on a skin flap from little finger to feet; the second depend on the same sort of patagium over all fingers to feet. With the evolution of feathers, birds kept their legs free for efficient locomotion and shock absorbing.

The pelvic or hip girdle of a bird depends on the fusion of 10 to 23 vertebrae; the top two may contribute ribs to the thorax. These vertebrae—the synsacrum—fuse with three pairs of bones (ilium, ischium, pubis) to form a powerful ring, to which is articulated by ball and socket joint the femur or thigh-bone. Below the knee, which is often hidden in the feathers, the upper long bone usually visible is the true shin or tibiotarsus, equivalent to the tibia and fibula of reptiles; and the lower is the tarsometatarsus or "tarsus," a fusion equivalent to part of the ankle and upper ends of three toes. Birds have no fifth toe; and their first or big toe usually turns backward.

Lowermost in the backbone are 4 to 9 free caudal or tail vertebrae and a final fusion of 4 to 7 vestigial vertebrae called the pygostyle, in which are firmly inserted the quills of the tail feathers, the rectrices. Usually there are 12 of these, but their number may vary from 6 to 20.

A typical feather consists of a main stem whose quill (calamus) is hollow and top part or rachis solid. From both sides of the rachis stretches the vane, which is composed of parallel barbs angled toward the feather tip. To these barbs are attached barbules; and those barbules that point toward the feather tip have hooks along the middle of their undersides that catch on to their opposite numbers, interlock, and make the vane firm and elastic. Ordinary contour, or body-covering, feathers tend to have downy, non-interlocking barbs on the inner part of the rachis, and below them grow downy plumules and hair-like filoplumes, special feathers whose function is

Air sacs of fowl, from front. c: *cervical;* i: *interclavicular;* ax: *axillary;* u: *upper thoracic;* l: *lower thoracic;* ab: *abdominal. (Lungs black.) Below: vertical cross-section of eye; brain seen from left.*

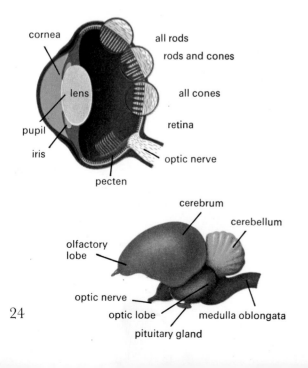

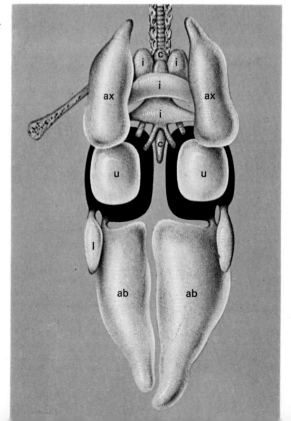

24

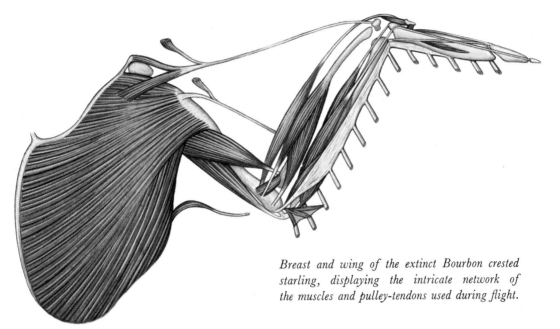

Breast and wing of the extinct Bourbon crested starling, displaying the intricate network of the muscles and pulley-tendons used during flight.

to give insulation. Once, twice, or even thrice a year, every feather is molted and replaced. A selection of fine feathers is shown on page 27.

Nearly all the larger bones of birds are pneumatic—hollow, with very little marrow. This is an adaptation for lightness; and the hollow bones also communicate with internal air sacs. Injected with plastic, these sacs reveal vast size and complexity. When a bird breathes in, air passes through its lungs into the sacs; when it breathes out, the sac air passes through the lungs once more. Oxygenation of the blood can take place at both stages, much faster than in an animal without air sacs.

Perhaps the two greatest bits of precision engineering in a bird's anatomy are its engine and its eye. By engine we mean the wing muscles that stem from its breastbone and produce all the movements of steered flight. The array often weighs more than a fifth of the whole bird, and involves a complicated pulley system, in which several tendons work over or through bone notches that can turn their pull through more than a right angle.

Bird anatomy: Australian aboriginal version.

Birds have the most highly evolved eyes in the animal kingdom. The eyes of many owls are larger than those of men. In basic structure bird eyes resemble those of other vertebrates; but in modifications they are refined. The retina—the sensitive back of the inner chamber—is so much more elaborately bestowed with the light-sensitive rod and cone cells than that of other vertebrates that a special avian organ has developed, the pecten. This is an auxiliary blood-tank that boosts the retina's nourishment. Some bird retinas have two especially sensitive areas that assist side as well as forward vision, the foveae. Nocturnal birds such as owls have only rods, which are most sensitive to light and are the only cells that work when it is nearly dark. The cones need more light for results, but give sharper resolution and can distinguish colors. A few diurnal birds have only cones; but most birds have both. Some birds have colored oily droplets in their cones, which filter blue light, cut down dazzle, and give better vision.

In general plan and relative size the bird brain equals or approaches a lowly mammal brain. But its cerebellum, which coordinates movement, is larger, as is its optic lobe. Its cerebrum is smaller, with the central part concerned with instinctive (unlearned) activities relatively larger, and the outer cortex, concerned with learned activities, rather small. Its olfactory lobe is small: birds have very little sense of taste and few much sense of smell.

Birds swallow morsels whole, after lacing them with saliva, down a gullet that in many broadens into a large storage bag in the throat—the crop. As soon as the gullet has passed behind the heart into the thorax it becomes a large bag, the stomach, of which the upper end is provided with acid cells for digestion and the lower part is usually a muscular gizzard, where rough or hard food is crushed.

After the stomach the food tube is continued as a loop—the duodenum. This is fed by ducts from the pancreas (a gland) with secretions that change starch to sugar and break down proteins and fats. Ducts also run to the duodenum from the liver, a huge storage organ that hoards sugar and keeps the blood constitution constant. Most material emptied into the duodenum from the liver is waste, but some of it helps digestion.

Now comes the small intestine, which can be very long, with many loops, in plant-eating birds. Here the main absorption of the digested food takes place. Waste products, dead bacteria, and unabsorbable food are finally discharged into the wide short rectum, which leads to the cloaca. The cloaca is the final passage, and leads to the only opening in the lower part of the bird's body. It receives the waste-ducts from the kidneys and the ducts from the reproductive organs. In birds the male organs or testes are held internally and lie over the kidneys; the ovary is a single one, which lies between the kidneys.

A bird's heart and blood system is more reptile-style than mammal-style, but highly efficient. One fortieth the weight of a high-altitude hummingbird is heart. Few birds have a temperature of less than 100°F, and some rate 114°F. Birds are the nervous athletes of the animal world.

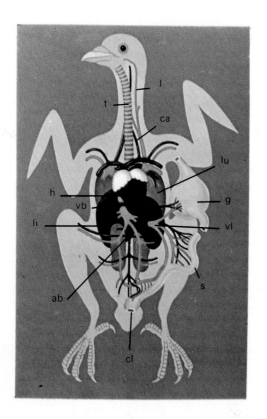

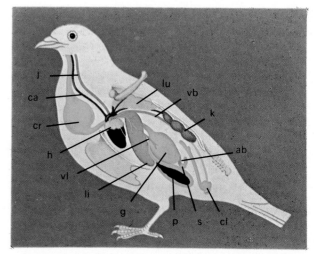

Blood and digestive systems of the pigeon, simplified. ab: *main artery of body;* ca: *carotid artery;* cl: *cloaca;* cr: *crop;* g: *gizzard;* h: *heart;* j: *jugular vein;* k: *kidney;* li: *liver;* lu: *lung;* p: *pancreas;* s: *small intestine;* t: *trachea (windpipe);* vb: *main vein of body;* vl: *main vein of liver.*

Opposite: Feathers from 30 species (identified on p. 183).

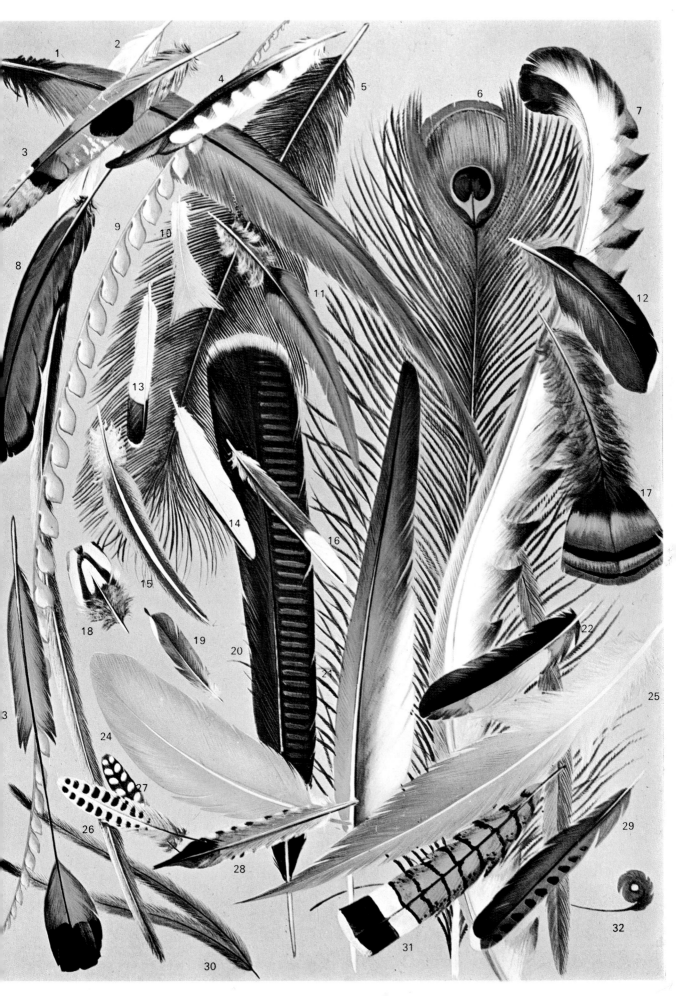

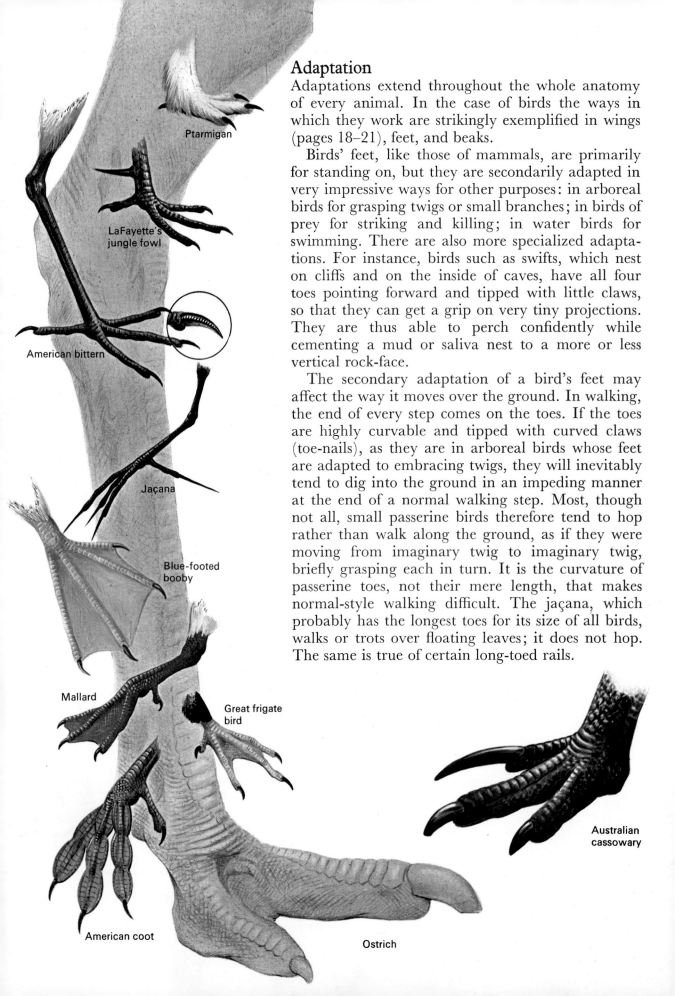

Adaptation

Adaptations extend throughout the whole anatomy of every animal. In the case of birds the ways in which they work are strikingly exemplified in wings (pages 18–21), feet, and beaks.

Birds' feet, like those of mammals, are primarily for standing on, but they are secondarily adapted in very impressive ways for other purposes: in arboreal birds for grasping twigs or small branches; in birds of prey for striking and killing; in water birds for swimming. There are also more specialized adaptations. For instance, birds such as swifts, which nest on cliffs and on the inside of caves, have all four toes pointing forward and tipped with little claws, so that they can get a grip on very tiny projections. They are thus able to perch confidently while cementing a mud or saliva nest to a more or less vertical rock-face.

The secondary adaptation of a bird's feet may affect the way it moves over the ground. In walking, the end of every step comes on the toes. If the toes are highly curvable and tipped with curved claws (toe-nails), as they are in arboreal birds whose feet are adapted to embracing twigs, they will inevitably tend to dig into the ground in an impeding manner at the end of a normal walking step. Most, though not all, small passerine birds therefore tend to hop rather than walk along the ground, as if they were moving from imaginary twig to imaginary twig, briefly grasping each in turn. It is the curvature of passerine toes, not their mere length, that makes normal-style walking difficult. The jaçana, which probably has the longest toes for its size of all birds, walks or trots over floating leaves; it does not hop. The same is true of certain long-toed rails.

Ptarmigan

LaFayette's jungle fowl

American bittern

Jaçana

Blue-footed booby

Mallard

Great frigate bird

American coot

Ostrich

Australian cassowary

The two main foot-adaptations for swimming—the fully webbed foot with three skin-flaps stretched between four toes, and the palmate foot with lateral lobes of skin on individual toes—are the result of separate evolution on parallel lines, and neither of them necessarily impedes walking. Good web-footed walkers include gulls and ducks, which can even run. Among palmate birds, coots and moorhens are also good walkers as well as fair runners.

Birds' feet are usually arranged with a back-pointing first (big) toe or hallux, and forward-pointing second to fourth toes. But the swift-running ostrich has lost all but its third and fourth toes; most other big flightless birds, bustards, and some water birds have lost the first.

Most swimming birds have feet modified as propellers or steering organs. The pelicans, cormorants, and boobies have a "totipalmate" foot in which the first toe is brought around to the side and a web embraces all four. A more normal "palmate"-footed duck has just the three front toes webbed. Frigate birds have reduced webs. Other water birds, such as coots, have toe lobes, not webs. In one small family, avocets have webbed, ibisbill lobed, and stilt plain feet.

Several orders of birds have the claws of their third toes modified as preening combs: examples are boobies, herons and bitterns, and nightjars.

The "standard" foot, with four rather equal toes, could be that of a crow, which spends time both on the ground and perching. More terrestrial and less arboreal species, such as the skylark, often have long hind claws to help their stance on flat ground.

Nearly all the birds of prey kill either by striking

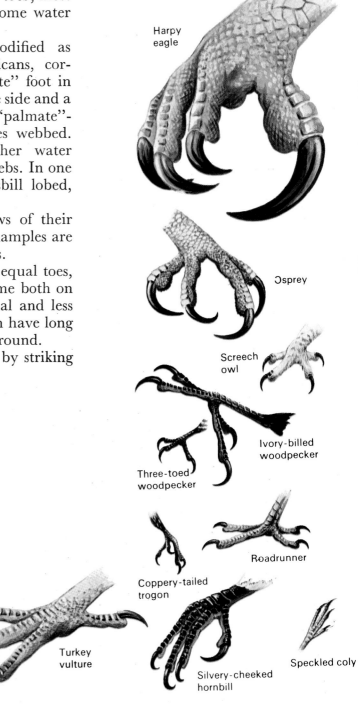

Whip-poor-will

Skylark

Fish crow

Harpy eagle

Osprey

Screech owl

Ivory-billed woodpecker

Three-toed woodpecker

Coppery-tailed trogon

Roadrunner

Turkey vulture

Silvery-cheeked hornbill

Speckled coly

Black-winged stilt

American avocet

Ibisbill

Black skimmer

Giant fulmar

Horned puffin

Red
crossbill

Hawfinch

Common kiwi

Red-breasted
merganser

or clutching with heavy sharp claws (talons); but the Old and New World vultures never strike and have weaker feet. Some grouse that live much in snow have deeply feathered feet; pheasants and fowl have a horny spur above the first toe, used in fighting.

Often diagnostic of families are the dispositions of the toes. In a condition known as zygodactyl the fourth toe lies aft with the first; this is found among climbing groups—toucans, parrots, cuckoos, and woodpeckers. One ground cuckoo, the roadrunner, is still zygodactyl. A few woodpeckers have lost the fourth toe altogether. Other birds (owls, touracos, rollers) are semizygodactyl—can move the fourth toe forward and aft. The osprey can do this and has its soles studded with spines to grasp fish. One family alone, the trogons, *appears* to be zygodactyl; but their second toe, not the fourth, has migrated aft—a condition known as heterodactyl. Colies and swifts, which hang from small projections, can bring the first toe forward (pamprodactyl). Kingfishers, todies, motmots, hornbills, and rollers are syndactylous, with two toes fused for part of their length.

The primary purpose of beaks is to eat with, and the reason why they have evolved into all kinds of shapes and sizes is that different birds eat different types of food and need different beaks to deal with it. Mammals, as a class, have a similarly extensive dietary range, but they have retained their teeth, and their adaptive radiation to deal with different foods manifests itself mainly in widely differing dentitions. However, except for Archaeopteryx, the oldest known bird, which dates back to Jurassic times, no bird outside the Hesperornis genus of the Upper Cretaceous Period is proved to have had true teeth; and only a few have ever had false teeth.

The order Odontopterygiformes, of Eocene, Oligocene, and Miocene times, included sea birds that had their mandibles (the bony edges of their upper and lower beaks) serrated with very sharp points at intervals, which presumably helped them to take a firm hold on the fish they caught. Among living birds, ducks of the genus Mergus, such as the red-breasted merganser, still have tooth-like serrations on their mandibles; and inside the beaks of flamingos—birds of extremely ancient lineage—there are serrations not unlike the whalebone system inside the jawbones of whalebone whales.

Birds, then, got rid of their teeth at an early stage of their evolution, and since then even false teeth have been something of a rarity. The great adaptive

radiation of beaks is therefore reflected mainly in
their outward and visible shapes.

Birds' bills may be flattened sideways or upward,
very long or short, curve up or down or even sideways. The ends of the two mandibles cross in
opposite directions on the conifer-seed-eating crossbills. Bills may have their cutting edge serrated or
notched as in mergansers and puffins. Spoonbills
have the broadened bill-ends full of nerve-endings, to
feel for animals when mud-grubbing. Some bills have
sensitive tips, such as those of kiwis, woodcock, and
snipe; and the nostrils are at or near them. Petrels
have tube-nostrils through which salt is excreted.

The odd bill of the flamingos is an adaptation to
algae-feeding; that of the skimmer to bringing food to
the water surface as it cuts it with its lower mandible.
The function of the huge bills of toucans is mysterious,
though they may help them reach fruit in prickly
places. The chisel-bill of the woodpecker is more
easily understood, as are the nut-cracking bills of
hawfinches and macaws.

Many secondary beak-adaptations have nothing to
do with feeding. The coloration of certain bills, for
instance, is essentially for display and recognition
purposes. Such is the puffin's highly colored beak
shield; worn throughout the summer as a sexual
signal and as a means of cementing the pair-bond, it
is shed when winter comes. In most birds of prey the
main killing tools are the feet, but a powerful beak
often serves to administer the *coup de grâce*. And in
most fish-eating birds other than ospreys (whose feet
have special tubercles on the under-toe to enable
them to seize and kill slippery fish), the beak is the
primary killing weapon as well as the eating
instrument.

Sulfur-breasted
toucan

Hyacinthine
macaw

Magellanic
woodpecker

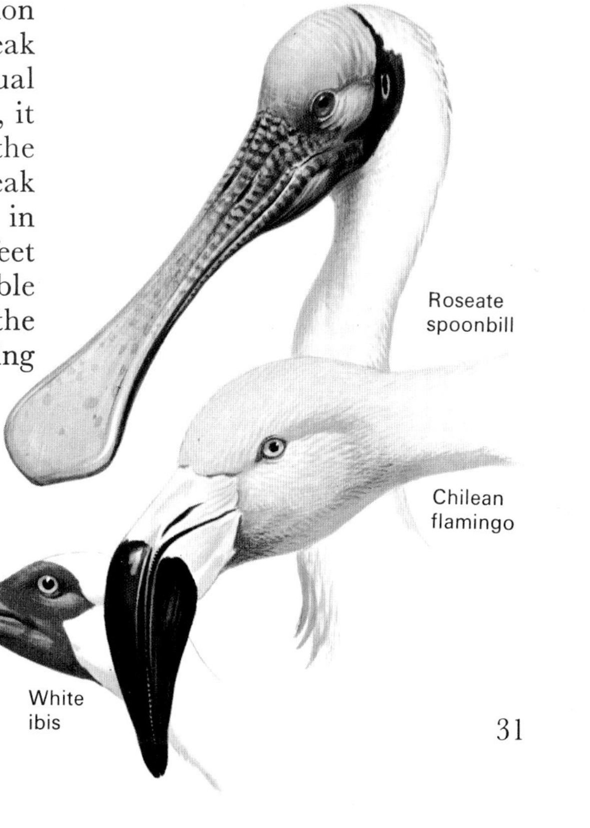

Roseate
spoonbill

Chilean
flamingo

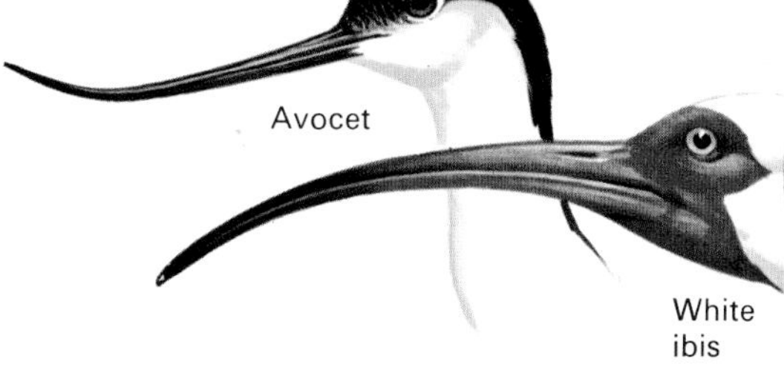

Avocet

White
ibis

31

Colors and Adornments

Every stage designer's trick to convey terror, companionship, love, alarm, meal-time, to conceal, lead away, astray or on, has been incorporated, millions of years ago, in the avian makeup. Birds signal with their plumage, bodies, movements and voices.

A cryptic (Greek, hiding) resemblance to the environment is found almost throughout the bird class. Nightjars, woodcock, snipe, grouse, and pheasants incubating their eggs have disruptive or outline-breaking patterns that, though not so contrasting as those of a ringed plover, blend wonderfully with their environment. Tropical forest birds of almost clashing coloration can disappear from sight among the shadows, or even when sitting on open leafless branches in front of a background of foliage. On the forest floor the pittas have such gorgeous plumage that they are known as jewel thrushes; yet their rich contrasts can be concealing. In self-colored open country many birds have underparts light-colored in contrast to their mantles and use the concealing device of countershading.

Some birds have few enemies because they are distasteful to eat, or peculiarly aggressive, or both. In Africa the black korhaan, a bustard that has a contrasting pattern that draws attention to it, is distinctly distasteful to humans and almost certainly so to animals of prey. The contrasting plumage of many kingfishers and some honey-eaters, and the shiny black plumage of the aggressive drongos, may be a warning of distastefulness. Some birds with warning coloration even have a few mimics among gentler species of other families, which are spared by enemies because of their resemblance to the models.

Some birds use adornments and voice to produce bluff or false warnings. Some kingfishers and owls have false eyes at the back of their head. Many birds have displays that confuse enemies, and involve snake imitations and the flashing of strange patterns of bars and eye-like spots.

Many birds, notably among the game birds and the waders, have nidifugous offspring—offspring that go from the nest very soon after they are hatched, and form little flightless flocks ranging about the territory, feeding and learning to feed in the care of their parents. Among such birds the young

Contrasting or conspicuous plumage like that of the black korhaan (left) may be a warning of distastefulness. Highly edible Rüppell's korhaan (right) has protective coloration.

Ptarmigans have white plumage in winter, go brown or gray when snow recedes. Cock molts white plumage after hen, deflecting predators from her at incubation time.

commonly have extremely adaptive plumage, cryptic in coloration, which, when they crouch, makes them almost unnoticeable to predators. Even so, they very often *can* be found if the predators have time to search for them. To minimize this danger, the parent birds—usually the mother, but sometimes the father—have evolved distraction displays designed to withdraw the attention of predators from the camouflaged but otherwise helpless young.

Often, while striding over the Arctic tundra, J. F. has disturbed a purple sandpiper not far from its flightless young. More than once the bird has mistaken him for a dangerous intruder, and has given a classic example of its distraction display. It has run away in a very tilted fashion, with wings outstretched and drooping, as if it had lost the power of flight. The unconscious object of the exercise was to draw his attention to it, so that he would chase it, thinking he could catch it; only when the bird had drawn him to a safe distance from its young would it fly away, as if cocking a snook at him. Yet such a behavior pattern is not consciously motivated but instinctive, triggered off solely by the presence of a disturbing animal.

Ptarmigans go white during the Arctic winter and a cryptic brown or gray, depending on the species, when the snow-cover disappears. The females undergo this change while still incubating their eggs, but the males retain their white plumage for a considerable time after the young are hatched. Being conspicuous against the summer coloration of their habitat, they draw the attention of predators away from the biologically more valuable females and young.

A few birds have developed special methods of alluring prey. In the Americas the eastern kingbird and the royal flycatcher have been said to attract insects within reach with their flower-like crests. The Australasian frogmouths can open their huge gapes to disclose a colored inner mouth surface that may possibly also act as an insect trap.

Much of the high coloration of birds has an aggressive function, or a courtship function, or both. The great train of the male quetzal is a badge of territorial ownership, and a courtship organ besides. The spread train

False eyes on back of American pigmy owl's head prevent daylight attacks by enemies.

Three forms of concealing coloration. Left: Disruptive pattern of incubating red-necked nightjar; center: Back of sand lark matches desert, underparts grade lighter toward belly to cancel shadow; right: The ringed plover, conspicuous on plain ground, melts on a pebble beach like the Cheshire cat in Alice.

The countershaded willet is inconspicuous at rest but ceases to be so once it takes off. In flight broad white identity patches flash on its wings and tail.

of the peacock is used primarily in courtship; other game birds, such as grouse, reach their full glory in territorial aggression. Among the most extraordinary display organs of all are the courtship dresses of pheasants and ducks, though some passerines (such as umbrella birds) run them close.

All plumage and adornment, of course, enables birds to recognize each other. Male and female may be equally bright or dull; those of about half the birds of the world are outwardly indistinguishable, except from their behavior. In most of the rest males outshine females, though a few females outshine males. In some cases, such as eclectus parrots, each has a special rich plumage of its own. On some cryptic birds the badge of identity is shown only at takeoff, when the flock is in danger, or in display.

Recognition marks are essentially interspecific, enabling a bird to distinguish those of its own species from those of otherwise similar-looking species of the same family or order. However, Peter Scott's study of the 200 or so Bewick's swans that winter each year at Slimbridge, in Gloucestershire, England, suggests that they may also be intraspecific, enabling birds of the same species to identify each other individually. Scott and his daughter Dafila have compiled a dossier of side-face and full-face portraits of several hundred Bewick's swans, and have discovered that in no two individuals are the black-and-yellow recognition patterns on the beak identical. They themselves can identify a great many individuals on sight; and the swans, whose interest must be at least as great, can presumably do the same.

Above: Male quetzal, finest of trogons; pair of eclectus parrots, male in front; displaying peacock.
Below: Umbrella bird in display; black-backed pitta; mandarin drake in courtship posture. As explained
in the text, the splendid colors and adornments of all these birds are functional as well as ornamental.

Cretaceous

Pteranodon ingens
(a reptile) 27′

Gigantornis
eaglesomei c. 20′

Eocene

N

Osteodontornis
orri 16′

Miocene

California

Teratornis *
merriami 12′3″

Pleistocene

California

Marabou
c. 12′

Modern

Africa

Wandering
albatross 11′6″

Modern

Southern oceans

Old World white
pelican 10′4″

Modern

South America

Dalmatian or
gray pelican 10′2″

Modern

Old World

Andean
condor 10′

Modern

Old World

* Teratornis incredibilis of the Pleistocene of Nevada may have spanned over 16′

Size

The range of size among vertebrates is one of the most spectacular results of evolution. The largest known reptile, *Brachiosaurus*, a dweller of the East African swamps in Jurassic times, weighed something like 50 tons; the smallest of living reptiles, the Malagasy chameleon, measures well under 2 inches and weighs a mere matter of grams. Among mammals the extremes are even wider apart. The smallest, *Suncus etruscus*, a shrew of north Mediterranean coasts, measures about $1\frac{1}{2}$ inches and weighs as little as 3 grams, whereas the blue whale, the biggest animal the Earth has yet known, can measure more than 100 feet and weigh well over 100 tons.

At the upper end of the size range, birds can scarcely begin to compete with either reptiles or mammals. In fact, the largest known bird of all time, *Aepyornis*, almost certainly weighed under half a ton—about one hundredth as much as *Brachiosaurus*, and less than one two-hundredth as much as the blue whale. But at the lower end of the scale there are birds that weigh in at even less than the Malagasy chameleon or the pigmy shrew.

The smallest living bird is the bee hummingbird of Cuba. Healthy adults weigh one eighteenth of an ounce—about 1.6 grams. If we could persuade 100,000 of them (which must be more than there are in the world) to sit still on a balance, they would just weigh as much as one large ostrich. The bee hummingbird is only $2\frac{1}{4}$ inches from beak-tip to tail-tip, with a wingspan under 4 inches.

Although all other members of the hummingbird family are larger, even the largest weighs well under an ounce. Nearly all of them suck nectar from flowers. They consume about half their own weight daily, mostly sugar; and some species go torpid at night to save energy. A bird less than 2 inches long would probably need more fuel than it had time to get, even in the

Pigmy
flowerpecker

Some of the world's smallest birds compared with eye of an ostrich (here shown to same scale).

White-browed
rufous piculet

Least pigmy
parrot

Short-tailed
pigmy tyrant

Pigmy tit

Locust finch

tropics, where food is abundant. It is therefore understandable that most of the smallest birds do live in the tropics; those shown in the illustration are each from a different family.

The upward limit to the size of any flying animal is linked with the mechanics of flight, and is of the order of 60 pounds. Some 30 years ago, work on the fossil flying reptile *Pteranodon* suggested that it may have weighed between 60 and 70 pounds, but two New York paleontologists have recently made a recalculation, and come to the conclusion that its weight was probably under 50. On the available evidence there is still room for argument. But the fact is that in order to fly, an animal weighing much more than 60 pounds would need a higher proportion of its weight as muscle for takeoff and (more especially) for landing than it could afford, consistent with maintaining all its other functions.

All the biggest of today's flyers are water-landers, dwellers in open plains, or soarers; and heaviest of all is the mute swan, which can tip the scale at about 50 pounds.

Larger flying animals than any living have been found as fossils. Only a few thousand years ago *Teratornis*, a great soaring bird of prey, lived in California and probably weighed over 50 pounds. A gigantic bird was recently found in Miocene deposits in California (about 10 million years old) and named *Osteodontornis*. In an order between the pelicans and the storks, it had a 16-foot wingspan and must have been very heavy. All we know of *Gigantornis* is a fossil breastbone from rock of Middle Eocene age (between 45 and 49 million years) in Nigeria. It was probably an albatross, and if so, had long narrow wings of span as much as 20 feet—nearly twice that of the largest living albatross.

Smallest of all, bee hummingbird – with eye of ostrich, natural size

The largest, though possibly not the heaviest, flying animal ever known to have lived was not a bird, but a reptile, a pterosaur. Flying reptiles flourished in the Jurassic and Cretaceous periods, for over 100 million years, with skin-wings stretching from vastly elongated little fingers to their ankles. Greatest of them was *Pteranodon,* which soared over the waves of a sea that covered what is now Kansas. Its fossils are found in chalk deposits 80 or 90 million years old. *Pteranodon*'s wingspan reached 27 feet; of its very considerable total weight—still a subject of discussion—more than a quarter was skin.

The biggest birds are (or were) flightless. The heaviest lived in the recent past: *Aepyornis,* the elephant bird of Madagascar, stood 9-10 feet high and probably weighed about 965 pounds. The New Zealand moas (*Dinornis*) stood taller (to 13), weighed less (about 520). The African ostrich can stand 9 and weigh 345; compare this with the Australian emu (5, 88) and cassowary (5, 74), and the South American rhea ($4\frac{1}{2}$, 44).

Diatryma, a curious bird between cranes and waders, from the Lower Eocene of Wyoming (around 50 million years ago), stood nearly 7 feet. The living emperor penguin stands $3\frac{3}{4}$ feet and weighs up to 94 pounds; but the fossil penguin *Anthropornis,* from the Lower Miocene of the Antarctic (about 24 million), stood about 5 and may have weighed about 240.

One of the few safe generalizations connecting size with way of life is that a bird of prey must be big enough and strong enough to catch and kill the prey in which it specializes. Thus in the Philippines there is an ecological niche for a monkey-eater; the monkey-eating eagle that evolved to fill it is a very big bird. It could not live as it does and be otherwise.

Within one family, and more especially within one species, birds living in cold climates tend to be bigger than those living in warmer climates, thereby gaining an advantage in weight-to-surface-area ratio. The arctic-breeding puffin, for example, weighs almost half as much again as the temperate-breeding puffin that nests off the coast of Portugal.

HEAVIEST LIVING FLYING BIRDS

– all reliable record weights we could find of 22 pounds (10 kilograms) or more

Mute swan (male)	50.6
Great Indian bustard (male)	40
Trumpeter swan (male)	38
Manchurian crane (male)	33
Kori (giant) bustard	30
(Dalmatian) gray pelican	28.6
Old World black vulture (female)	27.5
Wandering albatross (male)	26.75
Griffon vulture (male)	26.4
Royal albatross	26.25
Old World white pelican (male)	24.2
(Wild) turkey (male)	23.8
California condor (male)	23
Andean condor (male)	22.7
Pink-backed pelican (male)	22.4
Asian white crane	22
Stanley bustard (Denham's race, male)	22
Arabian bustard (male)	22

1. **Anthropornis nordenskjöldi**
2. Emperor penguin
3. **Diatryma steini**
4. Common rhea
5. **Dinornis maximus**
6. Emu
7. Australian cassowary
8. Ostrich
9. **Aepyornis maximus**

Left: Restorations of three extinct New Zealand flightless birds: Giant woodhen (l.); great moa, Dinornis maximus (center); a goose, Cnemiornis, (r.) Below: Three other flightless birds: Great auk, Atlantic sea bird (top); a cormorant of Galápagos Is. (center); common kiwi of New Zealand (bottom).

2 How Birds Live

Flightless Birds

The flightless birds are probably all descended from birds that once flew—even the great extinct elephant birds and moas and the living "ratites" (ostrich, emu, cassowaries, kiwis and rheas), as well as those superb swimmers, the penguins. All these families lost flight many millions of years ago.

The ratites have shown tremendous parallel evolution in widely separated parts of the world that their remote ancestors must have colonized while they could still fly. The elephant bird of Madagascar, which became extinct in 1649, and the moas of New Zealand, whose last representatives succumbed to human hunters by the end of the 18th century, had a great deal in common anatomically with their living relatives—the rheas of South America, the emu and cassowaries of Australia, and the ostrich of Africa; and living ratites share a number of behavior characteristics, such as the considerable role the male plays in incubating the eggs.

All these big, flightless birds occupy or occupied the same ecological niche as grazing mammals. Before the first invasion by *Homo sapiens* of New Zealand, about a thousand years ago, those that probably did best were the moas, which proliferated into 27 known species. Theirs was a particularly favorable environment because New Zealand, never having been connected with any other land, had no grazing mammals to compete with them—and indeed no mammals at all other than two species of bats and a few small rodents that must originally have arrived on driftwood. The rest of the great ratites have all met strong competition—the rheas and the ostrich from large, swift-running placental grazers, the cassowaries and the emu from no less efficient marsupial grazers such as kangaroos; and all have met this competition very successfully.

Exceptional among the (mainly graminivorous) ratites are the three living kiwis, all of which evolved in New Zealand and all of which are nocturnal worm-eaters with (for birds) an acute sense of smell.

The penguins are the descendants of flying birds perhaps closely related to those of the Order Procellariiformes (albatrosses and petrels). Indeed, their wings—long and not very broad—are still somewhat reminiscent of those of an albatross, though they are much reduced in size as an adaptation to a swimming life. In all 15 living species of penguins these reduced wings, moving in much the same way but less swiftly than they would have done in aerial flight, provide the main means of propulsion through the water.

The wings of flightless birds seldom have such an important function as they do in penguins, but they are equally seldom wholly functionless. In many such birds, including the ostrich, the reduced wings are used to help maintain balance while running; they are also equipped with feathers that are of display value.

A high proportion of flightless birds live, or lived, on islands. Most peculiar is the fruit-eating family of the dodo (p. 98) and solitaires, derived from pigeon-like ancestors that colonized the Mascarene Islands, probably a few million years ago.

The flightless grebe of Lake Titicaca may be a degenerate cousin of the bright-cheeked grebe of the Andes. A cormorant in the Galápagos Islands has reduced wings and is flightless; and the extinct spectacled cormorant of the Bering Sea was nearly so. The extinct great auk of the North Atlantic had a wing about the same size as that of a razorbill, which is only half its length. The three South American steamer ducks all have the same size wings, but the two flightless species are about twice the weight of the other. Among the ducks, also, two outlying island races of the brown teal of New Zealand have lost the power of flight.

Falkland flightless steamer duck

Titicaca grebe, also flightless

Kakapo, flightless N.Z. parrot

Flightless race of brown teal, Auckland I.

Weka, flightless N.Z. rail

Zapata rail, very weak flyer

One of 15 living penguins, all of which are flightless, the gentoo breeds on subantarctic and antarctic islands.

In New Zealand the kakapo cannot truly fly, though it uses its wings to help it hop. The extinct Stephen Island wren was never seen to fly; it belonged to a small New Zealand family. Four queer relict families are almost if not entirely flightless: the roatelos of Madagascar, which have normal wings but rudimentary collarbones; the kagu of New Caledonia; Australia's scrub birds; and the wattled crows of New Zealand, which include the extinct huia.

It is perhaps significant that of these four families one evolved in Australia, where there were few predatory land mammals, and another in New Zealand, where there were none. They could therefore fit into what might otherwise have been mammal niches; and becoming sluggish flyers, or even losing the power of flight completely, involved them in no danger of mammalian predation.

Of the 119 living species of rails, 16 show every stage of flightlessness. All of these are island birds; 12 rails have become recently extinct. In New Zealand the takahé (p. 100) has practically no keel on its breastbone and a reduced wing; the weka has a scarcely reduced wing with which, nevertheless, it just cannot fly. Cuba's Zapata rail has a normal wing but is a weak flyer.

Forty-six living and 16 recently extinct birds are or were flightless. Most have become so on small and more or less remote islands. On such islands, where mammalian competition and mammalian predation are less exacting than elsewhere, flightlessness offers little disadvantage, and one obvious advantage: birds that do not fly cannot get gale-blown away from home; birds that do, can. It is therefore no wonder that almost every remote island of consequence has, or has had, its own flightless bird or birds. But when Man arrives on the scene, the disadvantages of flightlessness soon outweigh the advantages, and species after species is driven to extinction.

Rufous scrub bird, Australia (top), and extinct huia, N.Z.

Left to right: Rockhopper (subantarctic islands); yellow-eyed penguin (N.Z.); king (subantarctic and antarctic isles); blue (Australia and N.Z.); jackass (South Africa); chinstrap (antarctic isles).

Game Birds and the Like

All six families of true game birds belong to the Order Galliformes, named from *Gallus,* the domestic fowl. They are the megapodes of Australasia, including New Guinea and the Celebes; the guans and curassows of South and Central America; the grouse of northern Europe, northern Asia and North America; the quails, partridges, and pheasants whose distribution is worldwide; the African guineafowl; and the turkeys of North America.

Some, especially among the pheasants, have plumage of rare beauty, which makes them an ornament to parks and gardens everywhere. All, being highly edible, attract the interest of numerous predatory mammals and birds; and Man has hunted and snared them since the Old Stone Age.

Most of them are very fleet of foot, run under cover, and burst out of it when disturbed by predators with short and often noisy bursts of highly accelerating flight. The American tinamous (game-like but not true game birds, related to the rheas) make a quick getaway in very similar style; but spurts of high acceleration apart, they are not particularly good flyers.

Among true game birds migration in the strict sense is rare. Some live in open country and make fairly prolonged flights, often in little flocks and groups, but most such movements are seasonal and relatively small. Exceptions are to be found among the Old World quails, one of which regularly migrates from North Africa to northern Europe, covering distances of up to a thousand miles.

In addition to the tinamous, four other families have a superficial resemblance to game birds. The bustard quails and plains wanderer of the Old World look like true quails. The trumpeters of tropical South America run fast, fly poorly. The bustards of Old World plains run very fast indeed, and can fly strongly.

Left to right: Martinetta, a swift-running tinamou, Argentina; Senegal bustard, Africa south of Sahara; vulturine guineafowl, dry tropical East Africa; satyr tragopan, a pheasant, Himalayas; capercaillie, biggest of grouse, northern Europe and Asia; mountain quail, US West and northern Lower California.

Large birds, from left to right: James's and Andean flamingos, Andes of South America; African saddle-bill; scarlet ibis, South America; Old World little egret. Smaller birds, from left: King rail, eastern US and Cuba; pheasant-tailed jaçana, Southeast Asia; stilt, cosmopolitan; whimbrel, subarctic/arctic breeder; red-wattled lapwing, Asia; painted snipe, Old World.

Water Birds

Over 600 living birds, belonging to 27 families, are adapted to life in the wetlands. So wide is their range of adaptations that there is scarcely a wetland in the world, except on some very remote islands, where at least one family is not represented. The fact that they tend to be more migratory, percentage-wise, than most birds gives them a tremendous additional advantage, enabling many of them to utilize the extensive wetlands of the Arctic, which are opened up for only a few months of each year.

The loons and many of the grebes, which pursue fish under the water, and two of the three phalaropes become sea birds in the winter. Some of the ducks are also to be classed among the sea birds. But the vast majority of long-legged marsh birds, waders, and wildfowl are paddlers or swimmers in lakes, rivers, streams, and marshes, or on shores and estuaries.

The five living flamingos, specialized to sifting algae from water, are confined to tropical or subtropical lakes, including some salt lakes, that have a very big flora of algae, especially the blue-green algae (Cyanophyceae). The limpkin of the New World, sole surviving member of a family that lies between that of the cranes and that of the rails, is adapted in the structure of its beak, and in its habits, to eating giant snails of a single genus. But it has by no means colonized the whole of their range. In Africa its ecological counterpart, the open-billed stork, lives on giant snails of the same genus.

Most herons are stalkers of the shallows and catch fish or frogs with darting lance-like bills. The 17 living storks, with a collective geographical range embracing more than half the earth's land surface, have many differing animal diets. Ibises are fishers and shrimpers and, with their long downcurved bills, worm-probers; in the same family, spoonbills are mud-sifters. The rather short-billed cranes are omnivorous.

With the exception of the coots, which swim in the open, the large rail family is more often heard than seen. At night marshes the world over resound with eerie groans, barks, gobblings, gabblings and shrieks as these undercover birds seek water animals and plants.

Nine Anatids from eight different tribes. Swimming in back row (from left to right): Red-crested pochard, Europe and Asia; shelduck, Europe and Asia; black-necked swan, southern South America. Swimming in front (from left to right): Ruddy duck, North America and West Indies; African pigmy goose. On land (from left to right): Goosander, northern world; Baikal teal, breeder in eastern Siberia; red-billed whistling duck, Texas, Central and South America; pair of handsome red-breasted geese, nesters in arctic Siberia.

Left, from top down: Sun grebe, from central South America, one of the three peculiar finfoots ; Wilson's phalarope, breeder in highland north that winters in southern South America ; black-throated loon of northern world shown side by side with black-necked grebe, northern world and Africa. Above: Common oystercatchers, the European race of a cosmopolitan wader specialized in feeding on shore mollusks.

The shy finfoots of tropical America, Africa, and East Asia can run fast, swim well, and dive for fish or amphibians; the rare kagu, confined to the forests of New Caledonia, is a night bird and primarily an insectivore, though it may also eat worms and mollusks; the handsome sun bittern hunts small animals in forest streams of tropical America.

Oystercatchers, with their chisel beaks, deftly knock limpets off rocks and specialize in eating shore mollusks. The great worldwide family of plovers and turnstones have short beaks, and are adapted to turning over stones to find their prey, which consists almost entirely of small invertebrates; turnstones are primarily but not exclusively crustacean-eaters, while most ordinary plovers (not crab plovers) live mainly, but not exclusively, on insects. Curlew, whimbrel, godwits, snipe and sandpipers all have long bills, and probe in the sand mainly for worms, but also for other animals, including mollusks. Painted snipe, too, are probers.

The long-legged stilts wade in water above the leg-joint and pick animals from (or from just below) the surface, and their avocet cousins sweep the water-surface with their upcurved bills or duck for crustaceans and worms. Phalaropes spin while swimming to stir up animals from below. The unique crab plover specializes in large crustaceans. The jaçanas hunt insects, snails, and seeds across the water lily pads of tropical pools.

The swans, geese, and ducks belong to a family with just over a gross of surviving members, since four of the 151 modern Anatids have become extinct. A recent classification would divide them into 11 groups.

The strange magpie goose of the Australian swamps, anatomically rather close to the earliest known Anatids that go back some 44 million years, may

Gay birds among the perching ducks: Wood duck of North America (left) and mandarin duck of eastern Asia.

be the most primitive, and is primarily a grazing animal. The 6 swans, 15 true geese and the coscoroba are also mainly grazers. The 8 whistling ducks are goose-like, mainly vegetarian, and dive well. The unique freckled duck of Australia is a plant-eater. Long-legged and often highly colored are the 8 sheldgeese (grazers) and 6 shelducks (omnivorous). The 3 steamer ducks of S. America mainly eat marine mollusks. The 13 perching ducks, which include the pigmy geese and the gay wood and mandarin ducks, often nest in tree-holes and are mainly vegetarian. Also mainly plant-eating are dabbling ducks, a tribe of 42 living species—mallard, teal, shovelers and allies. The 15 pochards are a related tribe that feed under water, partly on aquatic animals.

In the true diving duck tribe of 18 species are the eiders and scoters, mollusk-eating sea ducks; the goldeneyes and their kin, and the saw-billed mergansers, which eat mainly fish. Typical of the odd tribe of 9 stifftails is the ruddy duck of the Americas, which dives and swims under water, yet eats mostly plants.

Sea Birds

Flying below the horizon in the above picture are (left to right) the snow petrel, which nests nearer the South Pole than any other bird; Leach's petrel of the northern seas; the great shearwater, which nests in some millions on the archipelago of Tristan da Cunha and is common off Newfoundland in our northern summer; and the red-tailed tropic bird.

Above the horizon (l. to r.) fly a northern gannet, largest sea bird of the North Atlantic; the black-browed albatross, whose dynamic soaring in the southern oceans is helped by rough weather; the sooty tern, a common sea bird of the tropics; the great skua, found in both subarctic and antarctic; a flock of herring gulls, a successful northern species; and (in front of cliff) the brown pelican of the Americas.

On the cliff (top down) are some handsome blue-eyed shags of the southern seas; the magnificent frigate bird of the tropics, most agile flyer of all sea birds; the rare red-legged kittiwake, an ocean-going gull; with a darker mantle the western gull, also from the North Pacific; and the red-footed booby, a tropical relative of the gannets.

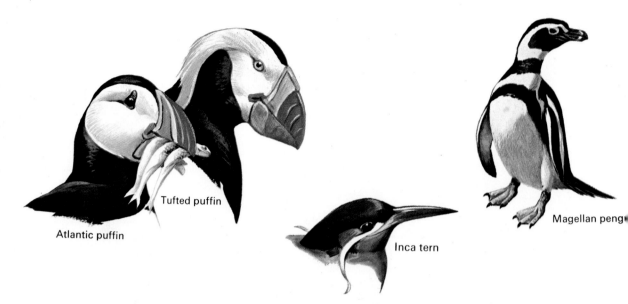

Tufted puffin

Atlantic puffin

Inca tern

Magellan peng[

In all about 260 species, or 3 per cent of all living birds, are adapted to life at sea, some as full-timers, some as part-timers. All belong to one or other of seven great taxa: albatrosses, petrels and shearwaters to the Procellariiformes; penguins (which share with them the distinction of being the most highly adapted sea birds) to the Sphenisciformes; pelicans, tropic birds, gannets, boobies and cormorants to the Pelecaniformes; skuas, auks, phalaropes, gulls and terns to the Charadriiformes; loons to the Gaviiformes; grebes to the Podicipitiformes; and a few waterfowl adapted to part-time marine life to the Anseriformes.

Most sea birds live on either plankton or fish or both. Some auks and small petrels are essentially plankton feeders; boobies live primarily on fish, some specializing in flying fish. Secondary sea birds (birds belonging to families whose members are for the most part wetland birds) may have different, and often more varied, diets. Some grebes and divers that live as freshwater birds throughout the breeding season go to sea in winter, where they pursue marine fish by diving and swimming. Eider duck are strongly adapted to eating mollusks, which they dive for to the bottom of relatively shallow seas. Two species of phalaropes spend summer in the north, nesting by the shores of tarns and living on insects and crustaceans; in winter they migrate south, often across the equator, and spend their time as surface swimmers in open oceans, feeding on plankton.

Many fully oceanic species feed as far from land as any animal can get, and drink salt water exclusively, or almost exclusively. Cormorants, gannets, boobies, albatrosses, and petrels get rid of excess salt by concentrating the sea water they drink into a still stronger salt solution in special glands in their heads, and then excreting it through their nostrils.

Some large albatrosses probably spend the first nine years of their lives without resting on the land at all. Sea birds on the whole tend to have long periods of adolescence before they can breed—time to learn to solve the problems of navigating the trackless ocean. Most breed slowly and live long, though just how long we can so far only guess. Most also have social breeding grounds, a practice that makes mate-finding easier and relieves pressure on the cliff-ledges and stack-tops available for nest-building.

Bateleur

Montagu's harrier

Red-thighed falconet

aracara

Fish eagle

Gyrfalcon

Long-crested hawk eagle

Red-tailed hawk

Swallow-tailed kite

Birds of Prey: and Owls

About 280 of the world's birds belong to the Falconiformes, or day-flying birds of prey; the day raptors.

A few, like the New World and Old World vultures, feed on carrion; and a very few like the palm-nut vulture and the honey-buzzards (which raid wasps' nests and bees' nests in search of grubs and insects as well as honey) have become mainly or wholly independent of flesh food. But most raptors kill prey by striking or clutching, hold it in their sharply clawed feet (talons) and tear it with their powerful hooked bills or swallow it whole.

The big broad-winged raptors, the condors, vultures, eagles and buzzards, all soar hundreds of miles a day with but little use of power. The largest are carrion-feeders, with naked heads and rather weak talons; these often patrol at a great height, watching not only the ground but their searching neighbors; when one descends on a find, others follow.

Eagles can dive fast and in one blow of their powerful talons clutch, kill and carry off an animal almost their own weight. Among their adaptations to this way of life are immense breastbones, wing muscles accounting for over a quarter—sometimes nearly a third—of their body weight, and wings large in proportion to their overall size.

Big falcons can strike bird prey in power-dives at speeds close to those of light aircraft. The goshawks are the most agile pursuit craft of all; the gabar goshawk of Africa easily overtakes weaver-birds when it comes to a chase through dense thorny thickets.

The Cathartidae, or New World vultures, include the condors and the turkey vulture (page 52), and are quite unrelated to the Old World vultures such as the Egyptian and lappet-eared (page 52), which belong to the Accipitridae. Also in the Accipitridae are kites; eagles and buzzards—of which the red-tailed hawk is an example; harriers; and harrier-eagles like the bateleur. The Falconidae include, besides the true sharp-winged falcons, the broad-winged caracaras and the tiny insect-hawking falconets, not much bigger than sparrows. The snake-catching secretary bird of the African veldt (page 52) is the sole survivor of a family that includes two extinct species. The fish-catching osprey (page 53) has a family all to itself.

Living by predation is no sinecure. Birds of prey often specialize in their quarry, and the population of the prey tends to govern that of the predator, rather than *vice versa*. Goshawks specialize mainly in smallish birds, up to pigeon size; larger hawks and some eagles in hares and rabbits; some smaller falcons in rodents; the African bat-hawk in bats; the osprey and, to a large extent, sea-eagles in surface-feeding fish; and several kites are snail specialists. The hobby (European falcon) shows a strong preference for members of the swallow family, and its own habits are geared to those of its prey. It nests late in the season, when it can best feed its own young on the young of swallows and martins, which are then plentiful and relatively easy to catch.

Birds that are predated have instinctive reactions to the outline of a potential predator, and instinctive patterns of cover-taking. Small song-birds often stop singing simultaneously with taking cover on the approach of hawks, falcons or day-flying owls.

Wherever herds of big game have lived there has been an ecological niche for scavenging animals ready to feed on their carcasses. Except for the hyena that niche is now occupied solely by carrion-eating birds. When bison, giant deer, elephants and rhinoceroses flourished in Europe carcass-eaters like vultures, including the lappet-eared vulture (now no longer in Europe) and the extinct giant Maltese vulture, were common. Europe may indeed be an ancestral home of vultures. The earliest fossils of the Accipitridae family, dating back to Upper Eocene times, were found in Europe; and even the New World vultures, now confined to the Americas, *may* have originated

Gabar goshawk
(black phase)

Secretary bird

Turkey
vulture

Lappet-eared vulture

Egyptian vulture

in Europe, since the earliest known fossil *Lithornis*, comes from England.

As the fortunes of the great grazing mammals have declined, so have those of the carrion-feeders. When the first human invaders set foot in North America, 15,000 or more years ago, a marked decline began in the mammalian fauna. Since then some 60 species have become extinct—more than 50 of them by about 5000 B.C. It is likely that many, if not most, were extinguished by hunting Man.

In the same period at least 25 species of birds suffered a similar fate, nearly two-thirds of them birds of prey. In all probability most of these died out because of the diminution and eventual disappearance of their food supply. Such were a species of horned owl; one of the two teratorns (very big New World vultures); the La Brea condor; the La Brea owl; the Santa Rosa owl; Willett's eagle; the western black vulture; Loye Miller's hawk; Woodward's eagle; the American neophron (last of the Old World vultures to inhabit the New World); Loye Miller's vulture; and the La Brea caracara, a falcon.

The order of owls (Strigiformes) is a gross of species strong. These raptors of dusk, night, and dawn are related in no way to the day raptors. They kill with powerful talons; but nearly all overtake their prey by stealth. With slowish wing beat, soft but robust and well-streamlined flight feathers, very soft contour feathers, and downy filaments at feather bases to cushion sound, they are all but silent on the wing. Their eyes, with retinas coneless but well endowed with dim-light functioning rods, are highly adapted for night vision. Their huge ears (*not* marked by feather tufts) are assymetrical and arranged for scanning the range and direction of sounds.

Barn owl

Spectacled owl

Long-eared owl

Short-eared owl

Osprey stooping on fish

Tropical forests abound in birds of brilliant plumage. From left to right: Fruit pigeon, Papua; chestnut-eared aracari, South America; orange-wattled bird of paradise, Papua; yellow-breasted fig bird, Australia;

Fruit- and Seed-Eaters

Over the tropical forests flocks of bright birds call in loud voices, swing through the air in long flights across broad brown rivers, turn in wide sweeps with yet louder voices, and suddenly drop and disappear in the tree canopy.

In the shades their violent patterns of purple, violet, blue, green, yellow, orange, red, white and black seem to vanish entirely. Down on the forest floor, 150 feet below, we can hear them only, shouting still. Then the shouts and hoots and shrieks die down, and all we listen to is the rustle of wings and leaves, and an occasional rushing noise as a dropped or loosened fruit tears down to earth through the layers of foliage.

The nomads of the forests are of many kinds, belonging to about 30 bird families. Each bird in the picture is a member of a different one. All roam in flocks, moving the year around in bands (sometimes of several species mixed) in search of fruit in season. When a crop of fruit on a clump of trees is exhausted they move to another crop; as one kind of fruit falls out of season they find another kind that is coming into season.

The success of fruit-eaters depends on certainty of supply; their bright

Cuban trogon ; crimson-backed tanager, Central and South America ; common touraco, Africa ; blossom-headed parakeet, south Asia ; double-toothed barbet, Africa. Below foliage colors blend with shadows and sunflecks.

colors are not just happy inventions of nature; they have a purpose, as has their raucous language. Clumps of fruit are sharable treasures, and often miles apart; so the fruit-eaters have it that the discovery of one becomes the prize of all. This they do by working in groups, and with the aid of vivid patterns and violent voices that enable them to recognize their own (and probably other) kinds at a distance in the open.

Under the canopy, however, their strongly contrasting plumage actually makes them blend with the shadows of the foliage and sunflecks so that they are very hard to find when they are quiet. Thus when they have discovered their food and are busy with it, or when they are nesting (often in holes in trees) they are safeguarded from some of their enemies.

It is only in tropical and subtropical regions that fruit of one kind or another is obtainable all the year around, or very nearly so; and it is only there that we find birds that are at once fruit obligates and residents. In northern lands very few families outside the waxwings are primarily fruit-eaters, and even they include insects as well as such items as cherries, berries,

Nutcracker and cone of Swiss pine. By habit this crow buries or hides pine seeds for winter use.

and cotoneaster in their diets. In temperate lands nearly all the birds taking advantage of summer and autumn fruit fall into two categories: residents that are seasonal fruit-eaters but whose food-spectra (see page 59) change when fruit is not in season; and migrants whose visits last only while the fruit lasts.

Resident starlings in Britain and the United States are omnivorous but become fruit-eaters first and foremost during autumn. Resident thrushes and quite a number of resident game birds of temperate lands have a broad seasonal band of berries in their food-spectra.

Most of the 28 species of Old World orioles (natives of Africa, tropical Asia, the East Indies, and tropical Australia) are tree-top foragers that also eat insects. In summer, while both fruit and insects are abundant there, the golden oriole visits Europe and western Asia from Africa. In a similar way the black-naped oriole winters in Malaysia and Indonesia and visits East Asia as far north as Manchuria in summer. The highly-colored tanager family of the Americas are mostly fruit-eaters, though other bands of their food-spectra include insects and berries. Quite a number of them visit temperate North America for the fruit season.

On the whole the fruit-eating birds of temperate lands are not fruit obligates and not specially adapted to fruit-eating. Only among the summer visitors from the tropics do we find the bright colors and raucous voices typical of the full-time fruit-eater.

Temperate lands tend to produce more seed than fruit, and certainly have more seed-eaters than fruit-eaters. In the grain belt of North America some grain-eaters have very big populations, notably the red-winged blackbird, whose winter roosts in southern USA build up to millions of birds. The rice-eating bobolink, a migrant from Argentina and other parts of South America, invades the rice belt of Louisiana in autumn.

Common waxbill

Blue-black grosbeak

European goldfinch

Red-billed quelea

Lapland bunting

Yellow-faced grassquit

Seed-eaters all

The Anseriformes—ducks, geese and swans—eat grain when it is to be had; most game birds are dedicated grain-eaters, though some of them also eat berries; and the most common bird in the world, the domestic fowl, is primarily a grain-eater.

Such seeds as those of wheat, millet and wild grasses, though small enough to be swallowed without preliminary breaking up or opening up, have a tough husk that must be dealt with somewhere in the alimentary tract. Birds that eat them must have highly efficient crops or gizzards, or both. Some graminivorous birds swallow stones that help the gizzard to mash up the grain (as some big grazing birds such as ostriches and rheas do, to help break up the tough cellulose of the grass stems they eat).

Among the numerous order Passeriformes seed-eaters, like fruit-eaters, are common. Some members of the crow family specialize not only in seed-eating but in seed-storing. The Old World jay, for instance, eats many things; but acorns—the big seeds of the oak—are its favorite food. It manages to eat acorns all the year round by burying them in the ground in chosen caches around its woodland beat.

Nutcrackers, too, are great storers of the seeds of conifers and other trees. The nutcracker of the forests of Europe and Asia, figured in the picture on page 56, hides pine seeds or nuts in all kinds of slits—for instance in the bark of trees and between stones; and tame birds in houses will put food between books or cushions, in the bowls of pipes or even in envelopes!

An eater of moderate-sized seeds needs a sharp-edged strong beak for splitting its food's hard jacket; a beak like that of a finch, in fact. This is one of the reasons why the classification of the finch-like birds is so difficult. When in the long, unhurried course of evolution members of different groups of birds, only very distantly related to each other, have taken to seed-eating they have quite commonly ended up looking very much alike in their general anatomy—and this is particularly true of the structure of their bills.

The finch-beak turns up in over two dozen groups of passerine birds belonging to well over a dozen families. Five of the six seed-eaters figured on page 57 belong to five different subfamilies of four different families. The sixth, a grassquit, *may* belong to the same subfamily as the blue-black grosbeak; but some authorities would put it with the buntings and others with the true finches. The evolutionary convergence of these birds is sometimes close enough to confuse the experts.

Almost all parrots, with their typically broad and immensely powerful bills, are seed-eaters, some of them eating seeds that are among the biggest and hardest on earth, such as brazil nuts. When cracking nuts—or when eating any food, for that matter—they use their feet as hands.

At Regent's Park Zoo, London, J. F. has seen budding child zoologists, equipped with nutcrackers, compete with a large macaw to see which could crack a brazil nut in the shortest time. The macaw, with its built-in nutcracker and its greater experience, has invariably come off the winner.

The avian world has an abundance of fruit-eaters and seed-eaters, and even a few flower-eaters, though no bird has (as far as we know) become specialized for eating flowers only. Some tits and finches will eat the blossom of fruit trees; sparrows and starlings will tear petals from low-growing garden flowers. But by and large the birds that show the greatest interest in flowers, such as hummingbirds, are not after the flowers themselves, but after the nectar they contain.

In a very real sense we can say that flowers have more interest in birds than birds have in flowers, for while comparatively few birds eat flowers many nectar-feeders play an important part in pollination.

These eat flowers occasionally: Long-tailed tit and bullfinch eat apple buds; house sparrow tears crocus.

These birds, all primarily fruit-eaters, readily take animal food when it is available: Red-fronted barbet (East Africa) eats ants and termites; king bird of paradise (Papua) takes eggs and young birds; crimson finch (an Australian waxbill) favors termites; cedar waxwing (North America) snaps up insects.

Omnivores

Although many birds prefer certain special foods, most also eat outside their speciality, some quite regularly. For instance, residents in temperate lands, other than the minority that eat solely animal matter, are bound to have a mixed diet, whatever their preferences may be, since the vegetation varies from season to season.

To find out what birds eat we must watch birds; collect the food they bring to their young; examine stomach contents; analyze the remains of food in feces and in the pellets of undigested stuff that many species regurgitate. And we must do so all through the year.

Each wild species has what we can call a "food-spectrum," with wide bands in it that represent favorite foods and narrow bands that represent less frequent, or less frequently available, choices. No two closely related species that live in the same place seem to have the same food-spectrum, except in times of the occasional superabundance of some special food. On the other hand, related species in different areas may have very similar spectra, such as the American robin and the European blackbird. Though each bird has its characteristic food pattern, this pattern may change very much with the seasons—especially at the time of feeding young—and from area to area within the species' range.

No birds have food-spectra more complicated than the omnivores: those that eat varied food, both animal and plant. Many animal-eaters switch to wild fruits in season. Nuthatches and creepers eat beechmast and seeds in the autumn. The carnivorous yellow-billed cuckoo of America eats elderberries, mulberries and grapes in season; in tropical Asia some

Acorn woodpecker (w. North America) finds or makes holes to wedge acorns, seek insects; sucks sap from holes earlier made by sapsuckers.

These birds are mainly fruit- or seed-eaters, but in breeding season eat insects and feed them to their young: snow bunting of the northern world; dunnock of Eurasia; rose-throated becard of Central America.

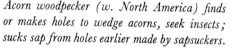

These birds are normally insectivores. But in fall the myrtle warbler of North America (l.) eats bay-berries; the Old World golden oriole (below) eats fruit; the Narina trogon of Africa takes berries.

Some birds eat nearly everything. Australia's spotted bower bird (left) has wide tastes, may be garden pest; North America's gray jay will rob camps, store biscuits in holes; the scarlet-rumped tanager of Central America eats bananas, berries, spiders, mice, eggs. Yet most such birds show distinctive food-spectra.

insect-eating cuckoo shrikes and babblers eat fruit when berries fall and guavas and figs are ripe; in Australia two insectivorous silvereyes are quite important orchard pests when the figs, grapes and soft fruits are ready for market. Both American and Old World warblers may take ripe fruit.

Many plant-eating birds switch specially to insects when they are rearing young, thus giving their offspring a high protein diet during growth. Others readily take animals whenever they swarm. Ants and other insects are snapped up by vegetarians ranging from barbets to blue grouse, from waxbills to waxwings.

Some birds like the gray jay have diets so mixed that they seem to eat anything they can get. But most with wide tastes still show a food-spectrum specially their own, even though it changes strongly from month to month. When the food of the mocking bird is measured through a whole year, it bulks about half animal, half plant on average, as does that of the skylark and the common starling. But in May the mocker's food is about 85 per cent animal, in December-January about 87 per cent plant. The others' diets vary as much, though not in the same way.

A bird that, through the year, eats mainly animal matter (82 per cent by bulk) is the common or black-billed magpie in America. Its plant food varies from hardly any in May to more than half from November to January. Conversely, the rook in wartime England averaged the same percentage (82) of *plant* matter.

An interesting and variable food-spectrum is shown by the great spotted woodpecker of Europe. In Finland its northern race is largely an eater of pine and spruce seeds in winter; only in summer does it have ants and the grubs of wood-boring insects as its main food. The British race, however, has larvae the year round, and acorns as a minor band in its pattern. Some (not all) great spotted woodpeckers make rings of holes around trees to get sap. In North America this is a speciality of the sapsuckers, and, at

Suspected bird pests have been investigated by measuring the percentage by volume of different foods in their stomachs. In Britain the skylark (center) eats 46% animal food, mostly insects, and 54% vegetable food, mostly weed seeds. Food of the starling (left) is much the same in Britain (51% animal, 49% vegetable) as in US (57% animal, 43% vegetable); over half its plants are wild fruits. In England much grain was grown during World War II; at that time the rook (right) ate 18% animal food, 82% vegetable. Highest animal food intake (54%) was in June, lowest (4%) in January-February.

European blackbird and American robin occupy similar niches. Food-spectra are also similar, though former eats more cultivated fruit than other thrush.

In Europe the start of the great tits' breeding season depends closely on the vagaries of the spring climate. Young ones, fed in nest hole during peak caterpillar fortnight, gain benefit of a high protein diet.

second hand, of the acorn woodpecker, which sucks from sapsucker holes. The acorn woodpecker bores holes itself, of course, and indeed may riddle trees with hundreds of them in which it stores acorns and some other largish nuts. The nut band is over half, the insect band under a quarter, of this bird's yearly food-spectrum.

The typical omnivore's adaptations are behavioral rather than anatomical. In general it is more of an opportunist, more ready to resort to trial and error, and more curious than the specialist feeder. Many of the jays all over the world are markedly opportunist in their feeding habits. Many of the tits are so adept at trial-and-error experimenting that in Britain they have now taken to robbing milk from the tops of bottles left on doorsteps. They will even occasionally rob from bottles still on the milkman's cart.

Populations of specialist feeders tend to fluctuate with the abundance of their chosen food, which in turn can fluctuate with climate. Populations of the omnivores tend, on the whole, to remain more stable, simply because in times when any one kind of food is scarce they can switch to another. In Britain four of the birds with the highest populations are blackbird, chaffinch, house sparrow and starling—all omnivores. And the common starling, prolific in both the Old World and the New, can do better than merely scratch a living in almost any habitat other than the sea: crowded city, uninhabited northern island, mountain-height, woodland, moorland, agricultural land, or even wetland.

62

Insect-eaters

Zoologists have described almost exactly a million full species of animals, of which no less than 700,000 are insects. Colossal though this total is, some expert taxonomists, or classifiers, have guessed that the insects so far named are far fewer than those that still remain to be named.

Only a handful of insects are marine: but the class absolutely dominates the planet's land surface in variety and numbers. It makes the solid base of the pyramid of life on land, being the most important prey of the animal-eating animals, including the birds. Big insects no less than small have their avian predators. Honeyguides are specialists in the nests of bees and wasps, eating the wax as well as the insects; some of the forest kingfishers eat centipedes and millipedes as well as large beetles; hornbills eat many kinds of large insects, but have a special taste for grasshoppers; and all kinds of birds, up to the size of storks, follow flocks of locusts.

Of under 160 living bird families, no less than 128 have insect-eating members. Of these 34 eat insects mainly, and another 10 eat insects and insect-like animals wholly.

It is no surprise, then, that we find nearly 20 bird families that hunt insects on the wing. The true nightjars, such as the nighthawk, can hover or sharply jink as they hunt at twilight or night. Fastest of all insect-interceptors

Four of the many birds that glean insects from leaves. From North America hooded warbler (top left), yellow-throated vireo (top right) and scarlet tanager (bottom right); from Europe the wood warbler (center).

Birds that catch insects on the wing. Flying (from left to right) : Nighthawk, North America; vermilion flycatcher, US to Argentina; swift, Eurasia and Africa; great racket-tailed drongo, Asia; white-fronted bee eater and rufous-chested swallow, Africa. Perching: Cuban tody and pied flycatcher, Eurasia.

are the narrow-winged swifts and their allies, many of which may log a thousand miles in a normal feeding day. Swifts and swallows make their long migratory flights at times when insects are nowhere uncommon along their flyways; and they pass through tropical areas during the spring and fall, when insects are plentiful and can be predictably expected even in the oases of the Sahara.

Nightjars and swallows seldom, and swifts and wood swallows never, use perches to make sallies from: but the rest of the flying insect-eaters do. The strange potoos of tropical America dart from favorite posts, on which they sit almost invisible, to snap up passing prey in their enormous mouths; the owlet nightjars, an Australasian family, have mouths nearly as big. These dusk birds have concealing coloration; but day feeders tend to be very brightly colored. The brilliant todies (a small family restricted to the West Indies) and the almost equally colorful motmots of tropical America have strict territories and hunting perches. In the Old World the handsome rollers often carry live prey to their perches for killing and eating; and many of the lovely bee eaters do the same. So do the slender, shining jacamars, long-billed dragonfly specialists of tropical America. The related but less highly colored and broader-billed puffbirds from the same area dive on flying prey from their watching-posts and sometimes take beetles on the ground.

Hunter of insects on the ground: Fairy pitta of East Asia and Australia, one of a 25-strong family.

Three more of the many ground insect feeders, all from more northerly latitudes and each from a different family. From left to right: Pied wagtail of Eurasia, fox sparrow of Canada, and Japanese robin.

Army-ant eaters (S. America) : Black-faced ant thrush; red-crowned ant tanager; chestnut-belted ant pipit.

Over a sixth of the passerine birds are air-catchers; the swallows and wood swallows are most aerial of all. A huge family of 364 species, the tyrant flycatchers of the Americas, has an unrelated counterpart in the rest of the world—the 398 Old World flycatchers, monarchs and whistlers. These are perch-darters, as are the aggressive drongos of the tropical Old World.

In the tropics most of the insectivores are residents or local wanderers. In temperate zones the only ones that can stay the winter are those adapted to living on hibernating insects and grubs, like the downy woodpecker in New England and the great spotted woodpecker in England; the rest—probably more than half—are summer and autumn visitors only.

So it is mainly in autumn that the authors' gardens resound with the sharp communication-notes of mixed flocks of insect-gleaning birds, working their way through the trees in search of insects and spiders under leaves and bark. Though the species are different in the two cases almost all those around R.T.P.'s home in Connecticut have their counterparts (in brackets) around J.F.'s home in Northamptonshire. Among the regular insect-gleaners of Connecticut are: black-capped chickadee (great tit or blue tit—occasionally coal or marsh tit); white-breasted nuthatch (common nuthatch); brown creeper (tree creeper, close species); golden-crowned kinglet (goldcrest); myrtle warbler—an American wood warbler (blackcap—an Old World warbler of a different family); downy woodpecker (great spotted wood-pecker). One insect-gleaner in R.T.P.'s New England garden, the Carolina wren, has no very good counterpart in England. England's common (and only) wren does its insect-hunting lower down, usually in the undergrowth, and is the same species as the North American winter wren.

About two-fifths of all the passerine species of birds are insect or small animal hunters among trees and bushes or on the ground. Some of the ground-feeders are specialists: thus on the forest-floor of tropical America whole groups of birds, of several different families, follow the big army ants and eat them and other insects they stir up: ant thrushes, ant pipits, ant tanagers belong to such gangs, as do some of the manakins and wood warblers.

Associates of African cattle: shoulder, piapiacs; neck, red-billed oxpeckers; horn, carmine bee eater; flying, wire-tailed swallow; last, cattle egrets, yellow wagtail.

Some Specialists

The army ant followers are not the only specialists that rely on other animals to disturb food for them. Wherever cattle range they have bird associates, for instance.

The oxpeckers that spend so much time on native cattle in Africa search their hosts for ticks. The rest of the African cattle club watch for the insects that the animals kick up as they graze, or seek beetle larvae in their dung: the noisy piapiac (a crow) and the carmine bee eater are members; present often are swallows, the yellow wagtail, the cattle egret, and sometimes plovers. In other parts of the world are other tick-birds, such as the fire-crowned tyrant and the smooth-billed ani in South America; and other snatchers of disturbed insects, like the common starling, the North American cowbird, the European jackdaw, the Asiatic king crow and a New Zealand member of the parrot family, the kea.

The five living flamingos—some people recognize six—are specialists of quite another kind, for all live on the minute plant and animal life that swarms in the water and bottom mud of warm freshwater and salty lakes. Most of this food they take by pumping the water or mud over filter-plates in their bills.

Although the flamingos are of very ancient design—the second oldest bird known was a proto-flamingo—and although the design was successful enough to enable them to establish themselves on every continent except Antarctica, they now have only a very fractionated and relict distribution. Extinct in North America and Australia, they are found only here and there in algae-rich waters in the West Indies, México, the Galápagos Islands,

Flamingos, birds of ancient lineage, feed on minute plants and animals in water and mud of warm lakes. In African lakes lesser flamingo feeds at surface, greater from bottom. Their tongues pump water full of plankton through filters in their bills. Right: As greater flamingo moves forward, water, sucked over filter plates, is expelled at nick of gape.

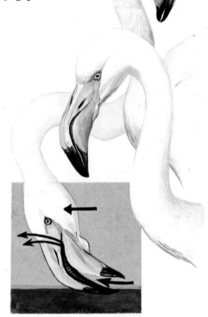

South America, Africa, west central Asia, India, Ceylon, France and Spain. All told there are not more than about 60 known colonies surviving in the entire world.

In some parts of the tropics giant water snails are abundant. Two storks, the open-bills of Asia and Africa, have a ridged gap in their bills that is a device to grip and crush the snails or take them to a hard place where they can be broken with the bill-tip. In the Americas, the quite unrelated limpkin (page 70) also has a bill-gap for the same purpose; and at least three species of kites are giant snail specialists, with fine hooks on their beaks. Other snail specialists use tools. The stagemaker bower bird of Australia uses stones to break large land snails. The song thrush of Europe and Asia and the ruddy kingfisher of the Philippines both smash land snails on favorite stone anvils.

The kingfisher family are not all fishers—one species in New Guinea digs earthworms—but the typical members are among the few land birds that dive for fish. Another is an American tyrant flycatcher, the kiskadee; though primarily an insect-eater, it varies its diet by diving for fish in estuarine mangrove swamps and similar areas. The members of the dipper family hunt animals on the beds of clear streams, walking below the surface by bending their bodies at an angle to the flow. Their prey includes all kinds of aquatic insects and, at the bottom of streams especially, the larvae of caddis flies and mayflies; they will also eat crustaceans, amphibians such as tadpoles, and small fish such as trout fry.

The kiskadee and the dippers are not so much food specialists as hunting-style specialists. The same is true of skimmers and turnstones. In the skimmers, related to the terns, the lower mandible is very prolonged. The bird cuts through the water with beak open, lower mandible just cutting the surface. When the lower mandible dips below small fishes or swimming crustaceans the upper mandible closes down on them. Turnstones, while on their nesting grounds in the high arctic, live mainly on insects; in their winter range, which extends well into the Southern Hemisphere, they hunt for crustaceans and other small animals of the seashore by turning over stones and bits of seaweed.

One of the most remarkable food-winning techniques is that used by the honeyguides in their quest for grubs and wax from the nests of bees and wasps. They lead the ratel, or African honey-badger, to the nest; the ratel breaks up the nest, eats the honey, and leaves the wax to the bird.

Heading the list of birds that specialize in offshore or near-shore seabed mollusks are the eider duck. Among the foremost of those adapted to hunting and eating shore crustaceans is the crab plover, a rare bird confined to the northern Indian Ocean and the Persian Gulf. Outstanding among the snake-eaters (which include the roadrunner of the American deserts, the secretary bird, some of the larger owls and some species of kites) is the snake-eagle of Europe and western Asia.

But perhaps the strangest specialized feeder of all is the oilbird, the only exclusively fruit-eating member of the otherwise insect-eating nightjar taxon. Nesting in dark caves in Trinidad and northern South America, feeding only by night, and finding its way to its nest by the use of sonar, it lives mainly on oily palm fruits. The oilbird exemplifies the broadly true rule that wherever there is a food supply of any kind some animal— often a bird and sometimes a specialist—will become adapted to eating it.

Plants and animals can also become adapted to each other, sometimes with tremendous evolutionary results. Flowering plants did not appear

In Old World brooks the common kingfisher hunts by diving for fish, unusual for a land bird. Dipper does its hunting in clear streams, walking under the water.

on our planet until the insects had already established dominance on the land. As these plants evolved, many produced honey-making organs that attracted insects; and moving from flower to flower to suck sugar, the insects pollinated them. Many flowers then evolved with insect-luring colors and smells; and many insects evolved with long sucking tongues.

About a fifth of the world's birds are now also involved in flower pollination. Red scentless flowers have evolved in the tropics very largely with honey-sucking birds—for birds see colors better than insects at the red end of the spectrum and have hardly any sense of smell.

The hummingbirds of the Americas do all their honey-sucking on the wing. They have long tubular tongues. The pretty Chilean fire-crown has been seen feeding at the red fuchsias of Tierra del Fuego in a snow-storm; the rufous hummer regularly summers in Alaska. Many suck flowers with long corolla-tubes; for instance, the sword-billed hummer of the Andes is the only bird whose (5-inch) bill is longer than the rest of it.

Several of the other nectar-bird families have tubed tongues, though the Hawaiian honeycreepers have trough-like ones with a fringed tip. Most important are the honeyeaters, sunbirds and flowerpeckers of the Old World; and a group of New World birds generally classed as the honeycreeper family, which includes the bananaquit and the flower piercers. Many other families, too, have a few members that are on the way to nectar specialization; for instance, among the American Icterids the oropéndolas and caciques suck tree nectar.

A large tribe of parrots, the honey parrots or brush-tongued lorikeets, have become rather crude nectar-feeders, for they grasp flowers with their beaks and specialized tongues, crush them and lick up the honey with the fringes on their tongues' ends.

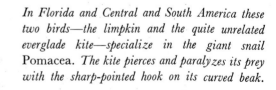

In Florida and Central and South America these two birds—the limpkin and the quite unrelated everglade kite—specialize in the giant snail Pomacea. *The kite pierces and paralyzes its prey with the sharp-pointed hook on its curved beak.*

*Lorikeets crush blossoms, lap up
nectar with fringed tongue (inset).*

*Most birds that feed on nectar also pollinate flowers. The nectar birds highest above are, from left to
right, the Méxican cacique; the ruby topaz and the helmet crest (South American hummers); a sunbird
of East Africa. Below them, left to right, are the bananaquit of Central and South America; the
scarlet honeyeater of Australia; the iiwi of the Hawaiian Islands; the rainbow lorikeet of Australasia.*

71

3   Birds of the Past

The Bird Ancestor

The bedrock of part of Bavaria is a fine slate, formed from mud-silt rapidly deposited at the bottom of a freshwater lake in late Jurassic times, about 140 million years ago. It is called Solnhofen limestone.

A slate-splitter, in 1861, found a fossil feather on a slab—with its impression on the counter-slab; and later in the same year the incomplete skeleton of a feathered animal was found in a Solnhofen quarry at Langenaltheim. It came into the possession of the district medical officer, Dr. Karl Häberlein, who sold it next year (with a fine collection of other fossils) to the British Museum in London for enough to give his daughter a good dowry. It was named *Archaeopteryx lithographica*—"the ancient winged creature of the stone for drawing"—in the year in which it was found.

In 1877 a second specimen turned up in another Solnhofen quarry at Blumenberg, about 10 miles away. Some researchers have thought it to belong to a species different from the London specimen: but it does not, and neither does the third, found at Langenaltheim in 1956, only 275 yards away from the site of the first. In September, 1970 a fourth specimen that had been overlooked was found in the collection of the Teylor Museum in the Netherlands. It had been collected prior to 1857, pre-dating the others.

Archaeopteryx is so far the oldest known bird—about 10 million years older than the next oldest certain fossil bird—the goose- or flamingo-like *Gallornis straeleni*, described in 1931 from Lower Cretaceous beds in France. The species seems to have survived unchanged for quite a time in the cycad forests of the late Jurassic period; and it may indeed have been one of the very earliest of birds, as we can judge from the large array of purely reptilian features it shares with no other known bird.

Among the reptilian features of Archaeopteryx, which are found in no other bird, are the long tail of twenty vertebrae; an uncomplicated backbone with no fusions of its vertebrae; three fingers with claws; no fusions of certain bones in the hand; simple ribs; and a simple brain with a small cerebellum (the part that coordinates muscular activities).

No reptile, however, has been found with feathers; and the structure of those of Archaeopteryx is identical with those of modern birds. The fossil's wing, with primary flight feathers (eight) attached to hand and wrist, secondaries attached to forearm, and covert feathers, is just like many a modern bird's wing. Only in birds do the collar bones join to form a wishbone,

Skeleton of Archaeopteryx, a mixture of reptilian and avian features

and those of Archaeopteryx so join; and some bones in the fossil's hip are arranged like those of birds only.

Archaeopteryx, then, was a bird; and a bird of forests, judging by the position of the "big" toe opposite the other three—an adaptation to perching. It had some hollow bones—an adaptation for lightness already present in the reptilian flying pterosaurs. Yet its powers of flight must have been limited: it had no keel on its breastbone, and could not therefore have had very powerful flying muscles. Further, with its small cerebellum it could not have been much of an acrobat. It was basically a powered glider, probably capable of rising flight from branch to branch, or from rock to rock, but quite unable to dodge or indeed to change direction quickly when in the air. It had teeth; but some later fossil birds also had teeth.

What sort of reptiles was this crow-sized early bird descended from? Archaeopteryx is doubtless of quite separate descent from the only successful flying animals that were true reptiles—animals of the order Pterosauria. The earliest pterosaurs belong to the Rhamphorhynchoid suborder, and the first of them, described by the pioneer English paleontologist Dean Buckland, in 1829, is *Dimorphodon macronyx,* from the Lower Jurassic Sinemurian deposits of Dorset, England; and these deposits, over 180 million years old, are far older than Archaeopteryx. The last known pterosaurs belong to the Pterodactyloid suborder, and were described in the 1950s from deposits probably of Maestrichtian age of the Uppermost Cretaceous time in Brazil and Jordan; and these deposits are more than 60 million but less than 70 million years old—far younger than Archaeopteryx.

An order of long-tailed lizard-like scaly reptiles of about the same size as birds lived from the Uppermost Permian to the end of the Triassic periods—that is from over 220 to a little under 200 million years ago. They are known as Thecodonts, and surely ran with their tails used as balancers. Ground-forms of these developed into two-legged runners with smallish arms; but (the theory is) tree-forms developed their arms equally as climbing and hanging organs. With their strong legs and balancing tails the tree-forms leaped from branch to branch; with their strong arms they climbed, caught and steadied themselves. Gradually their arms developed enlarged scales at the trailing edge, at first simple flaps, later flaps with joining hooks to enable them to work together when fanned out. The feather, in fact, is descended from a Thecodont reptile's scale, and evolved as an adaptation to increase its arm area, grip air and steady it in long leaps.

Fine feathers make fine birds; and it is certain that with the first feathers came the first birds. The feather was the great evolutionary breakthrough that gave rise to the class of animals that now, in species, outnumbers all other classes of vertebrates save the fishes. Birds owe their success as a class to mastery of the air conferred by feathers and by a design (better than that of pterosaurs and bats) that leaves their legs free.

Sea birds fossilized in the middle Upper Cretaceous Niobrara chalk of western Kansas which was, around 85 million years ago, a seabed: Left Ichthyornis victor; *on right rock* Hesperornis regalis; *swimming (l.)* Baptornis advenus, *(r.)* Hesperornis gracilis; *in distance another* Ichthyornis *species.*

Cretaceous

A rough calculation by Professor Pierce Brodkorb suggests that rather over 1½ million bird species have existed at one time or another in the 140 million years or more that have elapsed since the first bird appeared. James Fisher's own belief is that the number is rather under half a million.

Yet despite the great multiplicity they were to achieve, birds appear to have been slow to evolve in their early years. From the whole of the mild, long Cretaceous period, from about 136 to 65 million years ago, only 36 or 37 species are so far known. Gallornis, second in antiquity to Archaeopteryx, is the only bird as yet known from the lower part of the Lower Cretaceous; and only two species are known from its upper part. These two, known only from Albian deposits from Cambridgeshire in England, a little over 100 million years old, belong to the genus Enaliornis, and constitute a primitive family that is possibly ancestral to the loons.

All the birds presently recognized from the Cretaceous are water birds, swimmers or waders. Land birds must have existed then, but none of them has yet turned up in the fossil record, which is heavily weighted in favor of marine and estuarine deposits. The classic primitive sea birds come from the famous middle Upper Cretaceous Niobrara chalk of Kansas which was, around 85 million years ago, a seabed hundreds of miles from the shore. Over this sea the dominant flyers were huge reptiles like Pteranodon, the largest animals ever known to have flown (see wing span diagram, p. 36), but before the pterosaurs became extinct, at the end of the Cretaceous, sea birds were certainly also present.

Parascaniornis
Upper Cretaceous

Enaliornis
Lower Cretaceous

Elopteryx
Upper Cretaceous

Gallornis
Lower Cretaceous

Palaeotringa
Upper Cretaceous

All the Niobrara birds were described by the great American paleontologist Marsh, between 1872 and 1880. One of them was Baptornis, the first of a family that may have been ancestral to the grebes. Three of them were the biggish flightless sea birds Hesperornis, the only birds since Archaeopteryx proved to have had true teeth. The Hesperornithids show flightless specialization; their wings were reduced and they swam with their powerful legs and feet. The rest of the Niobrara birds comprise six flying sea birds of the genus Ichthyornis and another in the same order that has been called Apatornis; they represent two families that looked rather like gulls, and Brodkorb places them low on the branch of the family tree leading to the modern gull-wader order.

The last Ichthyornis species is known from a Texas deposit somewhat younger than the Niobrara. From a slightly later deposit in Alabama comes Plegadornis, in a family ancestral to the ibises. Later still are another Hesperornithid (Coniornis) from Montana and Parascaniornis from Sweden, a Torotigid in the same family as Gallornis; both of these are in Campanian deposits around 73 million years old.

The remainder of the Cretaceous birds come from its uppermost (Maestrichtian) deposits, of between 70 and 65 million years ago. The Upper Lance formation of Wyoming has an array of birds discovered by Marsh and Brodkorb: the last Apatornis; two species of Lonchodytes ancestral to the loons and in the loon order; the last Torotigid (Torotix); first of the wader suborder, three species of Cimolopteryx and Ceramornis, the only known members of the family Cimolopterygidae.

Lately bird-bearing deposits of New Jersey, previously thought to be Paleocene, have been positively identified as of Maestrichtian Cretaceous times, around 68 and 66 million years old. From the middle Maestrichtian Navesink formation comes the first member of the modern Scolopacid snipe-sandpiper family Palaeotringa, and the first known rail Telmatornis. From the late Maestrichtian Hornerstown formation come the first members of the modern cormorant family (two species of Graculavus), another species of Telmatornis and two more of Palaeotringa, and a mysterious bird Laornis whose family is uncertain though we can be sure it waded or swam. At the threshold of the Cretaceous and the lowest Paleocene (around 65 million years ago) comes Elopteryx, from the Transylvanian limestone of Romania—the first of an extinct family between the gannets and the cormorants.

Paleocene and Eocene

Sixty-five million years ago the Atlantic and Indian Oceans were formed, and much of the chalky sea-bottom of Cretaceous times was raised up to form land. Large parts of Europe and North America were tropical. The great reptiles died out; mammals and birds began their dominance.

The Eocene period (in the old sense) lasted until 37 or 38 million years ago. Its early period, until 53 or 54 million years ago, is now separated as the Paleocene period and has so far produced only eight bird fossils. They include early members of modern families, and land birds. From deposits in France, Germany, Belgium, and England, around 58 million years old, come the first of an extinct order of large flightless, land birds, the Diatrymiformes —Gastornis and Remiornis, belonging to the family Gastornithidae, and Diatryma, of the family Diatrymidae. Also present was the first known member of the modern diver family Gaviidae. In Wyoming the discovery of Diatryma in deposits about 55 million years old shows that North America shared at least one genus with Europe.

During the strict Eocene times that followed the Paleocene, birds flourished increasingly. In New Zealand's Lower Eocene deposits we find the first penguin; in Argentine deposits of like antiquity the first rhea, Opisthodactylus, and Telmabates, sole member of a unique family of the flamingo order. In deposits of the American West, around 53 million years old, a rail is found in Colorado, and in Wyoming the first Protostrix, belonging to an

Among fossil birds found in Wasatch, Lower Green River and Colton faunas of Lower Eocene Wyoming and Utah are (left to right) Paragrus prentici, *earliest true crane;* Palaeorallus troxelli, *an early rail; flying,* Coltonia recurvirostra, *earliest stilt; huge flightless* Diatryma steini; Protostrix mimica, *earliest owl;* Gallinuloides wyomingensis, *forerunner of chachalacas.*

Eocathartes
Middle Eocene

Neocathartes
Upper Eocene

Palaeotis, Middle Eocene

extinct ancestral owl family. Also from North America, of about the same time, come the first limpkin, Palaeophasianus, and the first true cranes—Geranoides and Paragrus.

In Europe, at the same time, England's London clay yields the first tropic bird, heron, and gull; a mini-condor of the living Cathartidae family; and Odontopteryx, a big sea bird with tooth-like growths on its jaws, in a special family of an order placed next to the pelicans. From the Ypresian deposits of France come a Diatryma, a Gastornis and a Remiornis.

In later Lower Eocene deposits in Utah, about 50 million years old, are found the first auks; two species of Nautilornis; and Presbyornis, placed in the family Presbyornithidae, between the avocets and the phalaropes. Coltonia, also from Utah rocks of similar age, is probably the only other known member of this extinct family. The first known Passeriform bird, Neanis, placed in the modern tapaculo family, comes from Wyoming's Green River formation.

Early Middle Eocene rocks give us the first known snake bird, in Sumatra, and the first albatross, Gigantornis, in Nigeria. A Wyoming formation about 48 million years old yields Gallinuloides, the first of an extinct family close to the modern Cracids. From deposits of the same age we find in Romania and Belgium last Elopterygids; in Switzerland the only representative of the extinct ostrich-like Eleutherornithidae; in Germany the last Diatrymid; a Cathartid; the first bustard, Palaeotis; the first painted snipe; and the first hornbill. From the Bridger formation of Wyoming, about 46 million years old, come three pre-owls, three cranes, two species of the snipe-sandpiper family Palaeotringa, and the first known motmot.

Birds from the Upper Eocene that we cannot more closely date include an auk from Oregon; from Wyoming Neocathartes, a long-legged bird of prey that is the sole member of a family close to the Cathartids; from Switzerland the first kingfishers; and from Egypt the first elephant bird, Eremopizus. Only one bird can be dated for sure as early Upper Eocene (about 44 million years old): the first known of the Anatids (duck family), found in Utah.

For middle Upper Eocene birds we must go to the Montmartre deposits of France. Here are found the first true hawk, Palaeocircus; the godwit Limosa gypsorum—possibly the earliest bird known of any modern genus; the earliest tit, Palaegithalus; and the earliest starlings. The Upper Headon beds of Hampshire, England are rich in bird fossils of the end of the Upper Eocene. Here, about 39 million years ago, lived a diver (loon); a cormorant; the first ibis, Ibidopsis; and the first modern flamingo, Elornis.

A few of the 48 Eocene-Oligocene birds of Quercy, France. From top down: Cypselavus, *true swift;* Archaeotrogon, *trogon;* Propelargus, *a big stork;* Plesiocathartes, *New World vulture;* Geranopterus, *a roller;* Amphiserpentarius, *secretary bird; sand grouse of the modern genus* Pterocles.

Oligocene

The Oligocene period lasted from 37 or 38 to about 26 million years ago, a warm dry time of mountain building, with an increase in grassland and a decrease of forests.

About 120 birds are known from it. From the Eocene-Oligocene threshold to about 31 million years ago, phosphorites were laid down at Quercy in France. Among 48 bird species found in them are a heron; the earliest storks; New World vultures; the earliest secretary bird; game birds of the extinct Gallinuloidid family; a crane; the last of the extinct Idiornithid family, near the rails; true rails; a wader of a modern genus; the first sand grouse of a modern genus; the earliest cuckoo; the earliest true owls; the first true swift; the first trogons; and the first roller.

In Argentina the Lower Oligocene has Cladornis, in a special Pelecaniform suborder; and the first of the seriemas, in the suborder Cariamae of the crane-rail order—a suborder that from the Oligocene onward produced big-headed flightless raptors. From North America come the first quail and the first New World Cathartid vultures. From France (not Quercy) come the first gannet and the first plover.

In Mongolia the first known Ergilornithids, near the cranes, are of Lower or Middle Oligocene age. The Middle Oligocene lasted from 32 or 31 to perhaps 29 million years ago. From North America it yields Palaeospiza, of an extinct family near the larks; and from Belgium the first petrel.

Australia's Etadunna formation, Upper Oligocene or Lower Miocene, provides the first pelican and Genyornis, the first of an extinct family in the same order as the emus.

79

Miocene

During the Miocene, 26 to 7 million years ago, the Alps and Himalayas were built; and it was warm.

About 277 Miocene birds have been named, and at least 40 remain to be named. Of the genera identified 36 per cent are modern. Notable extinct families found in the Lower Miocene are Cyphornithids (near the pelicans); Pelagornithids (near the gannets); Pseudodontornithids (false-toothed sea birds in the order of the Eocene Odontopteryx); the first Palaelodids (a flamingoid family); the last Gallinuloidids (primitive game birds); and the only Rhegminornithid (a primitive wader). Among representatives of families still living were the first grebes, oystercatcher, thick-knee, pigeon, parrot, barn owl, wood hoopoe, woodpecker, broadbill, wagtail, shrike, crow, Old World warbler (probably), and true sparrow (probably).

Families notable in the Middle Miocene are the first falcon and hoatzin, the last Brontornithid, the only Palaeoscinid (a passerine family near the dippers), and perhaps the first true finch. The Upper Miocene gives us the first storm petrel, the last Ergilornithid, the only Gryzajid (near the bustards), and probably the first known moas, in New Zealand.

The Miocene shows a progressive trend toward modernization of the avifauna. In the Lower Miocene (26 to 18 or 19 million years ago) just under a quarter of the birds identified are of known genera still living; for the Middle Miocene (18 or 19 to about 12 million years ago) the proportion is just over half; for the Upper Miocene it is just under two-thirds.

Lower Miocene species include many penguins in Antarctica and Patagonia, and in Patagonia the flightless Cariamans reached seven feet tall with Brontornis. The last Cyphornithids appear in South Carolina and Rhegminornis in Florida. The biggest avifauna, in Europe, was (still) of Ethiopian type (p. 105) and included a secretary bird, the earliest known parrot, a trogon, and the first broadbill.

In the Middle Miocene the sea bird fauna was generally modern, but that of California also had the last of the false-toothed Pseudodontornithids. The Helvetian fauna of Europe all belongs to modern Palearctic (p. 108) families, except for the flamingoid Palaelodus; the later Tortonian fauna is entirely of modern Palearctic families except for the last Pelagornithid, with several extinct Phasianid genera.

Europe's Upper Miocene bird fauna is close to the present Palearctic fauna, with a few additions like the only Gryazid and the last crane-like Ergilornithid.

Pliocene

From 7 to about 3½ million years ago mountain building died down, and the planet's surface stabilized. The Pliocene was cooler than the Miocene, warmer than the present; its temperate zone extended far toward the poles.

Of more than 110 fossil Pliocene birds known, three-fifths belong to modern genera, though probably none to modern species. We show here an early Pliocene fauna from Florida, which then had a desert rocky coast like modern Perú. The Bone Valley species (14 in all) were first described by Professor Pierce Brodkorb.

In South America the Pliocene was a time of change and invasion from the north. The Cariamans held on, and indeed reached their peak in the Lower Pliocene of Argentina. Here was five-foot Andalgalornis, and the king of all these flightless raptors, *Onactornis pozzii*, which reached no less than eight feet.

In the Lower Pliocene the first known buntings appear in Florida and Kansas; the first known lark of the modern genus Alauda, and the first known nuthatch in Italy; the first known ostriches in Greece, Russia, China, Mongolia and India; and the first known emu in Australia. Oregon had the last known Palaelodid flamingoid.

By the Middle Pliocene the number of modern genera represented had risen from under three-fifths to two-thirds, if we can judge from small faunas in Argentina and larger ones in México, the North American West and Italy. Bones from México of this age are probably of the first known mocking birds.

By Upper Pliocene times the fauna of the world was essentially modern in its pattern of families and genera. In Argentina the presence of the first known rhea of the modern subfamily and of the first known tinamous does not prove that these birds are not primitive; it is very likely that one day older fossils will be found. In Europe the earliest known fossil thrush, from the Astian deposits of France, was thought when found to be the blue rock thrush *Monticola solitarius*, which still lives. Doubtless thrushes are much older, and this Monticola belonged to an extinct species. All the "modern species" (well over a dozen) so far reported from the Pliocene have proved on re-examination to be extinct species. Thus a "sandhill" crane from Lower Pliocene Nebraska that has been referred to the living species probably belongs to *Grus conferta* of Lower Pliocene California, doubtless an ancestor of *Grus canadensis*.

In early Pliocene times Florida had a desert rocky coast like that of modern Peru. Bone Valley phosphates show that it also had limestone cliffs and big sea bird colonies producing rich guano deposits. Professor Brodkorb's Bone Valley birds include (top down): Australca, probably a direct ancestor of great auk; Wetmore's cormorant; guano booby; Elmore's gull, perhaps ancestor of ring-billed gull; Bone Valley goldeneye; Florida flamingo; and a species of godwit. These forms are now extinct. Inset is a bird not of the Pliocene but of the late Pleistocene – Titanis walleri, lately discovered in Florida by Brodkorb.

Much of California, not covered by the last glaciation, was then warm and rather drier than now. Above are some extinct animals trapped in the asphalt of Rancho la Brea 14 or 15 thousand years ago. From top: Imperial mammoth; great condor; Brea caracara; asphalt stork; Brea turkey; Brea blackbird.

Pleistocene

Something unusual happened to our planet about $3\frac{1}{2}$ million years ago; fluctuations in solar radiation, when at their minima, began to produce solid water, at first in the polar regions only. By half a million years ago the earth had permanent polar and alpine ice, and ice invasions began to strike large areas of continents that are at present temperate.

The first 3 million years of the Pleistocene were until fairly lately called Pliocene; but they are now called Villafranchian Pleistocene in the Old World and Blancan in the New. A forest régime in Europe and North America coincided with the first evidence of Antarctic glaciation around 3·3 million years ago. Next a steppe régime coincided with the first invasion of the Indian Ocean by Antarctic ice, glacial advances in Iceland and highland California, and the appearance of the oldest known man, probably of the genus *Homo,* in Kenya (about 2·6 million years ago). Next followed, in order, periods of forest, steppe, forest, steppe; and the last of these steppe periods marches with up to five minor ice advances detectable in Europe around 0·9 million years ago. Some 400,000 years later the great ice advances began, and of the four main ones the last ended about 10,000 years ago. Presently we are in what the Europeans call the Flandrian interglacial, for meteorologists are convinced that the Ice Ages are not over, and that we are still in the Pleistocene.

It is clear that before the first of the four great ice advances the Villa-franchian bird fauna of the world was essentially modern in genera; but its now-extinct species were more than twice those that survive. The combined known fossil avifauna of the world of that period is 64 species, of which at least 44 are extinct. This implies that around 2 million years ago the expectation of life of a bird species was nearly 3 million years. During the last half million icier years this life expectation has markedly declined, and by the end of the last glaciation it was down to about 53,000 years. Yet what has mainly changed in the intervening time has been the evolution rate of birds. With the great climatic changes, species have not only died out more quickly; they have also been replaced more quickly by forms better adapted to the alterations in the environment.

Over a thousand bird species are known fossil from deposits of the last half million years, and a quarter of these are now extinct. The last flightless Cariaman, Titanis, died out in the later part of this period, as did the flightless Dromornithids of Australia and the huge North American raptors, the Teratornithids. In historical times the last Aepyornithids (elephant birds) became extinct in Madagascar, the last moas (two families) in New Zealand, and the dodos in Mauritius. The demise of all these is due to hunting Man, who provedly began to overkill wherever he developed sophisticated tools and hunting methods.

Nevertheless, during the last great glaciation there was still a rich avifauna in some areas. In California the great fossil fauna at Rancho la Brea had an amazing community of giant mammals; and many of the fraction of its birds that has now become extinct were giants too.

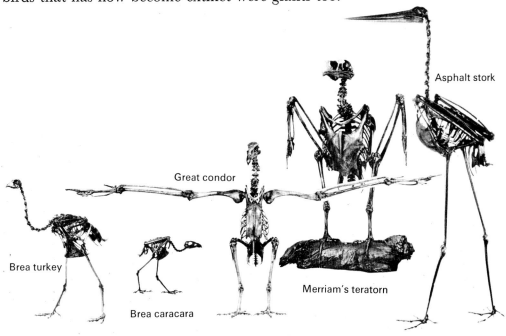

Asphalt stork

Great condor

Brea turkey

Brea caracara

Merriam's teratorn

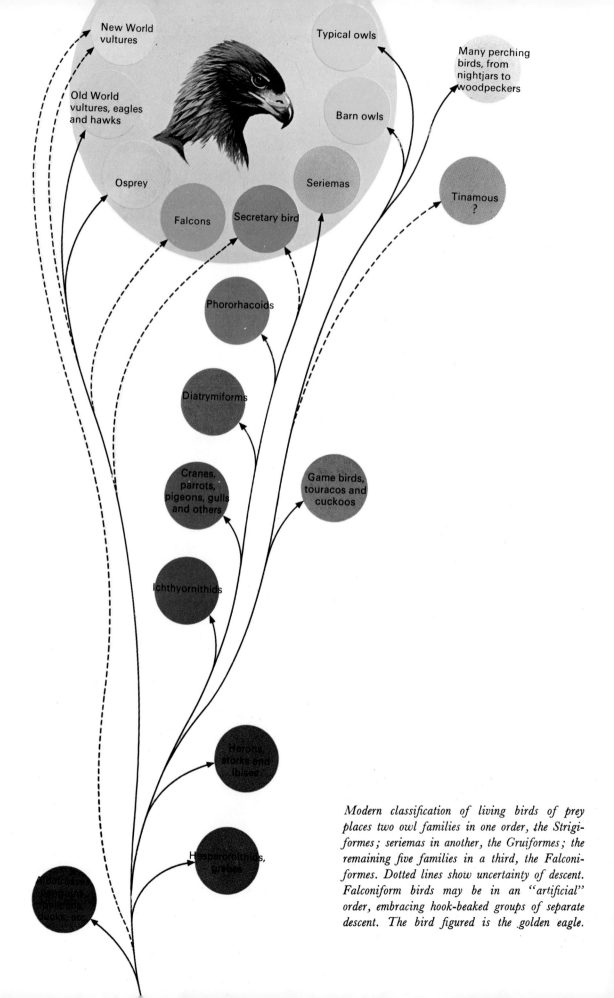

New World
vultures

Typical owls

Many perching
birds, from
nightjars to
woodpeckers

Old World
vultures, eagles
and hawks

Barn owls

Osprey

Seriemas

Tinamous
?

Falcons

Secretary bird

Phororhacoids

Diatrymiforms

Cranes,
parrots,
pigeons, gulls
and others

Game birds,
touracos and
cuckoos

Ichthyornithids

Herons,
storks and
ibises

Hesperornithids,
grebes

Albatrosses,
penguins,
pelicans,
ducks, etc.

*Modern classification of living birds of prey
places two owl families in one order, the Strigiformes; seriemas in another, the Gruiformes; the
remaining five families in a third, the Falconiformes. Dotted lines show uncertainty of descent.
Falconiform birds may be in an "artificial"
order, embracing hook-beaked groups of separate
descent. The bird figured is the golden eagle.*

4 Birds on the Tree of Life

Evolution

There is no other fossil fauna in the world so great as that of the asphalt tarpits of Rancho la Brea. For years at the time of the last glaciation (which did not cover that part of California) thousands of animals got trapped, embedded, and fossilized in bubbling pitch pools. The pits have been carbon-dated at between over 40,000 years and 14,450 years ago.

The Brea fauna lived in a warm climate rather drier than the California coast of today, among plains of grass and chaparral with thickets of live oak, cypress and pine. Some of its extinct animals were very big: huge ground sloths, a giant short-faced bear, a mastodon, two vast mammoths, a tall supercamel, a superbison over seven feet at the hump, the dire wolf and several great cats. Most of its small mammals and birds still live today. Among the birds, too, were giants; the ancestor of the California condor, a huge teratorn, the tall (4 ft. 5 in.) asphalt stork. Over 120 birds are known from the late Pleistocene of California, and most of the 22 extinct species among them are represented by many, many bones from which complete skeletons have been reconstructed.

As we will see, there are many ways in which the evolution and relationships of birds can be studied and deduced. The basic study is, of course, anatomy; from the arrangement of organs, the patterns of feathers, the insertions of muscles, the modifications of bones, anatomists can uncover similarities and differences that enable them to erect families, to gather families in appropriate superfamilies, suborders and orders. Fossil bones show the taxonomists, who strive for a classification based on true evolutionary relationships, the branches of the family tree that are buried in the past. About 9500 described bird species can be recognized; of these about 850 are known only as fossils. Of the 200 bird families a fifth are fossil only.

Since the first fossil bird was named in 1838, the list of them has grown at a rather steady rate. But bird fossil work in Africa, Asia, and even Europe has been lately neglected: a pity, since fossils are strong tools for reconstructing the true family tree. Though our chart on pages 88-9 is tentative, it could not even have been attempted without the work of the paleontologists.

Much remains to be solved by some new comparison in the dissecting room or by a lucky fossil find. The relationship of the birds of prey is a case in point. We can guess that the most primitive living day-flying birds of prey are the Cathartids—the so-called New World vultures whose earliest fossils are, in fact, Old World. Most taxonomists think they are on the same main branch of the family tree (the order Falconiformes) as are the other day-flying birds of prey, holding them to be a full suborder (Cathartae). The rest of the day-flying raptors are placed in a second suborder (Falcones).

By most classifiers the suborder Falcones is further subdivided into two superfamilies. One of these is represented by a single living species—the secretary bird—and dates back to the Upper Eocene or Lower Oligocene of Quercy (see page 79). The other superfamily embraces three living families: the Accipitridae (Old World vultures, eagles and hawks), which dates back to the Upper Eocene of Europe; the Falconidae, which goes back to the Middle Miocene of the Americas; and the Pandionidae, whose sole representative is the living osprey, none of whose fossils is probably older than 100,000 years.

Just when the branches of this part of the family tree branched from each other can presently only be guessed. Our guess is that the two suborders diverged at the very end of the Cretaceous period; that the secretary bird superfamily branched off in the early Eocene; that the Accipitrids diverged from the Falconids in perhaps the Middle Eocene; and that the osprey branched from the Accipitrids later. But the lines of descent have to be dotted, since there is a strong element of uncertainty.

Some good authorities are almost convinced that the secretary bird is related to the seriemas, which in turn are certainly closer to (for instance)

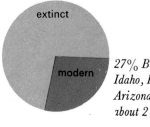

27% Blancan
Idaho, Kansas,
Arizona
about 2 million years

Teratorn descends on remains of superbison, is trapped in Brea tarpit.

78% Illinoian
Florida
184,000 years

85% Late Wisconsin
Florida, California
14–25,000 years

Left: Red areas show the percentage of modern bird species found in three Pleistocene faunas. Approximate ages of these faunas are indicated.

parrots than to hawks. And there are some who suspect that the joint ancestry of the hawks and the falcons may be farther back than we have guessed. Owls are more closely related to (for instance) nightjars than to any diurnal bird of prey; and the joint ancestors of hawks and owls may be no younger than the Lower Cretaceous.

Not all groups are related that appear superficially alike. In the course of evolution similar places in nature in different parts of the world have been entered by birds from different stocks which, through parallel adaptations, have come to resemble each other closely. This convergence can be quickly exposed by the anatomist, though it may be outwardly extraordinary. Besides the remarkable examples on this page, some members of the ovenbird family live in mountain streams in the Andes and look very like the unrelated dippers of the similar habitat farther north; and the seed snipe of southern South America occupy the same niche as the Old World sand grouse, which they strongly resemble.

Because classification bristles with difficulties, no one can as yet draw up a wholly certain family tree of birds. Our chart, on the following pages, does not profess to be more than a tentative sketch of what that tree may be like. In compiling it we have taken much advice, and have read hundreds of papers on fossil and living anatomy, on physiology, and on behavior. But the final judgment is ours, and many eminent ornithologists would not agree with us at every point.

Below : A remarkable instance of convergence. The eastern meadowlark (top) is an American Icterid; the yellow-throated longclaw pictured with it is an African Motacillid, quite unrelated to it.

Another example of marked similarity that does not betoken relationship. The little auk, above, is in the wader-gull-auk order, while Magellan diving petrel is in the albatross-petrel order.

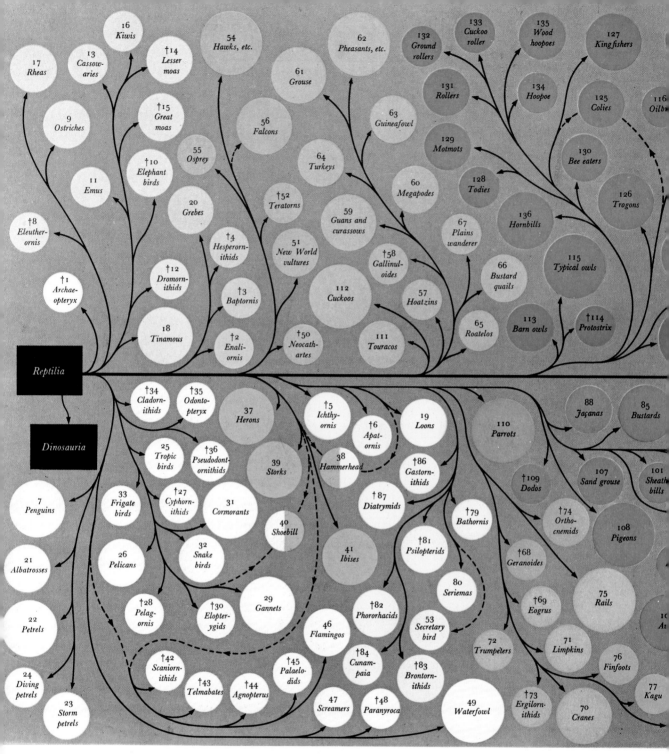

The Family Tree

On page 168 *et seq*. we list all the orders and families of birds. The families, fossil (†) and living, are numbered from 1 to 199. Three we subdivide into subfamilies, labeled a, b, c, etc. They are the Furnariidae, which embraces the woodhewers and the ovenbirds; the Muscicapidae, which has nearly 1400 species, including the thrushes and Old World warblers and flycatchers; and the Emberizidae, which has well over 500, including the buntings and American sparrows, cardinals and tanagers.

Here we plot these families and subfamilies in circles corresponding to their present size, represented as flowers upon a tree of life intended to show

1–5 species

6–25 species

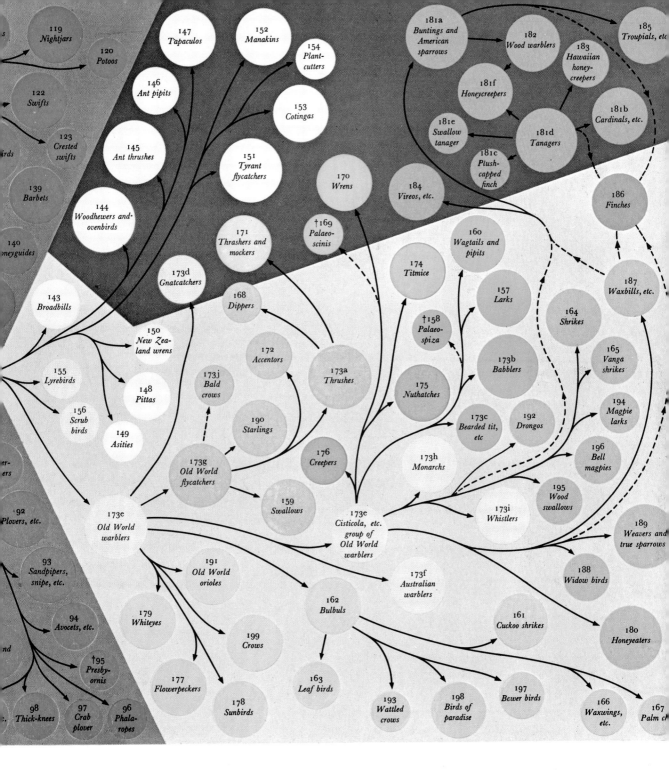

what is now suspected of their relationship and descent. Colors of circles help to pick out the branches of the tree. Among the giant Passeriformes order we have placed on light gray and brown the families or subfamilies that have probably undergone their main evolution in the Old and New Worlds respectively. Throughout, dotted branches (some shown as alternatives) represent relationships that are quite uncertain.

Our chart cannot remain fixed for all time. Indeed, in the few years since it was made new work has already found six whole new fossil families: †18A, †40A, †41A, †82A, †85A, and †87A. (See page 168 et seq.)

26–125 species

over 125 species

Relationship

There are a host of researches devoted to the solution of knotty problems of relationship. A novel biochemical investigation depends upon the apparent fact that no two species of birds have the same molecular protein structure. Proteins when compared show degrees of difference that may indicate distance of relationship. Thus Professor Charles Sibley of Yale University has shown that on egg-white proteins Old and New World vultures and eagles are close, but not close to falcons (see pp. 85–6); that penguins are near petrels; the gulls, plovers and auks all close; that the Pelecaniform order has well-related families; that the shrikes are very close to the crows; that the Old World warblers and flycatchers and accentors are closer to each other than to thrushes; and that the Hawaiian honeycreepers were probably derived from finches.

On Sibley's results it seems that the flamingos have proteins similar to those of storks and herons and unlike those of ducks and geese. But the question remains vexed, for in behavior flamingos resemble geese in many ways: and their parasites are far closer to those of Anatids than of storks. Miss Theresa Clay of the British Museum (Natural History) finds that flamingos share three feather louse genera with Anatids (not found on any other order), only one with storks and herons (found also on four other orders); storks and ducks share only one.

Within the family much can be understood about evolution by watching behavior, and in this field of research much pioneer work has been done in the United States. For instance, Dr. and Mrs. Nicholas Collias have shown a graded evolution of nest constructions in the weaver bird family, from simple cups to the huge colonial nests of the South African sociable weaver and to the delicate spheres and latticed snake-proof funnels of the tree-nesting malimbes (see page 92).

Another good example is the case of the wood thrush. This is the type species of a genus, *Hylocichla*, which for years has been used to embrace the other spotted thrushes of North America—hermit, Swainson's gray-cheeked, veery. Certainly the wood thrush *looks* more like these than the American

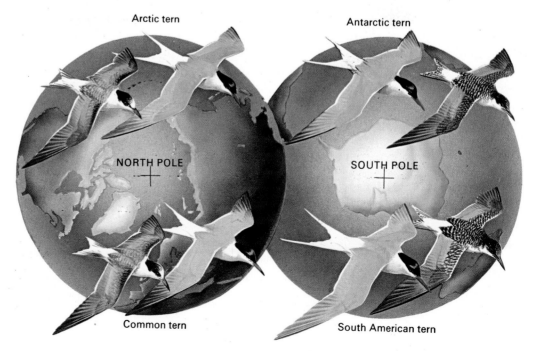

Arctic tern

Antarctic tern

NORTH POLE

SOUTH POLE

Common tern

South American tern

Wood thrush   Hermit thrush   Veery

American robin

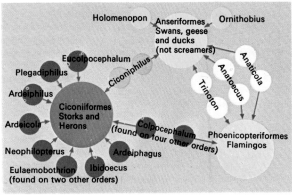

Bird louse genera shared between, and peculiar to, three water bird orders.

robin. But the American robin's big genus, *Turdus*, also includes many spotted thrushes in other parts of the world. Dr. William C. Dilger has found that whereas in most display behavior traits the wood thrush has a *Turdus* style, the other spotted thrushes have not. Based on Dr. Dilger's own fine drawings, hostile postures of medium intensity are shown here. The wood thrush's posture not only resembles that of the American robin but also that of Old World spotted thrushes like the song thrush. Most systematists now put the wood thrush in *Turdus*, and the other four spotted thrushes in the genus *Catharus* with birds from the rest of the Americas.

Sometimes useful systematic information comes from a study of birds' early stages—eggs, downy young, juvenals, immatures. Take the case of the bipolar terns. The arctic tern breeds in the north, and migrates to the antarctic, where the local antarctic tern very closely resembles it. The common tern breeds in the north, and migrates to southern South America, where the local South American tern very closely resembles it. It would seem reasonable to assume that the southern species were separately descended from the northern ones, or *vice versa*, but a glance at the immature plumage of all four shows a close similarity between the two southern species, and between the two northern species. Dr. R. C. Murphy of the American Museum of Natural History thinks the southern juvenal and immature plumage may represent a more primitive stage in evolution, lost in the north. Probably the southern species, including another, the Kerguelen tern, are of common stock, as are both the northern species; and the divergence of northern and southern stocks from each other was earlier than the similarity of the adults would lead us to suppose.

Without other clues, similarity or dissimilarity in appearance can often be misleading. For instance, the brown creeper of North America and the tree creeper of Europe look so much alike that until quite recently they were regarded as of the same species; but experiments in captivity have shown that when put together their voices, display, and other behavior traits are so incompatible that they would be most unlikely to interbreed in the wild. The black-capped chickadee of North America and the look-alike willow tit of Eurasia baffled classifiers in the same way. Conversely, many good species have races in different geographical areas which look so unlike that they were often (and excusably) classed as different species when first given their Linnaean names.

Cassin's malimbe

Spotted-backed weaver

The most advanced weavers build intricate nest, usually employing knots

Thick-billed weaver

Huge colonial nest of sociable weavers. Under a coarse straw canopy up to 300 pairs have own nest chambers, to side of top of upward tunnel.

Black-capped social weaver; semi-woven nest, two entrances

Buffalo weaver: large, thorny, compound nest (not shown)

White-browed sparrow weaver; domed nest, two entrances

Right: Welsh island of Skomer lies in overlap area of herring gull and lesser blackback. Nest sites differ ecologically: Herring gull favors rocky cliff edge, lesser blackback flat plateau.

House sparrow; nest, normally domed, may be domeless in cavity or box

Semi-domed nest

Ancestral cup nest

Probable evolution of nest types of the weaver family

Species Formation

The species, the basic building block of evolution, can be defined as an aggregate of interbreeding natural populations. This does not, of course, mean that because two kinds of birds can interbreed they *must* be of one species: for a true species in nature can be interfertile with others, yet have recognition marks, voice, behavior traits, even nesting seasons that effectively prevent it from breeding with them. And a species is ecologically specialized so as not to compete with its sibling (brother or sister) species.

How does a division start? Most ornithologists believe in a purely geographical origin of species. Bird species, in fact, are descended from subspecies or geographical races; and all have gone through a period in which they have been, as a race, isolated. In this isolation they have evolved separately in different environments, and after some success have often overlapped their sibling's ranges, and thus encountered a natural testing-time. The test is whether reproductively and ecologically the siblings are different enough. The mechanisms that can ensure reproductive and ecological isolation come into play. If they work, the differentiating traits will be improved by natural selection and the siblings will stabilize as two good species. If they do not, there will be a period of much hybridization and variation until a single species stabilizes again.

Nature provides us with tests under our very eyes. The gulls of the herring gull group were probably represented by one species until 10 to 15 thousand years ago. Since then five full sibling species have evolved, some so close to the threshold that several expeditions have gone to find out whether the isolation mechanisms are working: they are.

What evidently has happened is that the herring gull ancestor spread both west and east from the Bering Sea. In both directions the birds colonized new areas fast, and in various zones stabilized as races. Some of the successful races spread again.

North circumpolar map showing the "gull chain"—distribution of species and races: 1. Glaucous-winged; 2. Thayer's; 3. Iceland; 4. Herring; 5. Yellow-legged (race group of 4 or 6); 6. Lesser blackback.

Overlap ensued: the most spectacular is that of the herring gull, with its light mantle, which spread east across the Atlantic from North America, and the dark-mantled lesser blackback, which spread west in Europe from Siberia. End-members of the same race chain, the two in northwest Europe, behave as (and are) different species, with clear differences in color, food, voice, nesting site preferences, and migratory habits. Hybrids are very rare.

The only outstanding difficulty is whether to regard the yellow-legged, light-mantled birds of the Mediterranean and southern Russia as a race chain of herring gulls or of lesser blackbacks. They have by some been put in *Larus fuscus*, though they do not have black backs.

The other overlaps have taken much more sorting out, and indeed Thayer's gull has been restored to a full species as recently as 1961, when it was finally proved that it, a race of the Iceland gull and a race of the herring gull were sympatric; that is, shared a (small) breeding range in which they behaved as full species.

The scientific names of the species and races of the *Larus* chain on these pages are 1. *Larus glaucescens*; 2. *L. thayeri*; 3. *L. glaucoides*, races a. *kumlieni*, b. *glaucoides*; 4. *L. argentatus*, *argentatus* race group a. *omissus*, b. *argentatus*, c. *smithsonianus*, d. *vegae*, e. *birulai*; 5. *L. argentatus* (or *L. fuscus*), *cachinnans* race group a. *mongolicus*, b. *cachinnans*, c. *armenicus*, d. *michahelles*, e. *atlantis*; 6. *L. fuscus*, races a. *heuglini*, b. *antelius*, c. *fuscus*, d. *graellsii*.

Numbers and colored circles above key with numbers and colored lines on map opposite. In areas where species overlap the colors of the mantle, primaries, eyes or legs may all act as segregating mechanisms.

Most standard books regard the yellow-shafted flicker of northern and eastern North America and the red-shafted flicker of the west as different species. Certainly the red-shafted flicker with its red wing- and tail-linings, brown crown and red (not black) cheek-flash looks *very* different from the eastern bird: though the differences may depend on no more than a few hereditary characters.

There is reason, nevertheless, to regard these flickers as very well marked races. Clearly they must have evolved their separate ways in isolation: and equally clearly spread and met later. Now on a broad front their overlap zone runs for nearly two thousand miles along the edge of the Great Plains. Within it they hybridize: a typical hybrid looks like a yellow-shaft with a red cheek-flash. The hybrid zone has been of the same general extent for a couple of human generations; it is fairly stable, and though it is big the hereditary units (or genes) that control the recognition characters of the two species do not seem often to penetrate beyond it. Here then is a case where the forma-

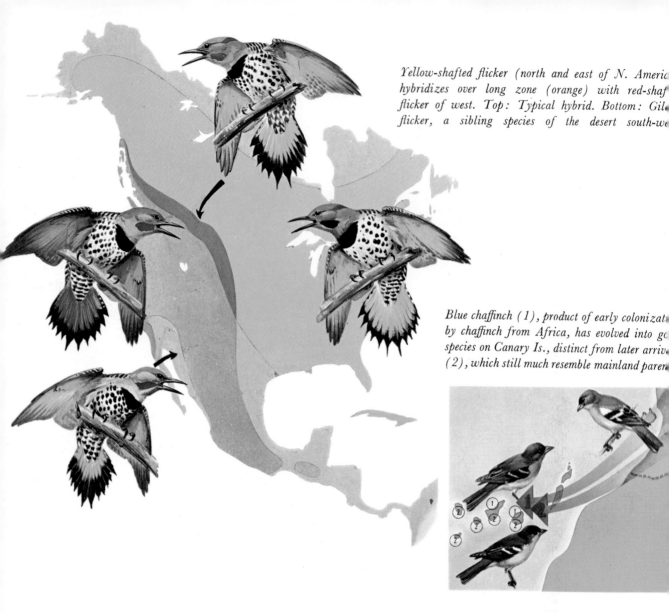

Yellow-shafted flicker (north and east of N. Americ
hybridizes over long zone (orange) with red-shaf
flicker of west. Top: Typical hybrid. Bottom: Gil
flicker, a sibling species of the desert south-we

Blue chaffinch (1), product of early colonizat
by chaffinch from Africa, has evolved into g
species on Canary Is., distinct from later arriv
(2), which still much resemble mainland parer

tion of species is not quite complete. We have actually caught it in the act.

Interestingly, in the southwest the boundaries between the red-shaft and a very close sibling species, the gilded flicker, are stable. The gilded, to look at, is nearly a red-shaft with yellow-shaft linings: occasionally it has a red-lined form but this is not certain evidence of hybridization. It must be regarded as a good species.

Many fairly remote islands, and some isolated mountains, have earned their bird fauna not by gradual but by sudden colonization, often as a consequence of winds and storms. A small population arrives by chance that can fit into an unoccupied niche. In isolation it may quite quickly evolve into a form unlike that of its parent species: and if the parent species survives, a second invasion from it after a time may settle down with the first, and both will behave like (and indeed will be) good, separate species. Sibling pairs from double invasions are found in many places, including the Samoan, Hawaiian, Galápagos and Canary Islands; quite large islands such as Luzon in the Philippines, Celebes, Ceylon and Tasmania; mountains like Borneo's Kina Balu and several mountain areas in Africa. Norfolk Island even has a sibling trio.

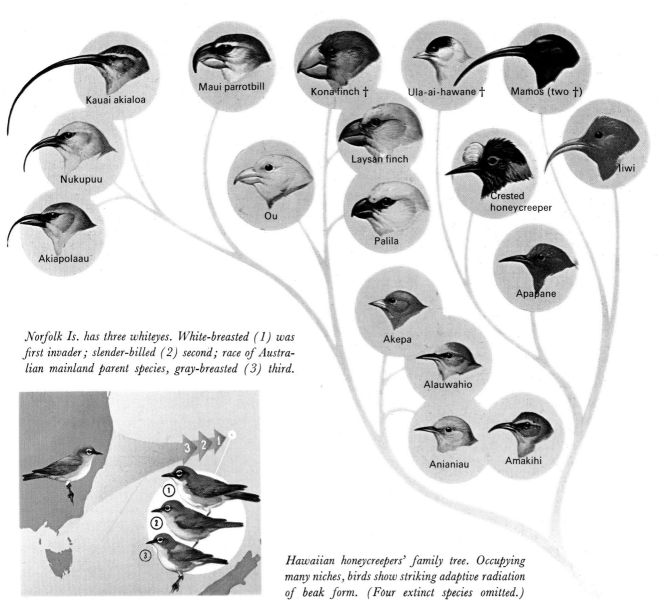

Kauai akialoa

Maui parrotbill

Kona finch †

Ula-ai-hawane †

Mamos (two †)

Nukupuu

Laysan finch

Crested honeycreeper

Iiwi

Akiapolaau

Ou

Palila

Apapane

Akepa

Alauwahio

Anianiau

Amakihi

Norfolk Is. has three whiteyes. White-breasted (1) was first invader; slender-billed (2) second; race of Australian mainland parent species, gray-breasted (3) third.

Hawaiian honeycreepers' family tree. Occupying many niches, birds show striking adaptive radiation of beak form. (Four extinct species omitted.)

The island colonists we have discussed and figured here show evolution at species level. Now island invasion may lead to higher evolution: for a whole, remote archipelago can be early colonized by an original stock that has time to evolve further and radiate into more niches than one or two. In the Galápagos and Cocos Islands a whole tribe of 14 highly differentiated species may be descended from a single bunting-like ancestor: Darwin, who first studied them, realized something of the sort years before he published his *Origin of Species*. The best example is in the Hawaiian Archipelago. At an unknown time these remote islands were colonized by finch-like American birds. The invaders gave rise to a whole special family, the Drepanididae, of which eight are now extinct and 14 survive.

The Hawaiian honeycreepers have had a remarkable adaptive radiation, forming species in at least a dozen major niches; though the most specialized have tended to be most prone to extinction. They have evolved into nectar-sipping, probing, seed-eating, nutcracking and even parrot-bill forms. One, the rare akiapolaau, has a strong straight lower mandible used for pecking wood; its curved upper mandible is used for digging; and it occupies a woodpecker niche.

1. *Laysan rail, extinct (†)*
   Midway I. 1944
2. *Carolina parakeet,*
   † in captivity 1914
3. *Leguat's starling,*
   † Rodriguez I. c. *1832*
4. *Passenger pigeon,*
   † in captivity 1914

5. *Cuban red macaw,*
   † c. *1885*
6. *Seychelles Island owl,*
   believed † 1906, returned
   from the dead 1959
7. *Hawaii oo, †* c. *1934*
8. *Mamo, † Hawaii, 1898*

9. *Crested Choiseul pigeon,*
   † Choiseul 1904
10. *Huia, † North Island,*
    New Zealand c. *1907*
11. *Tahitian sandpiper,*
    † 1777
12. *Dodo,*
    † Mauritius c. *1681*

13. *Crested shelduck,*
    † Korea c. *1943*
14. *Labrador duck,*
    † Long Island, N.Y.
15. *Great auk,*
    · † Eldey, Iceland 18·
16. *Riu Kiu Island kingf.*
    † 1887

5   The Distribution of Birds

Extinct and Rare Birds

All but one of the birds pictured opposite are almost certainly as dead as the dodo. No dodo was seen by anybody after 1681; and since then 85 other full species of birds have in all probability died out. Of that total at least 13 were done in by human hunting. About 11 were extinguished by predation (or possibly competition) of cats, rats, and other animals introduced into their living space. Another 14 or so can be proved to have died out after the direct destruction, by draining, tree-felling, fire, and agriculture, of their natural habitat.

Some of the remainder probably died out naturally; but others (as in Hawaii, where 14 have become extinct) should perhaps be added to those that have been driven to extinction by the competition of better-adapted species introduced into their habitat from elsewhere.

If we can assign a date to a fossil deposit we can work out the average life-expectation of species *at that date* by multiplying the age of the deposit by the number of species found in it and dividing the result by the number of those species that have since become extinct. On this basis J.F. has calculated that around 390,000 years ago the average species life-expectation was 2.03 million years; around 200,000 years ago it was 820,000 years; in the Upper Pleistocene of around 70,000 years ago it had fallen to 328,000 years; and at the end of the last glaciation, around 10,300 years ago, it had dropped to only 52,900 years.

An even more drastic decrease has come about since the start of Man's main civilizing mission around the world. Out of the 8663 species of birds estimated to have been living 350 years ago, 95 have since become extinct. This implies for recent historical times an average life-expectation of only 32,000 years.

When birds were never seen again after first being collected or described there is a strong case for believing they died out naturally. Among them we may number the Tanna ground dove, the Raiatea thrush, and the Raiatea kakariki, all reported in 1774 only; the Tahitian sandpiper (1777); the Samoan wood rail (1873); and the crested Choiseul pigeon (reported in Choiseul, Solomon Islands, in 1904). Cooper's sandpiper and Townsend's bunting (both 1833) may have been aberrant individuals.

Those extinguished by introduced predators or competitors include the Ascension flightless crake (1656); the long-legged warbler of Fiji (1890);

1. Cahow, Bermuda,
   24 pairs plus, 1966
2. Splendid parakeet, small
   pop., S. and W.
   Australia
3. Mikado pheasant, a few
   hundred, Taiwan
   mountains
4. Whooping crane, N.

America, 68 in 1968
5. Short-tailed albatross,
   23 on Torishima 1966
6. Kauai oo, Hawaiian
   Islands, just survives
7. Ivory-billed woodpecker,
   perhaps 6 Cuba,
   just survives USA
8. Noisy scrub bird, 50–80

W. Australia 1966
9. Puaiohi, perhaps 30
   Kauai
10. California condor,
    around 50 1969
11. Nippon ibis, Hokkaido,
    Japan, 11 1969
12. N.Z. laughing owl, last
    unconfirmed record

South Island 1956
13. Néné, Hawaii and
    tivity, over 500 19
14. White-breasted thr
    may be extinct St.
    Lucia and Martini
15. Takahé, South Isle
    N.Z., about 200–
    lately

the Stephen Island wren of New Zealand (extinguished by a lighthouse keeper's cat in 1894); and the New Caledonian wood rail (1904).

Although habitat destruction is hard to pin down as the agent of extinction, we can be sure it played a major part in ending the careers of such birds as the São Thomé grosbeak weaver (São Thomé, West Africa, 1888); the four-colored flowerpecker (Cebú, Philippines, 1906); the Laysan miller bird (Laysan, 1923); and the Carolina parakeet (whose last representative may have died in Cincinnati Zoo in 1914).

Birds that men have hunted to extinction in three-and-a-half civilizing centuries include the broad-billed Mauritian parrot (1638); the great elephant bird of Madagascar (1649); the dodo (Mauritius, c. 1681); the flightless blue rail (Rodriguez, 1730); the Réunion fody (1776); the Dominican green-and-yellow macaw (1791); the spectacled cormorant (Bering Island, 1852); the Labrador duck (Long Island, 1875); and the once-prolific passenger pigeon which by 1914 was reduced to a single individual that died in captivity.

The last bird provedly to become extinct was the Wake Island rail, which was undoubtedly wiped out by the Japanese garrison (probably for food) and has not been seen since 1945. The Laysan rail went in 1944.

One of the birds on page 98 was long thought to be extinct but is not quite so: the Seychelles Island owl. Other birds thought gone have returned from the dead, most famous, perhaps, being the flightless takahé rail of New Zealand, which was last collected in 1898, doubtfully reported as sighted in 1910, and eventually rediscovered in 1948. In Puerto Rico a nightjar known only from bones and an old skin was found again in 1961. Also rediscovered that year was the noisy scrub bird of Western Australia, thought extinct since 1920.

Probably 11 of the 15 birds figured opposite have world populations under the 100 mark, as may about 8 others we could name. One of the rarest is the ivory-billed woodpecker. Its race in the southeast USA now barely survives; its Cuban race probably had but 6 in 1970. Other birds whose populations are currently below 50 include the Korean white stork, the Nippon ibis, the California condor, the Mauritius kestrel, the Réunion cuckoo shrike, the Seychelles magpie robin, the puaiohi, the Rodriguez warbler, and the Kauai oo. All told, about 80 birds are known to ornithologists from but one or a few specimens; and in some cases their status remains a mystery. More than 140 other species all have populations of under 2000.

To sum up, about 2 per cent of our planet's birds are very rare indeed. Not more than a third of these may be naturally toward the end of life. The rest may have Man to thank for their parlous state.

When the Survival Service Commission of the International Union for Conservation of Nature considers a bird to be in danger it circulates a sheet to all subscribers to Volume 2 of the I.U.C.N's Red Data Book. The sheet estimates the bird's numbers and breeding rate in the wild, outlines reasons for its decline, gives the number and breeding potential of individuals in captivity, and states the protective measures taken and proposed. Special green sheets give information on birds previously thought to be in danger but presently thought to be out of it.

Conservationists seek to restore the fortunes of rare birds simply because, like Mount Everest, they are (still) there.

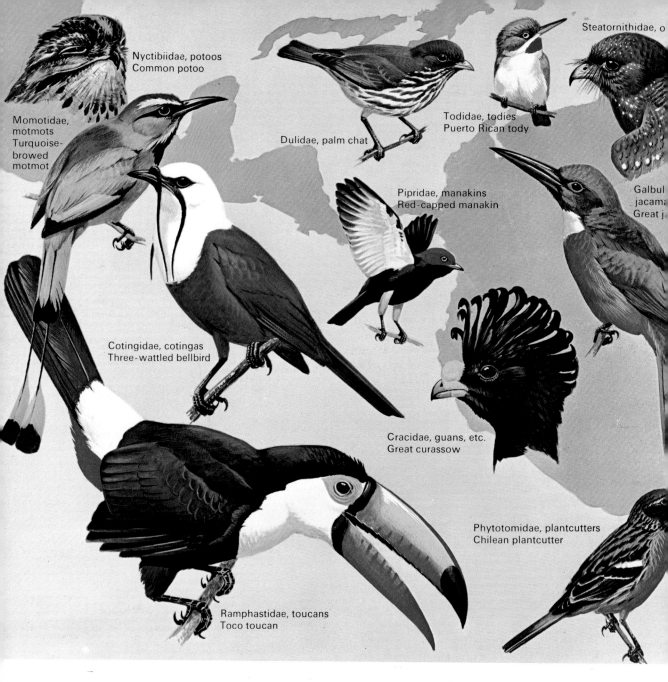

Nyctibiidae, potoos
Common potoo

Momotidae,
motmots
Turquoise-
browed
motmot

Dulidae, palm chat

Todidae, todies
Puerto Rican tody

Steatornithidae, o

Pipridae, manakins
Red-capped manakin

Galbul
jacama
Great j

Cotingidae, cotingas
Three-wattled bellbird

Cracidae, guans, etc.
Great curassow

Phytotomidae, plantcutters
Chilean plantcutter

Ramphastidae, toucans
Toco toucan

Great Bird Faunas: Neotropical

In 1858 Philip Lutley Sclater, Secretary of the Zoological Society of London, keen student of geographical ornithology, and close friend of that other great animal geographer, Alfred Russel Wallace, classified the world's surface into zoogeographical regions, largely from the study of birds.

Based on subsequent refinements, modern animal geographers now recognize six great zones of the earth, each of which contains a peculiar fauna or animal community—that is, one that differs markedly from the next. The present distribution of the great bird faunas is shown on page 109. Through the age of birds their borders have moved quite a lot, and some still move (though slowly) in our own times.

The world's richest, strangest, and most varied bird community is the Neotropical avifauna, which occupies the Americas from tropical México south, including the West Indies. It reaches its most multitudinous variety

Opisthocomidae, hoatzin

Psophiidae, trumpeters
White-winged trumpeter

Eurypygidae, sun bittern

Aramidae, limpkin

Cariamidae, seriemas
Crested seriema

Anhimidae, screamers
Crested screamer

Rheidae, rheas
Darwin's rhea

Bucconidae, puffbirds
Swallow-winged puffbird

Rhinocryptidae, tapaculos
Gallito

Thinocoridae, seed snipe
Small seed snipe

inamidae, tinamous
Martinetta tinamou

Furnariidae,
ovenbird subfamily
Hornero

in Colombia and this variety dwindles off greatly only well to the south of the equator. About half the species of birds of the world breed in the community, or visit its zone in winter.

If we include five extinct families, no less than thirty of all the known families of birds are peculiarly Neotropical. Examples of all living ones are figured above and on page 104. By "peculiarly Neotropical" we mean families that do not normally range outside the present zone, though the guans, limpkin, and cotingas just overlap the neighboring Holarctic (Nearctic) fauna. Besides all these, about a dozen other living families (like humming-birds, tyrant flycatchers, Icterids, and the bunting-cardinal-tanager family) that have penetrated into the Holarctic and often beyond, must have had their place of origin, their theater of evolution, in the Neotropical.

The word "Neotropical" was coined by Sclater, and though it strictly

Top : Barred woodcreeper, Furnariidae, woodhewer subfamily. Below, left : Cinnamon-chested ant pipit, Conopophagidae. Bottom right : White-bellied ant pitta, Formicariidae (family of the ant thrushes).

means "New World tropical" embraces Tierra del Fuego and the Falkland Islands, and may even extend to distant Tristan da Cunha, whose land birds seem to be mostly of South American origin.

The blend zone between the Neotropical and Holarctic, around the Rio Grande, is but 200 miles wide; so in May 1953 when we the present writers made our first Méxican trip together, as part of our 15,000-mile note-taking and photographing journey in preparation for writing *Wild America*, it took us only half a day to move fully into the Neotropical region. With us in R.T.P's big Ford station wagon was our good friend Bob Newman from the University of Louisiana, an ornithologist who knew the ground and could help us very much with the identification of birds that neither of us had seen before. In about 10 days J.F. saw 76 such birds and R.T.P. 60. During that Méxican trip neither of us broke our personal record for the number of species spotted in a single day (though J.F. did so in Texas in the same year); but seldom or never has either of us seen so many species that were wholly new to us in so short a space of time.

In another world we both saw or heard our first wild parrots, potoos, cotingas, tinamous, guans, motmots, honeycreepers, woodcreepers, trogons, and toucans. We both understood, for the first time, what it really meant to see a new fauna; how the word exotic (belonging to another country) has so much come to be used for animals and plants of unfamiliar and rich beauty; and why so many of the world's ornithologists have given the best years of their lives to work on the greatest galaxy of bird stars in the world.

Left: Representatives of nine specially Ethiopian bird families: 1. Ostrich, Struthionidae; 2. Shoebill, Balaenicipitidae; 3. Hammerhead, Scopidae; 4. Blue-naped mousebird, Coliidae; 5. Pin-tailed wydah, Viduidae; 6. Secretary bird, Sagittariidae; 7. Helmeted guinea-fowl, Numididae; 8. The cuckoo-tailed wood hoopoe, Phoeniculidae; 9. The common touraco, Musophagidae.

Above: Representatives of families special to Mada-gascan subfauna: 10. Philepittidae, asities (false sun-bird); 11. Vangidae, vanga shrikes (blue vanga); 12. Mesoenatidae, roatelos or mesites (Bensch's "rail"); 13. Leptosomatidae, cuckoo roller; 14. Brachyptera-ciidae, ground rollers (pitta-like ground roller).

Other Great Bird Faunas

Next in variety to the great Neotropical bird fauna, the Ethiopian fauna occupies the southwest corner of Arabia and all of Africa south of the Sahara. Though at its most varied, in the Congo Basin, it cannot match the richness of the Neotropical in Colombia, neither does it anywhere dwindle off as greatly as does the Neotropical in Patagonia and Tierra del Fuego.

It is the theater of evolution of many remarkable families. Besides the nine indigenous ones figured above, continental Africa probably nourished the world's first bustards, pratincoles, sand grouse, bee eaters, and some other arid country groups; probably also hornbills, bulbuls, and weavers, and certainly honeyguides; maybe the first larks. The Ethiopian fauna also has the distinc-tion of including the world's biggest living flightless bird, the ostrich; the biggest living bird of prey, the black vulture; and one of the world's biggest flying birds, the marabou stork, whose wingspan can exceed that of the wandering albatross.

In the northern winter, Africa south of the equator is further enriched by the many migrant birds that it attracts from areas of the northern world as far apart as Siberia, Greenland, and northeast Canada.

The island of Madagascar has been isolated from Africa at least since the Oligocene period—time enough for its fauna (which is primarily African in origin) to evolve in its own special way. Madagascar and its satellites have therefore rightly been considered to support a subfauna, for no fewer than five of its living bird families (see picture above) are indigenous; and in the

105

quite recent past—in historic times—the great elephant birds or Aepyornithids lived there and gave rise to the legend of the Roc. On the curious neighboring Mascarene Islands the Raphids—the dodo and the two solitaires—became extinct between 1681 and 1791.

The fauna of Australasia is nearly as rich as that of the Ethiopian zone, and representatives of 12 specially Australasian families are figured below. Several of these have only a very limited range, including the lyrebirds (confined to a coastal strip of Victoria, New South Wales, and southern Queensland) and the scrub birds (limited to a coastal strip of New South Wales and the southern tip of Western Australia). Both species of scrub birds are rare enough to be in peril of extinction.

New Zealand, with its satellite islands, where the two families of moas flourished until historic times, is often regarded as supporting a subfauna, and certainly it still has a few families that are specially its own. Also regarded as supporting a subfauna is the Antarctic and Subantarctic region, probably the evolutionary home of the best-adapted sea birds—penguins, albatrosses, and petrels—as well as of the peculiar sheathbill family.

The honeyeaters, which have one outpost in South Africa, are clearly of Australasian origin, as are probably those worldwide colonists of the tropics,

Representatives of specially Australasian families: 1. Australian cassowary, Casuariidae; 2. Emu, Dromiceiidae; 3. Kagu, Rhynochetidae; 4. Superb lyrebird, Menuridae; 5. Magpie lark, Grallinidae; 6. Rufous scrub bird, Atrichornithidae; 7. Green catbird, Ptilonorhynchidae; 8. Little owlet frogmouth, Aegothelidae; 9. White-backed "magpie," Cracticidae; 10. Wilson's bird of paradise, Paradisaeidae; 11. Collared hemipode, Pedionomidae; 12. Brush turkey, Megapodiidae. New Zealand families (inset): 13. Common kiwi, Apterygidae; 14. Saddleback, Callaeidae; 15. N.Z. rock "wren," Acanthisittidae.

Parrot family, too, is probably of Australasian origin. Above: Galahs—the roseate cockatoos of Australia.

the parrots (whose 317 living species include the handsome roseate cockatoos of Australia, pictured above), and possibly the now cosmopolitan pigeons. Hawaii's natural avifauna is Australasian with some Holarctic elements and an indigenous family, the Hawaiian honeycreepers or Drepanididae, which is probably descended from finches from the Americas.

The Oriental fauna is rather less rich than that of Australasia. Probably owing to its central position in relation to two other great faunas it has but one indigenous family—the leaf bird family whose 14 living species have a collective range covering almost all the Indian subcontinent, the whole of mainland Southeast Asia, Sumatra, Java, Borneo, and the Philippines. But within the Oriental zone most if not all of the following families have evolved to colonize and add variety to neighboring faunas: swallows, frogmouths, crested swifts, pittas, wood swallows, whiteyes, and flowerpeckers.

The Holarctic fauna, which occupies roughly the temperate and arctic northern world, is the one upon which the majority of the world's ornithologists have learned their business. Yet it is the least rich in the world. (Compare the faunal map on page 109 with the map showing distribution of bird variety, on page 14.)

This largest of all faunal zones divides well, at the Bering Sea and through the middle of Greenland, into a northern Old World (Palearctic) subfauna and a northern New World (Nearctic) subfauna. Of its five indigenous families the auks probably originated in the Bering Sea, the phalaropes, grouse, and loons in North America, the accentors in Eurasia. Families of probably Holarctic origin that have spread into other faunas are many. The New World vultures, pheasants, cranes, owls, barn owls, Old World flycatchers, shrikes, true finches, tits, creepers, nuthatches, and crows may have come from the Palearctic; the turkeys, waxwings, and dippers from the Nearctic; the sandpipers, skuas, and gulls from somewhere in the northern world.

We must reiterate that the present distribution of the world's great bird faunas, as depicted on the map opposite, is different from what it was two million years ago, and very different from what it was at different times in the 140 million years of birds' life on earth. Throughout history not only have the bird communities shifted, but the lands themselves have changed; indeed the continents themselves, and the poles, have most probably drifted great distances. The evolutionary changes of the birds have taken place upon an earth crust that has also been evolving and changing. The modern student of the distribution of birds (or any other class of animals or plants) needs to know his geological geography—his physiography—as well as his ornithology.

Representing the five specially Holarctic families: 1. Red-necked phalarope, Phalaropodidae; 2. Arctic murre, Alcidae; 3. Loon, Gaviidae; 4. Spruce grouse, Tetraonidae; 5. Alpine accentor, Prunellidae. The fairy bluebird (inset 6. right) represents the leaf birds or Irenidae — the sole family found exclusively in the Oriental avifauna.

Sheathbill belongs to the Chionididae, only family peculiar to Antarctic-Subantarctic.

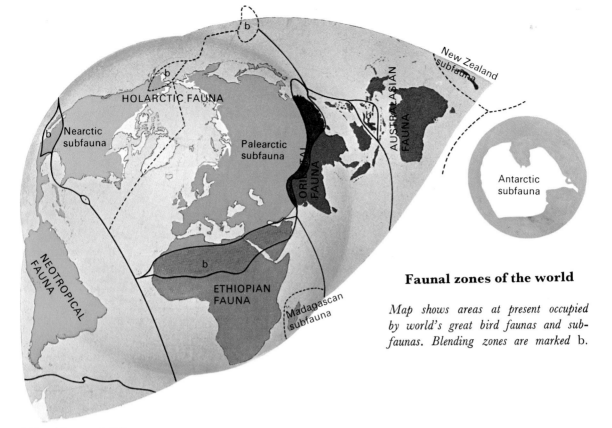

Faunal zones of the world

Map shows areas at present occupied by world's great bird faunas and subfaunas. Blending zones are marked b.

The Faunal Map

The blending zones in the map above are relatively small; outside them each great fauna has its own powerful individuality, its own special congregation of families and successful species.

The blending zones bear witness to the wisdom of using the expression "fauna" rather than "region." Each fauna has its own distinctive *spectrum* of families, some of which may be peculiar to it, but many of which, at different times in the earth's evolution, have occupied different areas of the earth's surface. Thus from late Eocene to at least Miocene times the Ethiopian fauna extended into southern France, as the fossils prove.

The present blend zones show that members of adjoining faunas often prospect into each other's territories. Thus the fauna of México has the south end of the range of numerous birds that are fundamentally Nearctic and the north end of that of even more that are fundamentally Neotropical.

In fact the blending zone between the Neotropical and Nearctic faunas is quite small, and may be slowly moving north. Bermuda is shown in such a zone because it is primarily Nearctic with a small Neotropical element. Tristan da Cunha and Gough Island are apparently mainly Neotropical with an Ethiopian element.

Over a broad and mainly desert band, North Africa and Arabia share Palearctic and Ethiopian birds; and south highland Asia and south China share Palearctic and Oriental birds. East of a line between Bali and Lombok, Borneo and Celebes, a number of Oriental birds have pushed into the Australasian fauna.

Hawaii's one peculiar bird family, the honeycreepers, is of American origin; the archipelago has also been naturally colonized by members of a considerable number of cosmopolitan families, as well as by honeyeaters of doubtlessly Australasian origin. The somewhat limited number of bird species in western Alaska are mainly Nearctic with a Palearctic element.

Altitudinal Zonation

Within each great bird fauna lesser communities are arrayed in orderly ways, in habitats or ecological zones.

In no other part of the world are such life zones better marked than in the North American West, where mountain ranges rise from the desert to around 10,000 feet. Here together one day the authors motored and climbed from a subtropical Méxican environment to that of Hudson's Bay—2000 horizontal miles in one vertical mile.

Roger Peterson has painted some of the birds we saw in each zone that are typical of it, and prefer it so much to adjacent zones that they seldom stray from it.

We started in the Lower Austral zone of the desert of Arizona. Around 3000 feet we found a land of mesquite and chaparral, cholla and other full desert plants, with willow and cottonwoods in the river channels.

The Upper Austral zone, around 5000 feet, had sycamore groves; hot canyon slopes with live oaks; yuccas, agaves, and semidesert plants, each with its typical birds.

Next, around 7500 feet in the Transition zone, Arizona pine ousted the live oaks and brought in new birds. In the Canadian zone at 8200 feet, the forest had become more fir than pine, with moist, open, flowery glades.

Over 9000 feet we were in yet another zone, the Hudsonian, dominated by the Engelmann spruce; and if we had made our climb farther north, in California, we should have found an Arctic-alpine zone above that.

Altitudinal zonation, most clearly marked in North America, is also very clear in the Andes, the mountain systems of Africa, the Himalayas, the central Asian mountains, and the mountains of tropical islands like Borneo. In the temperate mountains of New Zealand and Europe they are not so well marked, and indeed in Europe there are relatively few birds that can be called montane specialists.

Nowhere in Europe would it be possible to identify six well-marked altitudinal zones, as we can in North America. In the Alps, for instance, we can find at most a deciduous but not a desert zone in the valley bottoms, equivalent to the American Upper Austral zone; a coniferous zone above, on the middle mountain slopes, corresponding to the Canadian and Hudsonian zones; and an Arctic-alpine zone above the tree line, with choughs and snow finches (which are not finches but members of the weaver family).

Life zones to be met with in the mountains of Arizona, and some of the birds typical of each.

Black-throated gray wa

White-winged dove

Lucy's warbler

ARCTIC-ALPINE ZONE

Gray-crowned rosy finch

Clark's nutcracker

HUDSONIAN ZONE

Golden-crowned kinglet

CANADIAN ZONE

ove : further north high
cky Mountains bring in
other birds and one
re zone.

Evening grosbeak   Red crossbill   Mexican chickadee

TRANSITION ZONE

Pigmy nuthatch   Western bluebird   Broad-tailed hummingbird   Coues's flycatcher   Red-faced warbler

UPPER AUSTRAL ZONE

s oriole   Cassin's kingbird   Mexican jay   Acorn woodpecker   Virginia's warbler

LOWER AUSTRAL ZONE

w-breasted   Vermilion
flycatcher   Cactus wren

Black-chinned
hummingbird   Black phoebe

Tropical Forest Zonation

For his great study, *The Birds of the Belgian Congo,* Dr. James P. Chapin worked in the heartland of tropical Africa for many years, following the game paths worn by elephants and buffalo in one of the most luxuriant virgin forests in the world. In a smallish area as many as 70 different species of great tree could be found. Upon their trunks orchids, ferns, mosses, liverworts, and the beardy *Usnea* lichen grew profusely at all levels.

Dr. Chapin found that the birds of the Ituri Forest occupied three levels. A distinctive community lived on or near the ground; a different one lived around mid-tree level, "keeping low down enough to be in dense shade"; and a third group inhabited the tops of the trees. In other tropical forests we find much the same thing, though of course the *members* of the three communities are quite different. In the American forests, for instance, the singing birds that eat ants on the ground mostly belong to peculiarly Neotropical families such as the ant thrushes and the ant pipits, whereas the ant birds of Africa belong mainly to the bulbul and thrush-flycatcher families. Except for the Congo peacock pair (inset) all the birds shown opposite are birds of the Ituri Forest.

Typical treetop birds are the green pigeons; one of four is just alighting on an upper branch in search of fruit. Below it the gray-chinned sunbird feeds not only on flower-nectar but on red fruit and insects. Perched highest, the giant plantain eater (a touraco) is another fruit-bird, while the red-bellied malimbe under it is an insect-eating weaver. On the wing, a blue-breasted kingfisher snaps up flying termites. Another insect-eater, the golden-crowned woodpecker, hacks for larvae; and a male emerald cuckoo perches with a caterpillar in its beak. A small parrot, the black-collared lovebird, looks around for ripe figs. Two rare swifts—Chapin's spinetails—are hunting winged ants; and above all soars that great bird, the crowned hawk eagle, seeking monkeys.

Many of the mid-level birds hunt in the shade in mixed parties; and all those shown here are insect-eaters. From left to right we meet the gray-breasted paradise flycatcher, which usually moves rather nervously along about 30 feet from the ground; the abundant buff-spotted woodpecker that lives on little black ants that build earthy nests in trees; the shining drongo, member of a bold flycatching family that seldom leaves the 20- to 30-foot zone of the primeval forest; a pair of Jameson's antpeckers—these waxbills continually seek ants and other insects among the leaves and have never been seen on the ground; the common West African nicator, a bulbul that specializes in grasshoppers, katydids and the like; and the crested malimbe, a weaver fond of beetles and cicadas.

On the forest floor of tropical America we have encountered diverse ant birds (page 66) that follow army ants. Their African counterparts follow driver ants in the same way to eat them, or the insects that they flush or leave part eaten. Four of the birds figured opposite live this life: the bulbul on the left—the green-tailed bristle-bill; the fire-crested ant chat next to it, which is a thrush; the white-tailed ant thrush on the ground; and the partridge-like forest francolins. The blue-headed wood doves are looking for seeds or slugs, and the hovering waxbill (the chestnut-breasted negro finch) for caterpillars.

Zonation of birds in Ituri Forest (Congo). Inset: Not found in Ituri, but on floor of other forests of Upper Congo, is Congo peacock (pair), only peacock known in Africa, described by Dr. Chapin, 1936.

Swainson's hawk
S. America to U.S., Canada

Barn swallow
Argentina to Canada

Chimney swift
Perú to U.S., Canada

Common crane
N. Africa to n. Europe

Common cuckoo
S. Africa to Europe

Some champion long-distance travelers from various parts of the world as they appear in spring migration.

The Migrants

In the Arctic the winter makes life impossible for all but a few very hardy and specialized birds; but the short summer is a time of snow-melt, quick plant-growth and insect life: food is comparatively abundant.

In temperate countries there is always more food in summer and autumn than in winter and spring.

In many parts of the tropics there are wet and dry seasons, usually with a special abundance of food after the wet season.

This seasonal change in the abundance of food governs the life of birds. Nearly all fit their breeding season to the greatest supply of food. But many just cannot survive in their breeding place at the hardest time of year.

Quite a number of animals, it is true, solve the winter problem by hibernation—by going into a long sleep, with lowered temperature and breathing rate and thus little loss of energy during the period of food-shortage. However, only one bird (so far) is known to hibernate truly—the poor-will of the North American West, whose temperature may drop from a normal level of 42°c in activity to as low as 13.3°c during its long winter sleep.

The poor-will is quite exceptional. Birds normally solve the seasonal food-supply problem in quite a different way: by migration. Nearly half the birds of the world—over 4000 species—are animals with two addresses, a summer home and a winter home.

To understand the extent to which birds migrate let us consider an arctic country, a temperate Old World country, and a mostly tropical New World country.

Of the 64 species of birds regularly found in Greenland no fewer than 36 leave the great island entirely for the winter. Most of the remaining 28 migrate to south Greenland or to the seas off its shore. Perhaps only ptarmigan, black guillemot, snowy owl, fieldfare, and raven are true residents,

Blackpoll warbler, S. America to Canada

Pintail
México to Alaska

Gray-cheeked thrush
Brazil to Canada

Spotted flycatcher
Africa to Europe

Arctic warbler
S. Asia to Siberia, Alaska

White stork
S. Africa to Eurasia

Bobolink
Argentina to n. U.S., Canada

Common nighthawk
S. America to U.S., Canada

Rufous hummingbird
México to w. Canada, Alaska

Franklin's gull
Perú to n. cent. U.S., Canada

Gray-headed albatross
S. Oceans to Antarctic

Arctic skua
S. Oceans to Arctic

American golden plover
Argentina to Arctic

Sooty shearwater
N. Oceans to S. Oceans

Gray (red) phalarope
S. Oceans to Arctic

Wilson's storm petrel
N. Atlantic to Antarctic

White-rumped sandpiper
Argentina to Arctic

Penguins disperse far after breeding. Rockhopper breeds on far-south islands, swims thousands of miles from base in ocean tours.

birds of (almost) fixed address that winter near their nesting-places.

About 240 species of birds are regular in Britain and Ireland. About 55 (23%) are summer visitors only, 27 (11%) winter visitors only, 20 (8%) migrants that breed farther north and winter farther south and are seen only on passage Many others migrate within the countries.

About 950 species of birds have been found in México. Of these about 750 (79%) are resident; the other 200 (21%) are either winter visitors or passage-migrants.

Even in the tropics, then, a big minority of the bird community is migrant. Elsewhere the migrant species easily outnumber those resident.

Over 60% of all the families of birds have migrant members; each of the 22 bird species shown on pages 114–5, as well as the rockhopper figured above, comes from a different one, and is what Abel Chapman once called a "globe-spanner."

All the members of many modern genera of birds are very strongly migratory; and we may safely assume that when these genera appeared for the first time they were then at least capable of long-distance movement. Now fossils of modern genera first appear at the end of Eocene times. What may be a curlew, *Numenius,* is known from the Uppermost Eocene deposits of France, about 43 million years old. Birds from France at the threshold of Eocene and Oligocene (37 or 38 million) include four modern genera, of which the wader, *Tringa,* and sound grouse, *Pterocles,* are good migrants.

Another good migrant, the buzzard genus *Buteo,* is first found in the Middle Oligocene of South Dakota (about 32 million); and if we examine the swarm of modern genera in the Upper Oligocene of France (about 28 million) we find many excellent migrants, such as shearwaters, geese, ducks, kites, waders, gulls, swifts, wagtails, and Old World warblers.

Billions of birds belonging to nearly half the world's species pour along the flyways of the world each fall, and rather fewer billions pour back each spring. ("Billions" is here used in the American sense, to mean thousands of millions, not English fashion, to mean millions of millions.) Migration is often on a broad front, but more often by favored routes, along coasts, through mountain passes, along hill ridges where the prevailing winds give air-lift, over deserts where by day the hot air rises and saves the migrants' energy—for on protracted flights energy-saving is all-important.

All this has been going on for tens or scores of millions of years. The cranes flew and the swallows assembled in twittering bands long, long before there were any men to see them, let alone poets to sing of spring and fall, and ornithologists with binoculars and banding-stations to measure the great treks of the birds.

Great these treks are. Africa is a most hospitable winter home of migrants. Nearly a third of all the small birds that breed in Britain winter south of the Sahara desert. Nearly as many birds go to Africa from Central Asia as do from Europe. Some small land birds even go to Africa from the Far East; and the wheatear reaches it from Alaska, 7000 miles away.

Tiny birds, like the arctic warbler and the yellow wagtail, travel all the way from Alaska to tropical Southeast Asia and back. Between North and South America, and Europe and South Africa, the barn swallow can fly at least 7000 miles out, 7000 back.

Greatest globe spanner in distance covered is the arctic tern. Breeders in the Arctic and N. Atlantic area winter at the edge of the frozen Antarctic Continent or on the shores of the Indian Ocean. One arctic tern was banded as a nestling in West Greenland on July 8, 1951. On October 30 of the same year it was picked up dead at Durban on the east coast of South Africa, having flown over 11,000 miles in its first three months on the wing.

Another bird may travel farther, though perhaps not regularly. A Manx shearwater from Wales was not long ago found in S. Australia. This is the most distant recovery of any marked bird—about 12,000 miles by the nearest sea route.

Albatrosses make vast wandering journeys, though they usually keep within their own hemisphere. The Tristan great and the sooty shearwaters, which breed far down in the south, spend a non-breeding time slowly circling the North Atlantic, 5000 miles and more from base, in our northern summer; and the little Wilson's storm petrel does the same.

These last three birds are examples of Southern Hemisphere breeders that migrate to the north. They are sea birds. The main reason why so few land birds breed in the south and migrate north is simply space. If we exclude

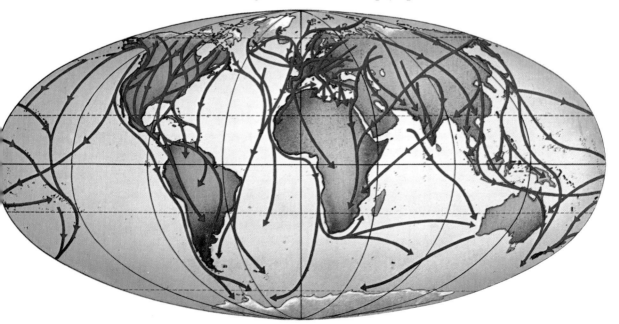

Some of the most important flyways used by migrants in September—northern fall, southern spring.

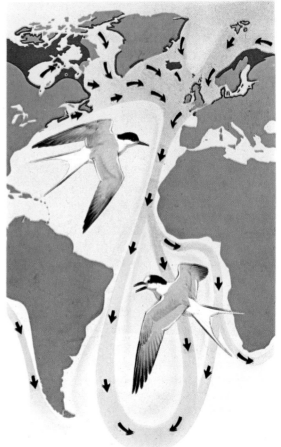

A small thrush, the wheatear, has three races. One nests in Morocco and Tunis; most widespread nests from Alaska through Eurasia—and migrates (Alaskan birds included) to winter in Arabia and Africa.

The third race, the Greenland wheatear, is the largest, but only weighs around an ounce. It nests (red) in Greenland, Labrador, and the eastern Canadian Arctic: and makes longest regular ocean journey of any small bird; for it winters in south-west Europe and West Africa.

Probably the wheatear was once a bird only of the Old World, which spread into the two corners of the New World. American birds have never lost their habit of migrating toward Africa in autumn.

From many ship observations it seems clear that in the fall the Greenland race normally makes a direct Atlantic crossing of 2000 miles. Apart from prevailing winds, the birds depend only on their own power. Against the winds, on the spring return, the Greenland wheatears "island-hop" via Scotland—Faeroes—Iceland—Greenland.

Atlantic flyways of arctic tern, greatest of all migrants.

the Antarctic, where there are practically no land birds, there is five times as much land in the Northern Hemisphere as in the southern; but the share of little birds from Patagonia that moves north in winter is just as big as the share of those in New England that moves south. Only a few Southern Hemisphere land bird breeders are known to cross the equator to winter, but some of these birds travel at least 1000 miles.

Perhaps the most remarkable transocean passages by birds that do not normally swim are made in the Pacific. The regular ocean-hop between Alaska and the Hawaiian Islands, flown by the western race of the American golden plover, exceeds 2000 miles. The bristle-thighed curlew, which breeds only in Alaska, winters over Pacific Oceania from the Hawaiian Islands south and west. Some of the wandering tattlers from the American northwest have a similar winter range. The banded plover of New Zealand regularly crosses to Australia; and two New Zealand cuckoos, the shining and the long-tailed, regularly make the long ocean journey to New Caledonia, the Solomons, and Polynesia.

Migration involves risks; yet it is worth the steady toll of bird lives lost by exhaustion and the perils of changed weather. It is the most remarkable adaptation that the most mobile of the world's animals have won. Millions of years of evolution by natural selection, on the basis of the muscled wing, have secured that no rock in the loneliest ocean, no oasis in the broadest desert, is unvisited by birds.

Typical day migrants of North America: 1. Chimney swift, winters to Peru; 2. Barn swallow, to Chile and Argentina (same species as Old World swallow); 3. American robin, to Guatemala; 4. American goldfinch, to México; 5. Blue jay, to southern United States; 6. Red-winged blackbird, to Costa Rica.

Bird Navigation

Men have recognized the homing ability of certain birds—notably pigeons—since the dawn of civilization. Yet, oddly, until quite recent times it was hard to prove that birds can be true navigators. For many years pigeon fanciers trained their birds to home from one direction only, increasing step by step the distances from which they were released. Experiments in the early years of this century showed that pigeons trained to home, say, from the north often tended to start flying southward when released from, say, east or west of their lofts. Further, when homings from unaccustomed directions were timed they often showed that journeys were slow, leaving open the possibility that the birds spent much of their time searching for familiar landmarks.

Today there are ample proofs of birds' prowess as navigators. Some 30 years ago our friend R. M. Lockley sent two Manx shearwaters from their nesting burrows on Skokholm Island, in Wales, by air to Venice, where they were released at once. The Adriatic Sea is outside the range of the Welsh race of shearwater; the Alps intervened between the birds and home; yet one homed in 14 days. By sea (which shearwaters prefer) the journey was 3700 miles; by land 930.

In June 1952, another Skokholm shearwater was released at Boston airport in Massachusetts—also outside its normal range. Its shortest Atlantic passage home was close on 3100 miles; and it was back in 12½ days.

Many other homing experiments have now been made with results almost as spectacular. They prove that birds have wonderful homing ability, even when homing involves crossing large tracts of land or sea utterly strange to them. All migrants are natural navigators; most non-migrants are provable navigators, too.

Night migrants of North America: 1. Red-eyed vireo, winters to Peru; 2. Swainson's thrush, to Argentina; 3. White-crowned sparrow, to México and Cuba; 4. Black-throated green warbler, to Panamá and Greater Antilles; 5. Rose-breasted grosbeak, to Ecuador; 6. Great crested flycatcher, to Colombia.

In the last three decades Matthews in England, Kramer and Sauer in Germany, and many other experimenters have shown that although bird navigation is still mysterious, at least the mysteries are now probably limited.

Birds navigate by sight, with a built-in "chronometer" or innate time sense; and as guides they use the sun by day, the stars and doubtless the moon by night. That they can sense magnetic forces, or forces at work in their internal ears due to the earth's rotation, seems to have been effectively disproved. Birds do not learn the basic techniques of navigation. These are born with them, though they may be improved by experience.

Geoffrey Matthews and the late Gustav Kramer have positively established sun navigation among birds. Matthews has suggested that a bird may be able to extrapolate the sun's movement, forward or back, to its highest point of the day, and by its in-built time sense get both latitude and longitude. This possibility depends on the fact that at any given latitude there is a sun-arc that is inclined to the horizontal at an angle that is characteristic of that latitude only. On any given day the highest point of the sun-arc, marking the sun's noon position, is thus different in every latitude. So if, from a brief sighting of the sun and an innate awareness of time, the bird can establish the highest point of the sun-arc in the place where it finds itself, it will be aware of its present latitude. By comparing how far the sun has traveled along the local sun-arc with how far it would, at the moment of observation, have traveled along the home sun-arc, the bird will also "know" its longitude.

With his ingenious planetarium experiments and other observations Sauer has gone far toward proving that birds are born with an innate knowledge of the constellations, and that the night-flying migrants use them normally, and naturally, and unconsciously in a style that Captain Cook could only attain with the help of a sextant and the newly invented chronometer.

Birds no doubt employ other techniques that experience may contribute more to than instinct. They learn the map of their neighborhood and, after they have lived a year or two, their flyways. They may exploit the set of sea-currents, use changes in temperature as guides, watch other birds of their own or other kinds, or other animals. What we can be quite certain of is that birds, without instruments, can often do better than humans with them. In overcast, though, when sun and stars are clouded out, the compass-less birds are much inferior to man. They stop migrating, if they can. Yet in complete darkness a very few flying creatures *can* navigate.

In 1940 Donald R. Griffin and Robert Galambos made the first of their wonderful proofs that bats emit a succession of high-frequency clicks and can detect the echoes of these sounds from very small or moving objects with their ultra-sensitive ears. They find their roost in the dark, and catch their insect prey by sonar.

By 1954 Griffin had proved that the oilbird—a relative of the nightjars that belongs to a family entirely of its own—also uses sonar, at a considerably lower frequency than that of bats: indeed its chirps are well within the range of human hearing. Soon others had discovered sonar among other birds of dark caves—the edible-nest swiftlets of the Philippines and East Indies. Probably our typical swifts use sonar, possibly nightjars and nighthawks do too; though it is not yet proved.

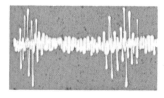

Each dot shows 10 seconds of activity pointed to a bearing by a starling Kramer caged at time of westerly migration in Europe. Movements were random in overcast (l.), directed in clear sky (r.).

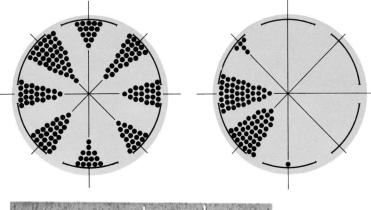

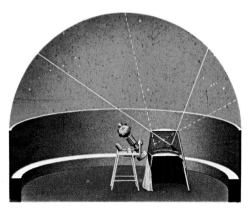

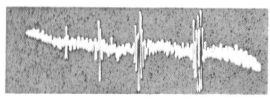

Studying night orientation in planetarium, observer in tent under cage watched bird's position as projector rotated artificial night sky. Solid line, sector visible to bird from right of perch; broken line, from left. (Diagram adapted from Sauer.)

Right: Oilbird. Above: Oscillograph records (adapted diagram) from tape recordings made by Griffin as bird flew out of a cave. The six sonar clicks appearing were uttered in a period of only one fiftieth of a second.

Population

Over half a century has elapsed since J. H. Gurney realized that it was possible to count the world population of a bird. His bird was the northern gannet; and he believed that all the colonies of this bird were known, and that it was possible to count or estimate the number of nests at each. His own guess that about 55,000 gannets' nests were occupied in 1912 was probably not far short of the truth.

Since then quite a few birds have been world censused, usually by counting nests but sometimes by counting winter flocks. Aerial photography has been used on sea bird cliffs and the feeding grounds of grazing birds. And a principle, worked out by Dr. F. C. Lincoln in 1930, enables banders who catch and mark large numbers of some birds to arrive at estimates of total populations from the number of marked birds they recapture.

All the same, very few birds with large or even average populations have been censused. One of us organized, during World War II, a census of the nests in every rookery in two thirds of the area of England, Wales and Scotland. There were nearly a million nests, and to count and plot them about 400 volunteers thoroughly covered an average of 150 square miles each. The survey was spread over three years. To extend it throughout the rook's wide range in Europe and Asia would be a major, almost military, operation.

It can thus be understood why the only birds with a population of over a million that have been fully censused are a few sea birds: it is usually much

Birds among c. 60 whose world population has been recently estimated. (Geese and crane counted in winter flocks, rest from nests occupied annually.) Few sea birds have estimated populations exceeding puffin's, but arctic murre and Wilson's petrel are doubtless far more numerous. Numbers of piquero and guanay (Perú, Chile) fluctuate widely. Estimate for royal albatross (mainly Campbell I, N Z.) includes adolescents.

Atlantic puffin 15,000,000

Northern gannet 330,000

Tristan great shearwater 4–5,000,000

Piquero 4–?40,000,000

Sandhill crane 170,000

Barnacle goose 30,000

Guanay 5–30,000,000

Ross's goose 2–3,000

Royal albatross 19,000

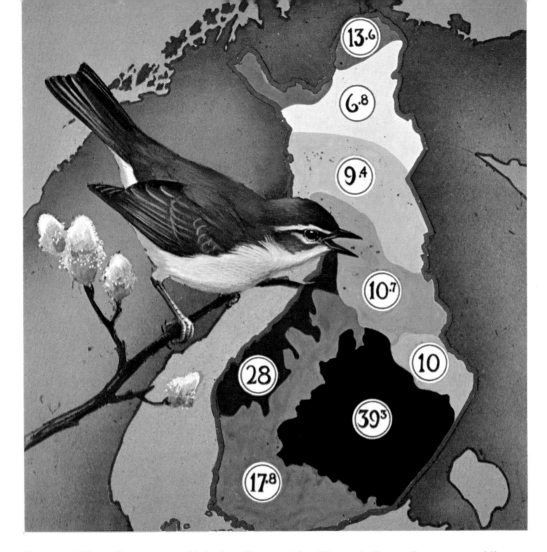

Density of Finland's commonest bird, the willow warbler. Figures indicate pairs per square kilometre.

easier to find and estimate the number of a sea bird's nests than those of an equally numerous land bird. The most abundant bird that has been the subject of a really careful and repeated census is the northern gannet. There are now 32 colonies, and the total number of nests around the late 1960s was about 166,000. The Cape gannet of Africa, from a photographic survey, had about 225,000 nests in 1956, and as this book goes to press may have nearly half a million. The Australasian gannet had about 21,000 in 1946-47 and about 27,000 in 1967.

About 60 birds have had their population estimated with more or less certainty, 14 of them sea birds, and 40 of them rarities (page 101) with numbers under 2000. Some of the more exact censuses have been of birds with small numbers. One of the best was the census of Kirtland's warbler in 1949 and 1961. This bird nests only in 32 square miles of central Michigan and nowhere else in the world. A band of good field men found every singing male in the state in both seasons (432 and 502). The world population of this bird in the spring cannot be much over 1000.

Early in the present century field workers in North America and England began to measure the density of spring breeding birds on sample areas of different kinds of land. What they did was to plot all singing males, and find as many nests as they could, so as to arrive at figures for the number of

After 5000 years of domestication fowl is by far the most numerous bird in the world today.

Starling and house sparrow. Introduced by Man into country after country, they are now probably the world's commonest wild birds.

territories of each species per unit area. This method has, through the years, been very much refined. Different habitats have been found to house very varying populations of land birds. Deserts, tundras, moors, and certain kinds of conifer forest support less than 1 bird to the acre; most agricultural land between 2 and 4; most temperate deciduous or mixed woodland 4 or 5. Gardens, orchards, parks, and open suburbs—habitats tailor-made for man's aesthetic pleasure—support anything between 6 and 20 (and in certain cases many more); tropical forests up to 20; some kinds of tropical grassland with bushy cover up to 40. Ponds and lakes support up to 2 birds per acre, sometimes more.

With suitable samples measured, and the national statistics on the total areas of each habitat to help them, ornithologists have been able to calculate the population of whole countries. Thus England, Wales, and Scotland may have about 120 million breeding land birds in a normal May, Finland about 64 million: and rough figures for all but the most scattered species can be arrived at. Probably the commonest birds in the British area are starling and blackbird, around 10 million; the house sparrow around $9\frac{1}{2}$ million; the robin and chaffinch around 7 million. In Finland the commonest bird is the willow warbler, over 11 million, followed by the chaffinch, over 10 million. Two separate estimates for the present spring land bird population of the United States have been made—at around $5\frac{1}{2}$ and 6 billion. When the passenger pigeon was in its heyday it was possibly half as much again.

The total bird population of the world, including sea birds, may be of the order of a hundred billion. By far the most abundant species now living is the domestic fowl, whose numbers may now approximate to the human population of the world, which is over 3 billion. Widely introduced by man into new countries, the common starling and house sparrow must be the most numerous wild species. It has been estimated that there are now about 150 million house sparrows in North America. One sea bird, Wilson's storm petrel, which breeds in the Antarctic and Subantarctic in formidable numbers, may be next in order of abundance.

Changing Numbers: Cycles and Irruptions

All animals vary in number: and some variations are remarkably, oddly regular. For instance, the voles, lemmings, and mice of the northern world have a rather regular four-year cycle. In some years of abundance the little animals wander in droves, cross water, and are followed by foxes and several kinds of weasels and by skuas, buzzards, harriers, and owls. In a big rodent year there is plenty of food for them to rear extra young, so the animals of prey usually have peaks of number in the next year.

The snowy owl is a rarish winter visitor to the United States from the North American Arctic. But after most of the big rodent years—that is, about every fourth winter—the lovely white birds invade south in unusual numbers. In the winter of 1926/27 so many snowy owls were shot in New England that a Boston bird stuffer had to cable to Europe for 250 extra pairs of glass eyes. Fortunately, sportsmen do not shoot so many now.

In Norway the changes in the numbers of the willow ptarmigan often go for many years with the four-year rodent cycle. This may be a coincidence, for ptarmigan and grouse do not depend on, or indeed ever eat, rodents, though some of the animals that eat them also eat rodents, and part of what they eat is also eaten by rodents. Not all grouse cycles are of four years, though. The cycles of the British red grouse (a race of the willow ptarmigan that does not go white in winter) vary from 3 to 10 years, with an average of 5·3. Black game cycles seem to average about 4½ years. In North America the grouse cycle is about twice as long as that in the Old World, and for several species runs between 9 and 11 years.

Other population changes seem to be quite irregular. In 1863 and again in 1888 a strange bird arrived along the whole east coast of England and Scotland and spread west as far as Ireland and the Hebrides. In 1888 Pallas's sand grouse even nested in Denmark, England and Scotland. Since 1909 it has invaded western Europe now and then, but never so far west from its nearest regular home in the half-desert scrub of southeastern European Russia.

In England we are finding that stocks of quite common birds like blue and great tits invade now and then from the Continent. Some of the more usual irruptive birds (as we call them) of the northern world are red- and white-winged crossbills and the Bohemian waxwing. While writing this book, both

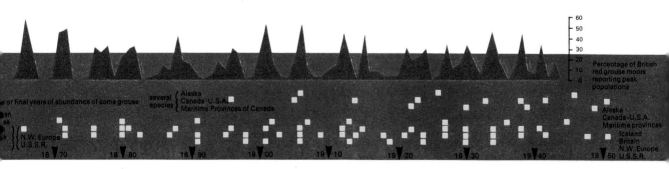

Numbers of most species of grouse show rhythmical fluctuations. Over a long stretch of time such as that dealt with above, cycle's period may average 4⅔ years in Old World, twice as much in New World.

125

Snowy owl and brown lemming

of us watched invasions of red-breasted nuthatches and boreal chickadees in North America. In England it was a waxwing winter, and waxwing invasions have been getting more common lately. Among the finches a frequent invader in North America is the pine siskin, in Europe the brambling. Western Europe is irregularly visited in summer and autumn by the rosy starling, which normally ranges no farther than rocky plains in Hungary.

What makes bird numbers change? A partial answer is food-supply. Many of the irruptive birds are driven to travel by bad weather or the failure of a food-crop, or both. Many of the cycle birds are so because their food has cycles. One of the causes of the regular cycles may be the lag period between the abundance of food and the abundance of the eater. Lemmings go up: and in the *next* year snowy owls are common. The lemmings increase, push up the owls' numbers; the owls increase, push down the lemmings' numbers; the lemmings decrease, push down the owls' numbers; the owls decrease, push up the lemmings' numbers. Like a see-saw, the owl-lemming relationship may produce a rhythm. But this cannot be the whole story, for we must bring in weather-cycles and other natural rhythms.

Meteorologists have found weather-cycles of various kinds ranging from 41 months through $3\frac{2}{3}$, $7\frac{1}{2}$, $9\frac{2}{3}$; $11 \cdot 2$ and $22 \cdot 3$ (these two linked with sunspots); 35, 45, 68, 90, 170 to 510 years—and some much longer periods. Our planet is full of cycles of change, which may support each other or cancel each other out, and some of which affect the birds.

A winter of unusual severity can deplete bird populations enormously. During the exceptionally hard winter that Britain suffered in 1962-63, at least a quarter of the indigenous species had their numbers reduced by half or more; and birds which in Britain are near the northern limit of their breeding ranges were among those to suffer most. Hardest hit were kingfishers, gray wagtails, goldcrests, stonechats, wrens, barn owls, snipe, and long-tailed tits.

When a high percentage of their numbers is wiped out, most birds show remarkable powers of recovery. Those that have large clutches, and especially those that also have more than one brood, tend to recover in two or three years. Slower-breeding birds, such as herons, may take four or five years.

White-winged crossbill

Rosy starling

Bohemian waxwing

Red-breasted nuthatch

Willow ptarmigan

Pallas's sand grouse

Changing Numbers: Long-term Trends

During the present century there has been a general improvement in the climate of late spring and early summer in Europe. New birds have settled as regular nesters in Iceland, the Faeroes, Britain, and Scandinavia.

Among land birds the most extraordinary spread over Europe was that of the collared dove (see map, page 131). This bird from Asia had an outpost in the Balkans till about 1912. It reached Hungary in about 1928. It enlarged its range by 1200 miles in 20 years, now breeds in a broad belt with its northwest end in the Scottish Highlands and Ireland, has been recorded in Iceland, and is still increasing fast.

The collared dove has little fear of man and likes places where there is waste grain, including zoos. The climatic change may have aided its spread, but this must also have been helped by the dove's natural attachment to human settlements and the Europeans' liking for birds.

Even more spectacular has been the saga of the fulmar. The spread of this sea bird from the Arctic has taken place in the wrong direction to have had anything to do with the improving climate, and is probably due to Man. Two hundred years ago the fulmars started founding new colonies, when the arctic whaling was at its height. Whales were stripped of their blubber at ship's side in the Greenland ice. The fulmars, which go mad about blubber, found free meals throughout the breeding season from bases in Iceland. And just when the whaling began to peter out, another industry—trawling—took its place in the North Atlantic. To this day, thousands of fulmars attend trawlers for offal, liver, unwanted fish, and squids. Although the fulmar

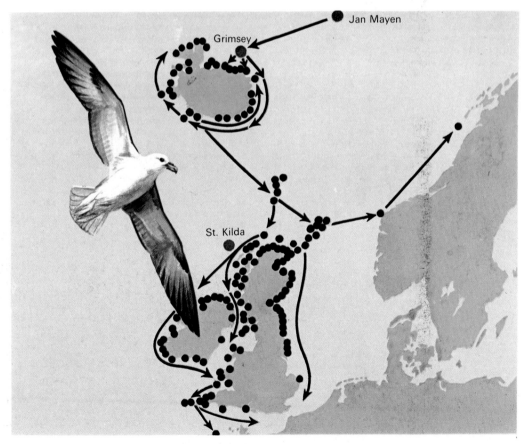

In 200 years the fulmar has established about 1000 colonies (black dots show main groups), some over 2000 miles from its two old northern bases (red). St. Kilda (also red) is a doubtful source of spread.

breeds slowly, it has multiplied throughout its new range, nested first in the Faeroes in about 1816, in Shetland in 1878, and in the Hebrides (apart from St. Kilda) in 1886. After 1900 it founded breeding colonies all around Britain and Ireland, in Norway, and in Brittany. The spread may continue as long as trawlers make waste.

Great spreads have not infrequently followed introductions by Man. The natural range of the common starling was Europe and western Asia: now, having been introduced into North America, Australia, Africa, numerous new areas of Asia, and many islands, it has a range that excludes no great landmasses other than South America and Antarctica. In North America introduced birds started breeding in 1890-91. After a short pause they made a wildfire colonization of the entire USA and much of Canada and México.

In New Zealand man-made introductions almost balance (though they do not extenuate) man-induced extinctions. When the Polynesians first discovered New Zealand, around A.D. 950, the archipelago had about 150 bird species, including 22 moas and other flightless birds. Since then a total of 45 native species have become extinct. But from the mid-19th century onward, when Europeans (urged on by acclimatization societies and private enthusiasts) started introducing birds, 35 new species have been successfully established. Among English passerine birds now flourishing in New Zealand are house sparrow, starling, goldfinch and rook (introduced in 1862); skylark and chaffinch (1864); blackbird (1865); hedge sparrow and song thrush (1867); cirl bunting (1871); bullfinch (1875); and siskin (1879).

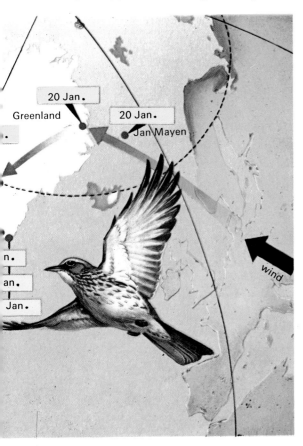 

Left: Fieldfare's wind-aided invasion of south-west Greenland in January, 1937. Right: Cattle egret's invasion of New World from W. Africa (which began a few years earlier) may also have been gale-assisted.

'55
'50
'45
'40
'35
.30
'25

1955
1950
1945
1940
1935
1925
1920
1910
1905
1915
1920

1925
1930
1935
1955

1935
1940

March of European starling's breeding range across North America from Central Park, New York City, where bird was introduced in 1890.

Several of the introductions into New Zealand have become self-spread from the main islands to outlying archipelagos—even as far as the Chatham Islands, 600 miles to the east. And since Europeans began keeping records at least eight *natural* colonists have reached New Zealand from Australia.

From their native Palearctic range house sparrows have been introduced over much of the world; and there is little evidence that they have anywhere done harm. Yet the story of introductions is not always as happy. It has certainly not been so in Hawaii, where 14 native birds became extinct between 1837 and 1945, while rather more came to face the danger of extinction. Although it is thought that the collapse of the native fauna is partly due to natural causes, partly to over-hunting and habitat-destruction, there is no doubt that it is also importantly due to competition from introduced species, and to the avian diseases that they have brought with them.

Not all introductions are purposefully made. Many birds have gone feral outside their natural range after escaping from aviaries or cages. The large number of budgerigars now breeding wild in Florida are the descendants of (ineffectually) caged pets. The goshawk, which became extinct in England as a breeding bird well over a century ago, has re-established a small population there since about 1938; this may be mainly or even wholly due to the nesting of escaped falconers' birds.

Similar accidental introductions into Britain (as elsewhere) have often been among the Anatids—much cherished birds of aviculture. The Canada goose, first kept by British aviculturists in about 1670, has been feral almost ever since; the mandarin duck from northeast Asia, kept in captivity since 1745 or possibly earlier, went feral in 1929 or 1930 and is now spreading. The ruddy duck of North America, which has been in British aviculture

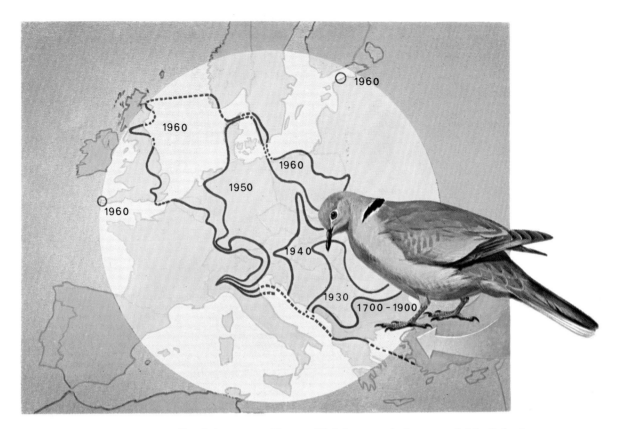

March of breeding range of collared dove across Europe. Bird has recently been recorded in Iceland.

since 1936, has now colonized Somerset, presumably from the Wildfowl Trust collection at Slimbridge, Gloucestershire; it also bred ferally in Hertfordshire in 1965.

In 1889 Lord Lilford, a keen aviculturist, reintroduced into England a bird unknown there since remote prehistoric times: the little owl. From his estate in Northamptonshire it has since spread to every English county, every Welsh county, and a few counties just over the Scottish border. Long hated by game sportsmen, it has now been recognized as having no adverse effect on the status of native wild birds, and has been given a clean bill.

Sometimes a bird has been brought to a new range that suits it by nature, not Man. A gale may have blown cattle egrets to South America from West Africa. They were first certainly seen in British Guiana in 1930, and in Florida in 1941 or 1942. Twenty years later their New World range ran from northeast Perú to the Caribbean and Atlantic states of the USA, and Ontario in Canada; and wanderers had been found as far as Newfoundland and the Midwest of the United States.

Everywhere throughout its New World spread the cattle egret has become an associate of cattle, previously introduced, of course, by Man. But there have been windborne spreads of birds whose success has had no man's help. Most of the bird species peculiar to remote islands must be descended from wind-blown ancestors.

A fine example of wind-colonization is the conquest of Greenland by the fieldfare. The actual strong gale from the southeast, which drove a flock of colonists across the Atlantic, is known. The survivors eventually found the only part of Greenland that grows birch-woods to their taste—down in the southwest—and their descendants live there naturally to this day.

Social breeder: On Bonaventure Island in Québec the gannet has its largest colony in the New World. On broad flat ledges nesters sit just out of beak range of neighbors, occupy just over a square yard.

6   Bird Society

Sociability

All successful and numerous birds appear to be in some way sociable, in their breeding life, their feeding life, or their traveling life. Perhaps the least sociable birds are some eagles, hawks, falcons, and owls.

All the true sea birds are sociable on their breeding grounds. Only on a few remote tropic islets are nesting birds crowded because the space is limited: and here the sea birds may even take turns and nest in "shifts." But most sea bird colonies are at places long favored by tradition, with unoccupied but suitable spaces between. The breeders gather because it is in their nature to gather.

Very much a social breeder is Wilson's storm petrel. When the famous American ornithologist Alexander Wilson first described it in 1813 he failed to give it a Linnaean name; he had discovered it on the North American coast, and thought it was the same species as the British storm petrel. In fact this bird spends the northern summer in the Indian Ocean, the Red Sea, the Pacific, and the Atlantic, commonly visiting the North American coast from April through September. In the northern winter (southern summer) it congregates in colossal breeding colonies in the Antarctic seas, where the vastness of its feeding flocks within range of the colonies gives rise to the wide opinion among ornithologists that it is the most numerous of all sea birds.

The pioneer student and mapper of the distribution of Wilson's storm petrel, our friend Brian Roberts of the Scott Polar Research Institute in Cambridge, England, started the field study that established the pattern of the bird's seasonal movements while in the Argentine Islands off Graham Land with the British expedition of 1934–37. But it has not so far proved possible to conduct anything approaching an exact census of this interesting bird. Like all members of the storm petrel family, it breeds in burrows and is very hard to count.

Among the auk family, the puffinry at St. Kilda, westernmost of the Scottish islands, has lately been of the order of a million birds; the combined puffinry and guillemotry of Bear Island, northern Norway, probably numbers over a million; and there are several auk colonies in Canadian Franklin that are as large or larger.

Around the Antarctic the *combined* rookeries of sea bird colonies on suitable capes and islands often number a million; many are dominated by penguins, such as the royal penguin on Macquarie Island, the gentoo penguin in the Falklands, and the Adélie penguin on or near the Antarctic Continent.

In temperate zones populations are not generally as big, though in South Africa there may be over half a million jackass penguins breeding on Dassen Island, off the Cape. In the tropics the biggest sea bird colonies are probably those of the sooty tern, which nests in hundreds of thousands in many archipelagos, particularly the Seychelles.

On land some social breeders have enormous colonies. Rooks are the commonest large birds in Great Britain. Rookeries usually contain a few score nests, often over a hundred, and sometimes thousands. But rooks have a second level of social organization—the autumn roost, to which thousands of individuals adhere, usually from within about 10 miles' radius. Rookeries, with all their members, "belong" to particular roosts: as populations grow, rookeries, and sometimes roosts, may "burst" and bud off new satellites, probably colonized by young birds.

But the record-holding social breeder among living land birds is the red-billed quelea of Africa, whose nesting colonies can outnumber even those of the guanays, of Perú's guano islands.

Within a social group of birds two forces or drives conflict. A social drive makes birds seek each other's company; an anticrowding drive makes birds repel each other when they get too close for comfort. Gannets' nests on flat rock are spaced evenly just beyond beak range. Starlings in a roost (some roosts can house over a million) jostle until they get out of touch. Swallows gathering on a wire have their individual distance. Waders on passage pack tight on small sandbars where food is abundant, then bicker till each has won room to probe undisturbed.

Social feeder: The marbled godwit, one of the largest waders of North America, probes the sands of California beaches in flocks as it passes north in spring. Flockers gain mutual protection from enemies.

Some social birds have a very low anticrowding drive. The passenger pigeon used to roost in huge solid masses, with typical nestings covering areas of rather more than 30 square miles; in 1869 over $7\frac{1}{2}$ million birds were sent to market from just one of them. This unfortunate bird may have been *too* sociable: when its great flocks were broken up by hunters its surviving groups quickly collapsed and faded fast to extinction.

The advantages of some kinds of sociability are easy to understand. Sociable flockers gain mutual protection from enemies, are able to find and share massed food-supplies evenly. The advantages of nesting sociability are less easy to prove. Large colonies tend to produce a higher proportion of young than small colonies; but many small colonies consist largely of inexperienced birds that are nesting for the first time: birds that have not bred do far more pioneering and colony-founding than old ones, which tend to be true to the site where they have already nested. Social breeders certainly find mates more easily than non-social breeders, and are more highly stimulated to go through their yearly cycle.

Many birds travel in flocks: the geese that nest in the north pack on their nesting grounds when the adults are in flightless molt and the goslings are growing their first flight feathers. All become full winged at about the same time and soon migrate south, sometimes across great distances of sea. The traveling flocks often adopt a V form, and may be led by experienced birds. When they arrive on their winter grounds they spread out evenly over the grazing, moving steadily under "pressure" from those at the back so that all get a fair sample; and within each moving group are lesser groups—the mated geese and ganders with their young of the year—showing that family ties are still strong in the broader community.

This is England, not New England; for no American crow nests in large rookeries like the Old World rook. This gregarious bird also has a second and much bigger social organization, the autumn roost.

Great frigate bird, courtship

Wallace's standard wing, aggression or courtship

Display

Above the roosts of European starlings, member flocks often indulge in beautiful aerial shows as they home in at dusk, the whole flock maneuvering around the roost place in a cloud with pulsating boundaries before finally settling. This is doubtless a social dance that keeps the flock together and celebrates its togetherness.

Every day of its life, a bird makes hundreds of signals, of many different sorts, in response to birds of its own or other kinds, to other animals, or to noises or light or other changes in its surroundings. It makes use of its colors, shape and adornments to produce patterns of enthralling beauty.

In short, birds display: and by display can hide from enemies, surprise prey or competitors, give signals to flee, approach, scatter, or band together, deflect or distract enemies from their young, mimic fiercer or more dangerous animals, recognize or find their own mates and families, court or intimidate or submit to their own kind, and make many other demands and statements. Birds talk as much with ritual movements of their bodies, with mime and dance, as with their voices.

The most wonderful of birds' displays are those of breeding time. Among a great many species bright colors and fantastic shapes and adornments have

Adélie penguin, greeting

White stork, greeting

been evolved solely for courting mates or for threatening sexual rivals.

On tropical islets the great frigate bird males attract the females to mate with them and start nest building by perching on a bush, opening their wings, rocking to and fro, inflating huge red throat-pouches to the size of toy balloons and trumpeting a loud greeting which one observer has written *trr trr trr kyu, kyukyu yu huhuhuhu.*

In courtship the little Adélie penguin has an ecstatic ritual in which the bird slowly upstretches head and bill, beats flippers in jerks, throws out its chest and makes a crescendo of drum-like noise whose climax ending has been written *Ku-ku-ku-ku-ku-kug-gu-gu-gu-gu-ga-aaaa.* Pairs bow deeply to each other in the early days of their mated life; and in the most typical mutual display face each other with up-pointed bills, eyes rolled down and back, crests raised and flippers at their sides, and sway with a raucous braying that can be heard half a mile away. Sometimes mutual display starts when a bird brings a stone to its mate at the nest-site.

On a pebbly shore the gift of a stone can have no utilitarian value, but to the Adélie it may well serve as a sexual stimulant. Gifts of food, common among many birds during courtship, also have more sexual than nutritional significance. A female herring gull fresh from feeding will beg food from her mate; so will a hen European robin surrounded by food and with her beak filled with insects. And while, during incubation, male birds will often bring their mates food *as* food, presenting it with little ceremony, many prefer, during courtship, to make a special occasion of the offering. Notable among them is the male tern, which holds a fish in his up-pointed beak, spreads his wings level with his back, erects his tail, and minces around his mate with precise steps before presenting his gift.

The greeting ceremonies of mated birds at their nests have been admired by writers back to the poets of ancient Rome. Petronius liked the stork with its "bill rattling like castanets." Sometimes, at the changeover, white storks bend their heads right back until their crowns nearly touch their backs and then bring them right forward and down, clappering their bills all the time.

Many birds have special display grounds. Male racket-tailed humming-birds assemble at certain spots and hover opposite each other with their bodies vertical, bobbing from side to side with clicking sounds, and curve their tails under themselves so as to frame their faces with the rackets at the end of them.

Male birds of paradise have meeting places where they spend much time bluffing their rivals with incredible postures, using all their colors and adornments, and eventually find mates. Wallace's standard wing has been described in its posturing as slowly raising and stretching as if it were in a fit. In another part of its display it back-somersaults from its perch and lands with closed wings.

One of the most beautiful waders has no two males alike. Ruffs in spring grow huge fans of feathers on head and nape that in full display rise to form circles of bright color around their heads. At the traditional "hills," the males crouch facing each other, shivering with erected ruffs, and bluff each other. Seldom do they really fight. The females, the reeves, are not even always present at the hill; but come there to choose their mates.

The display grounds of black grouse are known as "leks." The cocks can be found at them most regularly in March and April. They stimulate each other by crowing and jumping: stand with spread tail, swollen head-combs, head and much-swollen neck thrust forward, and shake as they make a

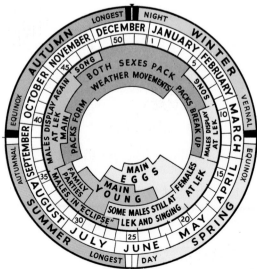

Yearly cycle of black grouse

Blackcock at the 'lek'

138

musical, bubbling *roo-koo* noise at rivals: and having thus carved out territories or "courts" for themselves on the lek they court the grey hens there with a circling, crouching dance ritual.

Birds sometimes transfer their aggressive displays to animals of other species; but this is comparatively rare, and is often caused by a superfluity of aggressive energy that is triggered off by the wrong signal. Avian aggression is mainly sex aggression, shown within the species.

In social birds there can also be food aggression. In a flock of such birds there is commonly a pecking order, developed by trial and error, which expresses the order of all-round prestige within the group. The dominant bird gains the right to peck all the rest; the most subservient is pecked by all.

Birds that establish a pecking order include chickens, swans, geese, ducks, waders, herons, storks, cranes, crows and even such social singing birds as sparrows, tits, finches and warblers. Among some species the decision as to which of two birds shall dominate the other is made as the result of a single fight, precedence going to the outright winner or the one last to show fear; among others dominance is achieved only after a whole series of minor jostlings and squabblings.

The pecking order is largely an order of sexual prestige, but also constitutes an order of feeding precedence. In the course of establishing it, most species make threat displays or threat sounds. And when two minor birds are trying to work out their place in the hierarchy a major bird may see both of them off.

Bird display constitutes a major part of total bird behavior; not only is it fascinating in its own right but it can also contribute much to our understanding of the evolutionary relationship between various bird families. This is one reason why many ornithologists, professionals and amateurs alike, devote much time and care to recording bird display with cinecamera and tape recorder.

Ruffs at the 'hill'

Territory

Chir'ri-tew! Ir'ri-tew! Wis'-yoo, Wis'-yoo! Wee'!-Swee'!-Tew-ay'! Tew, tew', tew, Psee'! Chirri-wee'! Tyo-to'! Se-Wis'sy-wissy, Wis'sy-wissy, Wee'!

Some years ago an English zoology professor, Walter Garstang, wrote an odd and charming little book, *Songs of the Birds.* This was one of his versions of the fall song of the darting, bobbing, bold, and tame little bird that all English-speaking Europeans call robin; not to be confused with that bigger thrush, the American robin.

The sweet song of cock robins begins at Christmas, trickles and tinkles like flickering waterfalls on a pebbly streambed nearly every day from late February to the middle of June. July is a silent month; but from August to October the song is doubled—hens sing as well and as strongly as cocks. November, again, is a rather silent time; but the robin probably sings on more days in the year, altogether, than any other European bird.

The red breast of the robin is its banner, and its liquid song its trumpet; for at seasons the robin is very warlike. It struts and sings to claim its possession of land. "One bush cannot harbor two robins" is an old saying.

Most birds hold territories in the spring, at the start of the breeding season. Many small garden birds have one or two acres to each warlike cock bird or mated pair. Rather few birds also have fall territories: but the robin is one, and among the browning leaves cocks and hens alike maintain their acres, by threat and song.

In the spring the hens hardly sing at all. But the cocks sing, chase, bob and weave with puffed red breasts at each other, until eventually each has carved out an acre or so for himself, with boundaries that mark where the aggressiveness of his neighbors is about equal. The red breast of the robin is not a courtship banner; a cock robin courts a hen by feeding her.

Birds mark their landowner's rights in many different ways. Hummingbirds often fly in flights so curved that they appear tied to their headquarters by invisible thread, their metallic throat-gorgets a signal of war to rival males and, in special short dives and swoops, of courtship to their females. Many wading birds have special territory flights; and snipe fly to a height from which they plunge in a fast fluttering dive, their outstretched tail-feathers sounding a humming, bleating war-cry—or rather, war-drum, for it is not a vocal sound.

Boundaries of four well-defined territories around small English farm, carved out by rival cock robins.

The territory system doubtless assists in the finding of suitable habitat. Young birds approaching their first nesting at the end of spring migration or dispersal may be attracted by the songs of experienced birds already there "to set up house next door." If they are driven away they will establish themselves in the nearest area of suitable habitat that is vacant. Thus the machinery exists by which a species is encouraged to colonize at the edge of its range and so increase that range. This probably explains why a successful species like the willow warbler can rapidly colonize new growth of suitable wood-edge scattered in isolated pockets all over the vast wilderness of the Scottish Highlands.

Territory is a fixed address that a migratory or dispersive bird adopts in response to the territorial behavior of the older members of its species during its first breeding season—and, as the banding records show, often keeps by annual homing and occupation for the rest of its life.

Yet some birds have such elaborate territory rituals that scientists often wonder whether the system can sometimes go beyond its usefulness. The male satin bower bird of Australia stakes a territory when the breeding

Aggressive European robin inflates throat and breast.

Spring battles between cock robins are often rough, seldom fought to finish. Below: Robin courtship, hen begging like fledgeling, cock feeding her.

Snipe drumming. In this fast-fluttering dive its outer tail-feathers vibrate noisily.

Left: On social breeding ground these elegant terns exer their anti-crowding drive, spacing out nests according to distance to which they can stretch their beaks. Above: Par satin bower birds at male's bower, in heart of his terri Below: Air fight between male ruby-throated hummingb

season comes, selecting a high branch from which he advertises ownership with a ringing *ee-oo* cry. In the territory he then quickly builds an extra-ordinary structure (usually north and south) of two parallel walls of arched dry twigs. Near one entrance of this he puts his collection of objects; for he will collect almost anything, particularly if it is blue or bluish—parrot feathers, blue or violet flowers of many kinds, bits of blue glass bottles or blue plates, blue paper, blue cloth, bluish or brownish snailshells, and even blue animals if any are around. He may steal blue-bags from laundries. He may also plaster and paint his bower with fruit pulp.

Now at the bower the male displays to the duller-colored female, with a whirring leaping display, with a specimen from his collection in his beak. But the bowers have a great attraction for the rival neighboring males. They raid. They steal. They sneak in and out by special hidden routes. Out of 100 bits of blue bottle put (by bird watchers) on runways and bowers, 76 were found in the collections of *neighbors* by noon next day!

Male mallee fowl tests temperature of incubation mound with beak; opens it up if too hot, piles on more leaves or loam if too cool. Below: Eastern crested tree swift on its acorn-in-cup type nest.

Male silvery-cheeked hornbill coughs up pellets of mixed earth and saliva; female uses them to seal up nest-hole entrance for months.

Nests

From his bathroom window in England J. F. has watched a hen goldfinch weave her perfect bowl-shaped nest on a side-branch of an old sycamore. The open cup is perhaps the commonest type of bird's nest. In the North American West the rufous hummingbird builds one of the most delicate bowls of all on a downward-bending branch, of cottony willow down all mixed and covered with green moss, cemented with spiderweb and decorated with bits of leaves and bark. The long-tailed tailor bird of Asia also builds a deep, soft nest-bowl of stems, wool, and down. But this nest is slung in a cradle of two or more large hanging leaves, which the bird sews together. It steals thread from spiders, moth-cocoons, or human housewives, punches holes in the leaves with its sharp beak, somehow ties stop-knots on the threads and draws them through until they are tight.

Remarkable among bowl nests are those of the tree swifts of Asia and the East Indies. A tree swift's nest is a tiny cup of bark and feathers into which the single egg fits like an acorn: it is gummed together, and to a horizontal

The ringed plover's "nest" is no more than a simple scrape on pebbly barren ground or on a beach.

The red-and-yellow barbet may excavate nest in termite-hills in the semidesert East African bush. Below: Bee eaters excavating a nest-burrow.

Rufous hummingbird's nest; inner diameter of rim one inch. Below: The tiny elf owl of the American desert breeds in old woodpecker holes.

Long-tailed tailor bird's nest-bowl is slung in cradle of hanging leaves which the bird sews together. Goldfinch's nest is woven of stems and roots with moss and lichens, and lined with plant-down and wool.

branch, by the bird's own saliva. When sitting the bird grasps the branch with a foot on each side of the nest and egg, which fit snugly among its belly feathers.

Many birds of many families nest in burrows or holes. In France we have watched pairs of common bee eaters quickly excavating their nest-holes in a sandbank. The birds dug with their bills and kicked spurts of sand out every few seconds. When finished, the burrow may run up to nine feet horizontally, and at the end of it the birds incubate on the bare sand.

In high trees in Africa the female silvery-cheeked hornbill finds her nest-site in a hole. To her the male flies with plaster for the entrance, with which she imprisons herself for up to four and a half months while she incubates her clutch and feeds her two young on fruit regurgitated by the male.

Some birds use second-hand holes. In the Arizona desert we have seen the world's smallest owl (no bigger than a sparrow) rearing its young in old woodpecker holes in the huge, stately saguaro cactuses.

In Australia at least three parrots and five kingfishers regularly burrow into occupied termites' nests. There are termite-hill-nesting birds, too, in South America. In Africa the red-and-yellow barbet is also an example. Oddly, the termites do not seem to molest the birds, and we have no evidence that the birds eat their hosts. Possibly the birds get some protection from enemies from this curious association.

Largest of all birds' nests are those of a family of game birds known as the mound-builders or megapodes. Each pair of mallee fowls in the Australian bush owns a vast mound of soil and loam scratched up mainly by the male. In it are many egg-chambers filled by the birds with fermenting leaves; and in the breeding season the male digs these out, the female lays in them and the male covers them up again. The eggs are then incubated by the heat of fermentation. When the chicks hatch, almost able to fly, their parents do not look after them at all, but continue attending to the mound.

Some birds have no nests, or practically none. The king and emperor penguins rest their eggs on their feet and cover them with a pouch. Some of the auk family hatch their single egg on bare rock. Many waders, like plovers and oystercatchers, lay their clutch on a simple scrape in the open.

145

Hen common pheasant, a prolific layer, lays an egg a day until the clutch is full, then incubates 3-3½ weeks.

Eggs

The array of eggs shown opposite belongs to 41 species in 34 families.

The largest egg known (14½ inches long, around 27 pounds) was laid by the largest extinct bird known, the elephant bird. In a good sense, though, it was a small egg, for it probably weighed under 3 per cent of the bird that laid it, far below the average. Yet smaller (1·7 per cent) is the egg of the ostrich, even if, at around 3 pounds, it is the largest now laid. In proportion, it is nearly the smallest: the smallest egg and egg output of any bird known are those of the emperor penguin, whose single annual egg weighs but 1·4 per cent of its body.

The emu's egg (1·5 per cent) is nearly as small: but the quite closely related kiwi lays an egg that weighs one third of its body—the largest known, in proportion. Though the eggs of hummingbirds are the smallest known, they are above average in proportion (usually 10 per cent). A bee hummer's egg-weight is, we believe, unknown; but judging by close relations, should be about 0·15 grams, or around five thousandths of an ounce.

Hummingbirds lay clutches of two: but most small birds lay many more, producing one a day and usually starting to sit when all are laid. In the wild, the mass-output record seems to be held by the little goldcrest, which produces 144 per cent of its own body weight in a ten-egg clutch. Most eggs in a year are probably laid by the common pheasant and partridge; if they lose their first clutch they can lay in all nearly 30.

Nearly all female birds have bare patches in the breeding season among their breast-feathers, to warm their clutches next their skin: and if the males share in the incubation most have brood-patches too.

Many small birds regularly lay two, and some even three, clutches in the year. The early and late clutches tend to be smaller than those in the full season. The size seems to depend on the food available.

There is enormous variation in the incubation period of birds—the time to hatching from the laying of the last egg, when most birds start to sit.

146

Osprey

Brown booby

Steller's eider

Red-throated loon

Madagascar sparrow hawk

Chilean tinamou

Ptarmigan

Peregrine

at horned owl

Great-tailed grackle

Sharp-tailed grouse

Great bustard

Little bustard

Senegal dove

mmon murre (guillemot)

Incubator bird

American black vulture

Guira cuckoo

Clapper rail

Catbird

Red-billed tropic bird

Black-headed jay

Common grackle

Emu

Yellow-bellied tyrannulet

Black-bellied (gray) plover

House wren

Ovenbird

Calliope hummingbird

Eastern kingbird

Veery

Great blue heron

Painted bunting

Jaçana

White-breasted nuthatch

Water pipit

Gray kingbird

Common nighthawk

ern tanager

Crissal thrasher

Martinetta

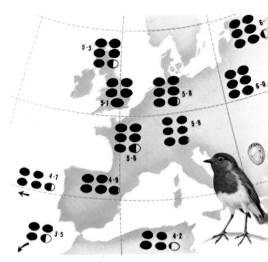

Left: In breeding season nearly all female birds have bare patches among breast-feathers, to warm clutches next to their skin. Laughing gull's three-egg clutch fits its mid and side incubation patches. Right: Map shows how average clutch size of eggs of European robin increases northward, with increasing length of summer days; also eastward, where May and June are warmer and there is probably more food.

Smaller singing birds and most woodpeckers usually hatch their eggs out before the end of the second week of sitting. Groups whose eggs mostly hatch in week three include rails, pigeons, nightjars and crows: in week four grebes, divers, game birds, cormorants, gulls, waders, herons and ducks: in weeks five and six ostrich, rheas, storks, falcons, most hawks, cranes, flamingos, larger geese, swans, auks and owls: in seven and eight cassowaries, penguins, petrels, gannets, vultures and eagles: in nine and ten emus, most albatrosses and the Andean condor. The longest incubation periods so far reliably recorded for any birds are 73 days for the wandering albatross, 80 days for the kiwi and 81 days for the royal albatross.

Most brightly colored eggs are laid where their owners can recognize them by daylight; their colors are doubtless badges of identity. Where the brightness of their colors does not match their surroundings, eggs tend to be laid in nests well hidden by foliage or in well-constructed deep nests. Such are the blue eggs of the hedge sparrow, or dunnock.

Eggs laid in open nests, particularly those on the ground, tend to have concealing or cryptic patterns of dark spots or splotches on a light background. Birds that nest in burrows or holes tend to have white or near-white eggs. Some open nesters (including some pigeons, sea birds and even hawks) have very light-colored eggs.

Coloration is laid upon a bird's eggshell by glands as it passes down the oviduct; the four main pigments are oocyanin, which produces a basal blue: oochlorin, yellow; ooxanthin, red or purplish (as on tinamou eggs); ooporphyrin, which often produces fine patterns, as on the eggs of waders.

Most eggs tend to be oval with one end rounder than the other. The most pear-shaped form is found among the eggs of auks, which can roll in a small circle and are not likely to fall off a ledge. The purest ovals are perhaps those of game birds, loons and some birds of prey, and most round are those of owls. The eggs of emus and tinamous are "biconical," tapering rather evenly toward each end.

Left: Paradise wydahs, cock melba finch. Hen wydah lays in nest of "finch" (a waxbill). Right: Brood parasite of New World; in México giant cowbird, near entrance to nest of Montezuma oropéndola, parasitizes birds of own Icterid family.

Brood Parasites

About 78 birds—less than one species in a hundred—lay in the nests of others, leaving their eggs to be hatched and their young to be reared by foster parents. The habit has probably arisen at least six times quite independently in the course of evolution, for the known brood parasites belong to six different families: the ducks, the honeyguides, the wydah family, the weavers, the cowbirds, and the cuckoos.

The fact that some members of a family are brood parasites does not necessarily mean that all are. Thus among the cuckoos, which are proverbial for the habit, only one entire subfamily, together with one species outside that subfamily, are brood parasites; the rest lay their eggs in their own nests. And many birds that are not full brood parasites may casually drop eggs in the nests of others.

The habit is common among the ducks, especially so in the tribe of ruddy ducks and their allies, whose eggs need little incubation after the first few days. The shy parents leave their nest on slight provocation; and the nest itself is poorly made. One member of the tribe, the white-headed duck of Europe, very often lays in the nests of coots. Another, the black-headed duck of southern South America, is a full brood parasite: no nest of it has ever been found. Its eggs, though, have been found in the nests of an ibis, a screamer, the swan-like coscoroba, other ducks, a caracara (a relative of the falcons!), the limpkin, rails, coots, and gulls.

All but one of the 14 members of the honeyguide family live in Africa, and it is probable that all are brood parasites of hole-nesting birds such as barbets, woodpeckers and starlings. Wholly African is the widow bird or wydah family; all eight of its members parasitize waxbills, a not-very-distantly related family of finch-like birds related to the weavers, and some of them also have other hosts. Although the large weaver family (95 living species if we exclude the 37 sparrows) is quite close in relationship to the wydahs, only one of the true weavers is a parasite—the African cuckoo finch, which specializes in Old-World warblers as hosts.

The most successful parasitic birds of the Americas are the cowbirds, eight members of the specially American Icterid family (New World orioles). The bay-winged cowbird of Argentina shows how the habit may evolve; for its pairs look for (or oust the owners from) nests of other species in which they lay eggs and feed and rear their own young. Next most primitive are the screaming cowbirds, which pair up in the spring as usual, but hold egg-laying until their bay-winged cousins' usurped nests are ready, when they lay their eggs exclusively therein and leave the bay-wings to rear the young. More advanced are cowbirds that have largely or entirely lost their mono-gamous and territorial habits: some, like the giant cowbird, specialize largely in other Icterids as hosts, but others have adopted a large variety of species, mostly smaller than themselves.

About 200 different fosterers have been recorded for the North American cowbird: its females watch hosts building and sometimes lay four or five eggs on successive days, each directly into a chosen nest, usually just after the first egg has been laid by the host.

Above: In Argentina the yellow-billed coot is among the many hosts of the black-headed duck. Below: Through its range cuckoo has gentes *that lay eggs (lower rank) wonderfully like those of their hosts.*

Meadow pipit	Brambling	Rufous-bellied niltava	Meadow bunting	Streaked laughing thrush	Great reed warbler
Cuckoo	Cuckoo	Cuckoo	Cuckoo	Cuckoo	Cuckoo

No family deploys brood parasitism more widely, more successfully, or in a more advanced manner than the cuckoos. Forty-seven out of the 125 living cuckoos are parasites—a single species, the striped cuckoo, in the Americas, and a whole subfamily comprising 46 members in the Old World. Cuckoos tend to parasitize several families, including passerines, not related to them at all. The most widespread and successful, the common cuckoo, is known to have at least 300 different hosts.

The female common cuckoo seems to be an even better nest-finder than the North American cowbird, for she can lay more than 15 eggs in a season, usually at two-day intervals, timing each to a fosterer's first egg. She holds this fosterer's egg in her beak while she lays direct into the nest, then flies off and eats the stolen egg. Her own egg has an incubation period of but $12\frac{1}{2}$ days, usually as short as or shorter than that of the host; and when the young cuckoo is quite newly hatched it wriggles in the nest until it has shoved the fosterer's eggs or young out.

Cuckoos are unrivaled at laying eggs resembling those of their hosts. Individuals tend to lay in the nests of the host species by which they themselves were reared; and by natural selection many *gentes* (that is, hereditary lines) have developed, each with eggs strikingly like those of their own fosterers.

The picture opposite compares eggs laid by six *gentes* of the cuckoo range with eggs laid by their six fosterers. In three cases (meadow pipit, brambling, and meadow bunting) the cuckoo's egg is noticeably larger than the fosterer's while the coloration is remarkably similar; in one case (great reed warbler), the cuckoo's egg is slightly different in shade from that of the fosterer, the size and marking much the same. In two cases (rufous-bellied niltava and streaked laughing thrush) the match is all but perfect.

Examples of directive and recognition marks in the mouths of nestlings. Left to right: Croaking cisticola, a warbler; yellow-throated longclaw, wagtail-pipit family; speckled mousebird. (All are from Africa.)

Young razorbills a fortnight hatched flutter from cliff when primary feathers are mere buds, continue growth at sea. Eider ducklings (below) leave nest when dry, tumble after ducks down steep rocky moors to the sea.

Nidifugous young of yellow-throated sand grouse appear boldly patterned against plain ground; but when they "freeze" in grass cover they are effectively hidden by outline-breaking colors.

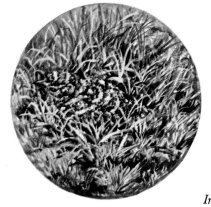

In distraction display parent bird raises one wing, drops the other, flutters as if hurt, drawing attention of predator away from young, which then rely on cryptic "freezing" for protection.

Pulli

The heading above means, in Latin, young animals. Pullus has been adopted as the official word to describe a bird that has hatched but cannot yet fly. As soon as a bird can fly it is a juvenal. Pullus is the only word we can use for both nestling and chick: a fledgeling is a bird that has just flown and is therefore juvenal.

Pulli are of two main sorts, if we exclude the young of flightless birds, whose transition to juvenals is hard to define. Most pulli are altricial, that is, helpless and often naked when hatched: these are also called nidicolous—staying in the nest—or simply nestlings. But many birds have precocial pulli fully downy when hatched, often called nidifugous because most run away from the nest when dry—in short, chicks, ducklings, or goslings.

If we call (as most do) the period between hatching and fledging the fledging period, then some precocial birds have short fledging periods indeed. Megapodes (p. 145) can practically fly when hatched, and spend the early juvenal stage in further growth. Other game birds like ptarmigan have fledging periods as short as ten days, and nearly all continue to grow after they can fly.

Many small singing birds fledge in under a fortnight; the majority of passerines in under three weeks; pigeons, nightjars, hummingbirds, trogons, bee eaters, and most woodpeckers in under four. Bustards, most owls, motmots, and some kingfishers, Icterids, and crows take up to five weeks; most waders up to six; herons, falcons, skuas, gulls, auks, and some toucans up to seven, though murres and razorbills (auks) flutter from their cliffs at about a fortnight. Storm petrels, some cormorants, darters, some bitterns,

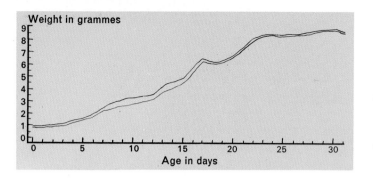

Weight in grammes

Age in days

Most hummingbirds rear twins. This day-by-day record, kept through fledging period of two young Estella hillstars, shows that both first grew evenly, then for a while lost weight when feather buds sprouted during their third fortnight.

storks, most rails, and some large owls and hornbills cannot fly until they are nearly eight weeks old. The tropic birds, pelicans, and secretary bird may take a week longer.

The birds with really long fledging periods embrace rather few families. Swifts may not fledge for nearly ten weeks in years of insect scarcity: other ten-week birds are cranes, the smaller New World vultures, the osprey and caracaras. Petrels, gannets, most eagles, and barn owls seldom fledge in under eleven weeks; big Old World vultures, like the griffon, may not fledge in under twelve.

With quite a different order of fledging time are the albatrosses, the largest penguins, and the condors. The smaller albatrosses and mollymawks have fledging periods of 20 or 21 weeks. The three North Pacific albatrosses and the three smaller Antarctic penguins spend almost exactly half a year in or near their nest. The California condor certainly, and the Andean condor very probably, cannot fly until 26-30 weeks hatched. The emperor penguin is fed by its parents on the antarctic sea-ice for 35-39 weeks before it swims off.

The longest fledging period absolutely proved is that of the royal albatross at 36 weeks, though there is evidence that its close cousin the wanderer may go to 44 or 45. But the king penguin spends from 10 to 13 months as a pullus.

The slow growth of albatrosses and penguins is bound up with the problem of food supply. In both families it is a very demanding job for parents to feed their young, which is why twins are rare among them. Although food is supplied fairly regularly to pulli, the amount is restricted by the difficulties of obtaining and transporting it; for an albatross may have to range over hundreds of miles to find food, and so (though less commonly) may a penguin. And the young bird's limited food intake is necessarily reflected in a limited growth rate.

Birds whose pulli remain comparatively helpless for a long time have special adaptations that help to safeguard them from enemies. Penguins have evolved a crèche system, by which the young band together in an enormous group, safeguarded from skuas by "nurses" while the parents are away fishing. Among the longer-lived petrels, such as the fulmars, pulli develop the ability to vomit almost as soon as they are hatched. Since most predators seem to dislike the habit intensely it serves as an effective defence against them.

The pullus period of a bird has adaptations of color and organ special to it. The young of many nidicolous birds have colored mouth markings which elicit parental feeding responses when they gape. Pulli of hole nesters often have horny spiked heel pads to grip the walls. Nidifugous pulli are mostly colored with patterns that conceal them from enemies when they lie still.

154

Flying: Wandering albatross, from first year (r.) to male of 9 (l.). Ground: Campbell I. adults and young. Right: A black-browed albatross lived to over 34 in Faeroes (record in the wild).

Adolescence and Longevity

Most birds breed in the first season after they are hatched, but quite a number breed later. Second-year breeders include the emu, diving petrels, geese, many hawks and owls, smaller gulls, some swifts, and a few large passerines. Frigate birds first breed in their second or third, the smaller penguins and storm petrels in their third, and the ostrich, pelicans, king vultures, most terns and gulls in their third or fourth year. Typical fourth-year breeders are gannets, the larger gulls, the Adélie penguin. Storks breed in their fourth or fifth year; many petrels and large birds of prey in their fifth; the king penguin in its fifth or sixth; the California condor in its sixth.

All birds so far known to breed first at seven or older are petrels and albatrosses. Male short-tailed shearwaters breed first at seven, females at five. The fulmar probably does not come to land until three or four, or breed till seven. No royal albatross known to be in less than its sixth year was seen at the colony watched by L. E. Richdale, and none provedly bred before its eighth year. One male did not breed until its eleventh.

What is long adolescence for? Some ornithologists believe it is inherited as a method of limiting the population: but we believe it is long for learning. The slow maturers have to learn a lot: the great vultures must get to know the topography, and all the air-currents, thermals and winds of thousands of square miles: the great albatrosses need nine years of experience to become masters of the trackless stormy oceans before being fit for parenthood.

The longest adolescents are the slowest of breeders. All lay but one egg. The king penguin, with its year-long fledging period, breeds only twice every three years, condors and the two great albatrosses every other year.

The five birds that have lived longer than any others known, all in captivity. Above: Eagle owl, 68 years; Asian white crane, 59. Below: Andean condor, 65; greater sulfur-crested cockatoo, 56; bateleur, 55. Parrot records of 69, 79, 80 and 120 years are not provable, through absence of reliable documents.

Pied flycatcher juvenal . . .
. . . and adult. Past juvenal stage, life-expectation is 18 months.

In spite of half a century of banding, we still know rather little about how long birds can live in the wild. But the records of some zoos and aviaries go back a century and a quarter; and from the studies of the late Stanley S. Flower and others we can say that the longest-lived birds proved are probably the five figured above.

The only lives the banding records can so far give us over 30 are herring gull (nearly 32), curlew (31½) and black-headed gull (31¼). (The albatross on p. 155 was unbanded.) But if banding cannot prove maximum wild longevity, it can already tell us the average *expectation* of life of wild species.

Expectation of life is a calculation of how long, on average, animals *do* live. In nature it is probable that only top-of-the-pyramid birds, like vultures and albatrosses, can die of old age. The rest die by being killed and eaten, of starvation, by drowning or migration, by accident, or from disease. All birds have a high mortality rate when juvenal. Once mature, their life expectation is about constant; indeed, it may even improve with longer experience of life.

Only one bird has been found with a life expectation less than a year: the mallard in Britain, where it is a major shooters' prey and rates 11 months. Apart from sporting birds, small birds rate lowest. Good figures are European robin, redstart, swallow, 12 months; American robin and European song thrush, 17; European starling, 18; European blackbird, 19; blue jay, 20. Over two years are European woodcock, lapwing, heron, marsh hawk, night heron. Some cormorants, geese, gulls and owls can expect over three, swifts over four, several terns over five. Banding has not gone on long enough to produce figures for really long-lived birds. We guess, though, that one day albatrosses, and a few other great birds, will be *proved* to have a better life-expectation than Man in middle age.

Instinct and Intelligence

Birds are creatures of instinct. Their lively intelligence operates in a field more limited than that of high mammals and quite unlike that of Man.

An instinct is a capacity to respond with special and often clear-cut patterns of behavior to stimuli in the environment—a capacity that is inherited, innate, does not have to be learned. A jay needs no tuition in how to hide nuts in the bark of a tree or acorns in holes in the ground; a year-old chaffinch that left the nest three weeks after hatching does not have to be taught how to build a nest of its own; an early-hatched swallow does not have to wait for its elders to show it how to make its first flight from western Europe to Africa.

In any bird there is a whole complex of innate drives that lead to what behavior students now call appetitive behavior. Under the appropriate stimuli birds express urges or appetites for certain kinds of activity, ranging from simple random searching to activities of extreme complexity (like starting breeding) that involve more than one instinct. Eventually the appropriate environmental circumstances (usually simple and special in pattern) may release the final consummatory act, the satisfaction of the appetite. A bird, W. H. Thorpe says, is "tuned to recognize without previous experience the goal of its instinct."

Birds fight their way out of the egg by instinct, hide by instinct, flock and forage by instinct, scratch and preen by instinct, sing and cry by instinct, migrate, orient themselves and navigate by instinct, take territories and display by instinct, feed and protect their young by instinct. Yet nearly all these activities can be, and often are, improved by experience, by learning; and the learning and memory abilities of birds can be marvelous.

Jackdaw opening correct box, according to number of dots on key card. In another Köhler experiment, this bird further learned to associate each number from 1 to 5 with one of 5 plain boxes, all differently colored.

157

In the wild, when a female mates with a male that has already established its territory, she can get to know the topography and resources of that territory within a few days—every tree, every branch, every food source, every water source, every good bit of cover. In captivity, a budgerigar can learn nearly as many English words as some Englishmen, and can even associate some of them with objects, sounds or times in its own environment, though it cannot ever understand their true meaning. Nor, perhaps, should we be surprised by the avian capacity to learn quickly, for birds in general have better sight, keener hearing, and a faster rate of metabolism than most other vertebrates, besides enjoying the ability to explore freely in three dimensions; and as families they have exercised all these advantages for millions of years.

Intelligence is still rather a loose word, so to tighten it a little let us confine the realms of birds' intelligence to those abilities of theirs that involve learning and insight. First, birds have a large capacity for habituation; for learning not to respond to things in the environment—such as scarecrows and noisy runways—that may frighten them at first but are found by experience not to be particularly unfavorable. Habituation sorts and simplifies a bird's mental pictures of the real and the bogus dangers around it, and saves energy.

A large element of trial-and-error enters into the learning of birds. Chicks peck by instinct, learn much about what is rewarding to peck by trial. Pigeons go through drinking motions by instinct, but have been proved to have to learn by several trials that water is the stuff to drink. Some (but by no means all) nest-builders are incompetent the first time, and have to learn the right sizes and shapes of twigs before they can do really well the kind of job their innate drive prescribes. (A highly skilled ornithologist who specializes in individual species can often distinguish between a first-year nest and a second-year nest; and if the builder of the nest has been color-ringed so as to prove its age his findings can be confirmed.)

Individual birds vary greatly in their capacity for successful trial: though

Köhler hid food in one of 5 boxes numbered by irregular blobs. Raven was shown key of 1 to 5 differently irregular bits of Plasticine. Arrows in diagram link keys with boxes bearing same number, which bird correctly opened every time.

  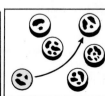 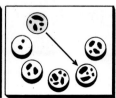 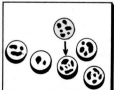

tits have a natural drive to make trials of all kinds only a few "genius" tits found out how to open milk-bottle tops and steal the cream when modern bottles were first introduced in England; and the habit spread in a very orderly way from rather a few original centers by imitation. Birds generally have a fair capacity for imitation, and a few families a propensity for the vocal mimicry of other species that is as remarkable as it is (at present) inexplicable. Birds also are very fond of play, adults more so than young. Play probably enhances their capacity for trial learning.

Experiments have shown that birds learn some lessons by insight. Presented with new problems, they sometimes appear to find the answers by a quick reorganization of their previous experience, without trials. Put another way, they have an inherent curiosity that sometimes enables them to cut corners, and meet new situations with a kind of drill that has been set up by old ones.

A few birds use tools: woodpeckers have their favorite anvils where they wedge acorns to split them: the woodpecker finch of the Galápagos Islands uses a long cactus spine to poke insects out of holes; the long-tailed tailor bird uses thread to stitch the leaves of its nest-cradle together. Some birds learn tricks in the wild and in captivity—string-pulling, drawer-opening, needle-threading, pulling sticks away to release nuts—that have no relation to natural problems and must be at least partly based on insight.

The counting ability of birds is about as good as that of a man deprived of the abstract concept of number: shown groups of marks on a screen for too short a time for deliberate counting, man can nearly always distinguish between four and five, only sometimes between seven and eight. Birds, which cannot name the numbers, get about as far—pigeons up to five, ravens and jackdaws to six or even seven.

Birds live in a world of which they themselves can have no abstract concept. Within it they have wonderful skills, based on a network of complex instincts, fine learning capacity and memory, a dash of insight. No philosophers they, they live and die in a drama of colors and shapes and music that makes philosophers of us.

Right: Blue tits can beak up over 2 feet of baited string to perch, placing foot on loops. At least 6 other families can solve problem; ability varies. Solution may come from insight, not through trial and error. Below: Rewarded with millet by Indian entertainers, tethered baya weavers can learn to thread an 8-inch tasseled cord with 8 or even 10 beads, holding a 3-inch needle half inch from the tip in order to gain maximum control.

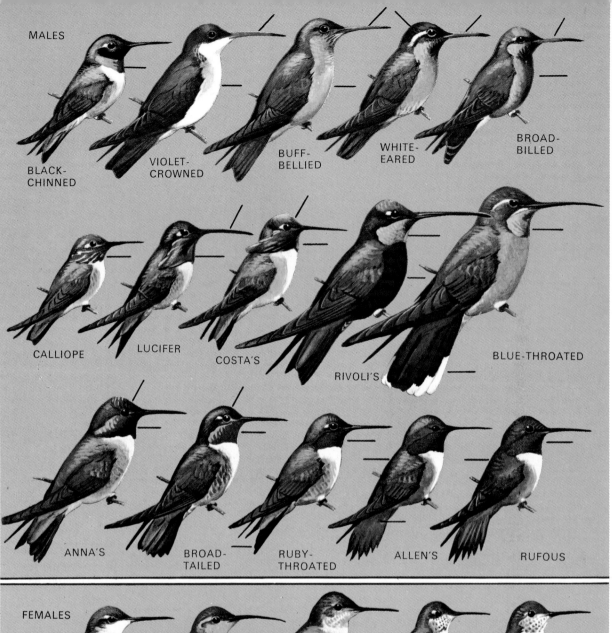

MALES

BLACK-CHINNED

VIOLET-CROWNED

BUFF-BELLIED

WHITE-EARED

BROAD-BILLED

CALLIOPE

LUCIFER

COSTA'S

RIVOLI'S

BLUE-THROATED

ANNA'S

BROAD-TAILED

RUBY-THROATED

ALLEN'S

RUFOUS

FEMALES

BLACK-CHINNED
RUBY-THROATED
COSTA'S (similar)

LUCIFER

BROAD-TAILED

CALLIOPE

RUFOUS

ANNA'S

BROAD-BILLED

RIVOLI'S

BLUE-THROATED

WHITE-EARED

7   Bird Watching

Both authors have often been described as bird lovers. While we readily accept the description, we agree that it is no good just loving birds. The person who wants to watch birds in a rewarding way must recognize that there are many facets to the hobby and must try to do something useful about those that he finds most interesting. His bird watching must be systematized until it becomes an array of clear targets to aim at.

His first step must be to master the identification of birds in the field, and for this the essential tools are the optical instruments that have now almost completely replaced the collector's gun; the notebook; and the field guide.

Good field guides are now published to the birds of almost every country in the world, and some countries have several excellent rival alternatives. But a field guide is not a textbook. It can best contribute to the recognition of birds only if it is used as part of a proper drill. Ideally the watcher should use his notebook and pencil during and after his observation, and *before* his field guide check; and he should write his notes as fully as possible.

Below, we offer the note-taker our field drill. For those who like mnemonics we start each heading with a bold capital. These spell out our objective: **WHICH IS IT?**

Where and when? (Locality and date.)

Habitat: is it in a wood, marsh, meadow?

Impression: what does the bird look like at rest, in movement? Note the general appearance.

Comparison: what is its size? Note this in relation to some well-known species, or better still some known species that your bird is in company with, if any.

Habits: how does the bird behave, move, when standing, walking, running, flying?

Identification flashes or field marks: many birds have diagnostic bars, patches or contrasting marks that readily identify them. See the amplification, below, of the important subject of *field marks*.

Sounds: hear your bird. Write down all you can of what it cries or sings. If possible listen to published sound recordings.

Important details (size, shape, color) of legs, feet, bill and, if possible, eyes.

Tail and wings: their shapes, length and patterns. (Identification flashes are often here.)

Plate from a Peterson field guide. Juxtaposing similar species facilitates comparison of patterns. Short arrows draw attention to key field marks.

Each of the above headings that deal directly with identification may demand an entry in the notebook if the record is to be reliable. To supplement them we suggest a secondary drill with the code: **DO IT!**

Distance: how far were you from the bird?

Optics: binocular or telescope; what power? Comment also on the light and its direction.

Instant of observation (time and duration).

Team: log the names of your companions, if any. Somebody may want to check with them.

Field marks: these have also been called "trade marks of nature." Below we offer a basic outline of the things to look for.

(1) *Breast:* is it plain (unmarked), spotted, or streaked, or striped?

(2) *Wings:* do they have wing-bars (one or two) or are the wings plain? Wings of water birds may have: (a) patches, (b) stripes, (c) solid color, or (d) black tips.

(3) *Tail:* does it have a band at the tip, bands across it, white sides, or spots in the corners?

(4) *Rump:* does it have a conspicuous rump patch?

(5) *Head:* does it have (a) a stripe over the eye; (b) a ring around the eye; (c) stripes on the crown, or (d) a patch on the crown?

As the note-taker gains experience he will find his drills improving, becoming second nature. The identification drill is the root of all bird watching; but many others must be followed before something new and valuable finds its way from the notebook into the corpus of our science and sport. One important drill is neatness; another consistency of style; paramount are completeness, accuracy and objectivity.

Field notes should be transferred to the permanent record *as soon as possible*, before the observer has forgotten his own abbreviations. What form this record will take depends on taste and experience. J.F. has now put the whole of his permanent research record on 5 × 8 in. (12.7 × 20.3 cm.) slips in loose-leaf binders, each of which holds over 600 slips. Two binders containing as many as 300,000 words will stow in an ordinary brief case.

The ordering of research notes in a binder demands a system. Fortunately there are two excellent numerical classifications of knowledge that the ornithologist can use: the system of the Library of Congress in the USA and the Universal Decimal Classification, more widely used in Europe.

Duck-counter's eye view from the A. W. Boyd Memorial Observatory, Rostherne Mere, Cheshire, England.

If pressed to divide bird watchers into two categories we would classify them as club men and individualists, or joiners and non-joiners. The non-joiner we are sorry for. Though he doubtless derives some pleasure from his hobby he misses much. He must find it hard or impossible to keep in touch with the current literature of birds; and he cannot get far without it, for textbooks alone are certainly not enough. He cuts himself off from the conversation and advice of other ornithologists, and misses the chance of becoming part of what is, in effect, an international brotherhood. And keen though he may be, his isolated work is unlikely to add much to ornithology as a whole.

We happily confess that we are joiners, and that between us we belong to close on a hundred natural history and ornithological societies all over the world. Many of these, such as the national and regional Audubon Societies in North America, and the British Trust for Ornithology and the Royal Society for the Protection of Birds in Britain, offer their members a tremendous amount of advice on the tools of bird watching, either in exchange for modest subscriptions or in cheap pamphlet form. Any member of these admirable societies can also get cheap and reliable briefing on what essential optical instruments to buy and where to buy them; and the latest and best information on how to build or where to obtain a hide (or a blind, as it is called in North America)—an essential tool for bird photography or for the field study of bird behavior.

Twelve emblems of famous ornithological societies. 1. British Ornithologists' Union's sacred ibis; 2. American Ornithologists' Union's great auk; 3. Royal Naval Bird Watching Society's arctic tern; 4. Society for Ornithological Studies' lark (France); 5. Netherlands Ornithological Union's black-tailed godwit; 6. Danish Ornithological Society's lapwings; 7. Cooper Ornithological Club's California condor (Pacific USA); 8. Italian Ornithological Association's and Royal Society for the Protection of Birds' avocet; 9. Royal Australasian Ornithologists' Union's emu; 10. South African Ornithological Society's ostrich; 11. Ornithological Society of New Zealand's takahé; 12. Scottish Ornithologists' Club's Scottish crested tit.

Serious bird photography dates back to nearly 90 years ago, when British pioneers started a portrait gallery that must now embrace over half the world's birds. Since 1962, when Eric Hosking, king of British bird photographers, and his friend Cyril Newberry published their *Bird Photography as a Hobby*, and Russ Kinne, king (or, if he prefers it, president) of American bird photographers, published his *Complete Book of Nature Photography*, all sorts of staggering improvements have been made in cameras and films; yet the advice these masters offer to the newcomer to bird photography remains entirely valid. However, those who want to keep up with ever-changing techniques and equipment simply must be joiners, and get their briefing from one or more of the splendid array of photographic clubs and photographic magazines to be found in every civilized country.

In our lifetime photography has evolved from a good hobby into an essential scientific tool. Cinematography, in particular, now contributes handsomely to the research files of every bird-study unit throughout the world. Not a day passes without a 16mm. projector shining golden research material on a screen watched by students of animal behavior at one university or another. Every day, too, tapes carrying the recorded voices of birds are listened to, or fed into a sound spectrograph, on one or another campus.

Nature sound recording began in 1889, when the great Ludwig Koch, as a boy, recorded the voice of a common shama on an Edison wax cylinder. Koch, who later founded the magnificent collection of recorded nature sounds of the B.B.C., is still happily active in England, and he and his pupils the world over have now recorded the voices of about a third of the birds of our planet. Today there are many professional bird-voice recorders, but as everywhere in ornithology there is unlimited scope for the amateur; and in this facet of our hobby amateurs still outnumber professionals.

Every enlightened nation now has its own sound-recording club, ready to welcome the joiner and give him good advice; and there is no lack of specialist magazines to keep him abreast of rapidly advancing techniques.

Here, for slow-motion flight pictures, Roger Peterson is shooting at 64 frames per second, using a gunstock. Use of Nydar gunsight makes accurate tracking easier.

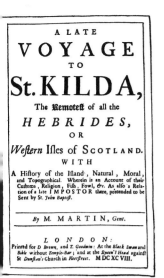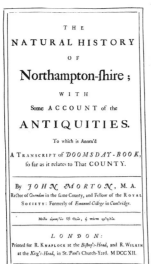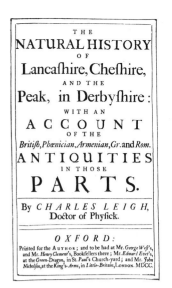

Title pages of seventeenth- and eighteenth-century British works, all containing good local avifaunas.

Bird watching has one great advantage over many other hobbies: almost from the start it offers the hobbyist splendid opportunities of making real contributions to knowledge. Below we list five spheres of activity in which he can play a useful part. His own ornithological or natural history society will be delighted to enlist his services for such activities in his own locality, or to advise him of opportunities of usefulness elsewhere.

Local Records: Every state of the American Union, every province of Canada, every department of France, every county of England has been the subject of published avifaunas; and many now have an annual bird report, published by their local ornithological or natural history society. Most other enlightened countries keep similar local records. All these taken together form the raw material from which the scientific analyst prepares his assessment of the global distribution of any bird species. Over the years they can also be amazingly valuable to biologists interested in the ecological changes of the world's fauna.

Compiling local records is such an immense task that without the help of many enthusiastic amateurs it could never be accomplished. Whenever a bird map is composed of dots, as it quite often is, it is safe to say that more than half those dots have been positioned as a result of amateurs sending in their note records to their local societies.

Census Work: Bird census work, with its basic unit the number of occupied nests or territories, was first put on an organized footing in Britain and America by the beginning of the present century. Today it has everywhere reached some degree of sophistication.

In 1969 the Sea Bird Group of the British Trust for Ornithology began a preliminary survey and census of all the breeding sea bird colonies in the British Isles. In Operation Seafarer, as it is called, well over 1000 census workers took part; and more than 90 per cent were amateurs, thoroughly enjoying a happy and useful holiday task. Already Operation Seafarer has told us with some accuracy the location and population (for Britain and Ireland) of every colony of the North Atlantic gannet and practically every colony of the fulmar, the kittiwake, most other gulls and terns, cormorants, shags and auks.

The keen amateur seldom need be at a loss for similar pleasant and rewarding work during his vacation.

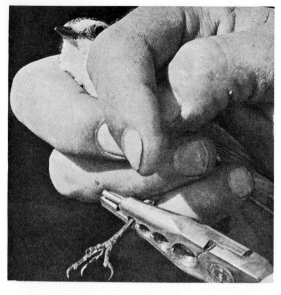

A whinchat, trapped at a British migration observatory, is held in the ideal position for banding; head is comfortable between first and second fingers, breast is not pressed. Special pliers squeeze band gently around leg.

Migration Studies: One of the happiest holiday tasks an ornithologist can undertake is to help man one of the many stations where the passage of migrant birds is observed, and where the birds are harmlessly trapped for study and for ringing (or banding, as it is called in North America).

There are now about 40 permanent or semi-permanent ringing points in Britain and Ireland and about 60 official banding stations in the USA. Most other civilized countries also have their own network. In each country the banding is coordinated by a national banding authority that issues its own ring series at cost.

Only the availability of an army of amateurs, who board at or near these stations for a week or a fortnight of their annual holiday, makes it possible for field migration studies to continue on their present scale. It is to the deployment of these enthusiastic amateurs that we owe much of our present knowledge of the migratory routes, longevity and life-tables of the world's globe-spanning birds. But in this facet of our hobby enthusiasm must be backed up by brief training. In every important national scheme we know of, nobody can become a bander until he has qualified under supervision, usually at an observatory.

Nest Records: During the breeding season of 1936 E. A. Billett, a keeper at Whipsnade Zoological Park in Bedfordshire, England, kept a record of all the nests in its nearly six-acre bird sanctuary, noting day by day the number of eggs laid, the number hatched, and the number of young fledged. Julian Huxley, then Secretary of London Zoo, analyzed his notes and realized that spread over the years, seasons and latitudes, similar records could provide valuable statistical data about clutch-size, breeding season, and breeding efficiency of bird species all over the world.

In 1939, together with J.F. who was then his assistant, he designed "hatching and fledging cards" (now known as nest-record cards) for the British Trust for Ornithology to circulate among its members. Today over 10,000 nests are watched every year in Britain alone, and similar nest-record schemes are operated in many parts of Europe, North America, South and East Africa, and in New Zealand. As a result many common birds have by now been the subjects of nest-card analysis, which has made it possible to link their seasons and breeding fortunes with climate and food supply.

The work continues and grows; and much of it—particularly the field work—is in the hands of amateurs.

Bird Behavior: No facet of ornithology can be adequately covered by field work alone. The amateur determined to be proficient must spend time studying, and this is especially true if his main interest is bird behavior. Before he can hope to add anything of value to the existing body of knowledge on this fascinating subject he must immerse himself in its literature, master its special vocabulary, and grasp its philosophical concepts. As he does so he will realize that the behavior patterns of bird species are as vital to an understanding of their evolution as are their anatomical characteristics; and he will appreciate just how much still remains to be learned on the subject.

His own contributions, when he feels prepared to begin making them, are most likely to come by way of careful field observations backed by meticulously accurate notes, and by his work with cinecamera and tape recorder in the shelter of a good hide (or blind). The *interpretation* of his sight and sound recordings may best be left to an acknowledged expert.

We could go on listing opportunities open to the keen amateur: specialist study of nests or eggs; detailed work on food spectra; life-history studies of single species (there is singularly little literature as yet on the hedge sparrow, the raven, the jackdaw, the pied wagtail, and quite a number of other common birds); but in fact the opportunities are virtually unlimited and whoever seizes any one of them seizes a lifetime of joy and interest.

Great crested grebe displays and rituals, mainly after the pioneer study of Julian Huxley (1914). 1. Seeking attitude of either sex; 2. Female assuming hostile attitude; 3. Pair in "cat" position; 4-6. Pair in stages of the shaking ritual; 7. The "penguin dance," a bond-cementing ritual involving presentation of nest material.

167

The Regiment of Birds

We here present a classification of the class Aves with a census of what we believe to be the acceptable genera and species named by 1969. It embraces all fossil, lately extinct, and living birds known to us. In all but three cases this regimentation is pursued through subclasses, orders, and families; the three large families Furnariidae (no. 144), Muscicapidae (173) and Emberizidae (181) we have broken down into subfamilies, shown as a, b, c, etc.

In the classification the symbol † before the name of a family means that it is fossil only and extinct by 1600. The phrase "lately extinct species" refers to species that have become extinct since 1680, the year before the probable extinction of the dodo. Birds recorded as "extinct before the dodo" were still living in the early 17th century.

The reader can work out the number of paleospecies and neospecies from the figures given under family or subfamily. Thus (family 108) 299 pigeon species are "known"—that is to say, accepted by us from a study of the literature. Of these 285 are living, 6 lately extinct, 1 extinct before the dodo and 37 fossil. The neospecies are $285+6+1 = 292$. As 299 are known, $299 - 292 = 7$ are paleospecies, and $37 - 7 = 30$ are neospecies also known as fossils. In the census of genera, the number fossil is of paleogenera (purely fossil genera) only.

An arrow after the name of a geological period (*e.g.* Eocene→) means that the family has persisted from that period to the present.

The system here employed is based on that of the first edition of *The World of Birds* (1964), but is here published without the family distribution maps. Revisions of the number of members of the families or other taxa (*e.g.* subfamilies of the bigger families) have been made, especially of the fossils; and some new families have been inserted (with "A" numbers). We have kept to the systematic order of 1964, and the family numbers ("A" numbers included) remain in sequence.

Silhouettes of families now extinct are shown in gray

CLASS AVES, BIRDS

SUBCLASS † SAURIURAE, DAWN BIRDS

Order † Archaeopterygiformes
(Family 1)

1 Archaeopteryx
Family † Archaeopterygidae, Upper Jurassic
Genus and species: 1 fossil (some authorities hold 2)

SUBCLASS † ODONTOHOLCAE, TOOTHED BIRDS

Order † Hesperornithiformes
(Families 2–4)

2 Enaliornis
Family † Enaliornithidae, Lower Cretaceous
Genus: 1 fossil
Species: 2 fossil
May be in loon order, before new family 18A

3 Baptornis and Neogaeornis
Family † Baptornithidae, Upper Cretaceo
Genera: 2 fossil
Species: 2 fossil
Earliest fossil, *Baptornis*, Kansas; may be i grebe order, before family 20

4 Hesperornis and Coniornis
Family † Hesperornithidae, Upper Cretace
Genera: 2 fossil
Species: 4 fossil
Earliest fossils, *Hesperornis*, Kansas

Family 4

UBCLASS ORNITHURAE, YPICAL BIRDS

der † Ichthyornithiformes
(amilies 5 and 6)

chthyornis
mily † Ichthyornithidae, Upper Cretaceous
nus: 1 fossil
ecies: 7 fossil

Apatornis
mily † Apatornithidae, Upper Cretaceous
nus and species: 1 fossil

der Sphenisciformes
amily 7)

Penguins
mily Spheniscidae, Lower Eocene→
nera: 6 living, 21 fossil
ecies: 47 known; 15 living, 36 fossil
igin: probably southern or even
bantarctic; earliest fossil, an as yet
named fragment from New Zealand

der Struthioniformes
amilies 8 and 9)

Eleutherornis
mily † Eleutherornithidae, Middle Eocene
nus and species: 1 fossil
own from fragmentary pelvis only. May
in Diatrymiform order, near family 86

9 Ostriches
Family Struthionidae, Lower Pliocene→
Genus: 1 living
Species: 7 known, 1 living, 7 fossil
Origin: possibly Palearctic; earliest fossils
Egypt, Greece, S. Russia, Persia, N. India,
Mongolia

Order † Aepyornithiformes
(Family 10)

10 Elephant Birds
Family † Aepyornithidae, Upper Eocene—
Recent
Genera: 1 extinct before dodo, 3 fossil
Species: 9 known; 1 extinct before dodo, 9
fossil
Origin: possibly Ethiopian; earliest fossil,
Egypt; survived in Madagascar until
historical times

Order Casuariiformes
(Families 11–13)

11 Emus
Family Dromiceiidae, Upper Pleistocene→
Genus: 1 living
Species: 3 known; 1 living, 3 fossil
Origin: doubtless Australian

12 Dromornis and Genyornis
Family † Dromornithidae, Pliocene to Upper
Pleistocene
Genera: 2 fossil
Species: 2 fossil
Origin: doubtless Australian

13 Cassowaries
Family Casuariidae, Upper Pleistocene→
Genus: 1 living
Species: 3 known; 3 living, 1 fossil
Origin: doubtless Australasian; only fossil,
race of living Bennett's cassowary, *Casuarius
bennetti lyddekeri,* New South Wales

Family 13

Order Apterygiformes
(Families 14–16)

14 Lesser moas
Family: Emeidae, Upper Miocene or Lower
Pliocene—Recent
Genera: 2 lately extinct, 5 fossil
Species: 19 known; 2 lately extinct, 19 fossil
or subfossil
Origin: doubtless New Zealand; survived in
South Island until late 18th contury; earliest
fossil, *Anomalopteryx antiquus,* Timaru, S.I.

15 Great moas
Family † Dinornithidae, Middle Pliocene—
Recent
Genus: 1 fossil (and extinct before dodo)
Species: 8 known; 1 extinct before dodo, 8
fossil
Origin: doubtless New Zealand; survived in
South Island until historical times; earliest
fossil, *Dinornis novaezealandiae,* Nukumaru,
North Island

16 Kiwis
Family Apterygidae, Pleistocene→
Genera: 1 living, 1 fossil
Species: 4 known; 3 living, 4 fossil
Origin: doubtless New Zealand

Order Rheiformes
(Family 17)

17 Rheas
Family Rheidae, Lower Eocene→
Genera: 2 living, 2 fossil
Species: 6 known; 2 living, 5 fossil
Origin: doubtless South American; earliest
fossil, *Opisthodactylus,* Patagonia, may merit
family status, before 17 (16A); if so,
Heterorhea dabbeni, Upper Pliocene,
N. Argentina, is earliest fossil

Family 17

Order Tinamiformes
(Family 18)

18 Tinamous
Family Tinamidae, Pliocene→
Genera: 9 living, 3 fossil
Species: 46 known; 42 living, 14 fossil
Origin: doubtless South American; earliest
fossils, Argentina. May be most primitive
typical birds; if so, before family 5

Order Gaviiformes
(Families 18A and 19)

18A Lonchodytids
Family † Lonchodytidae, Upper Cretaceous
Genera: 1 fossil
Species: 2 fossil
Origin: probably North American

19 Loons
Family Gaviidae, Upper Paleocene→
Genera: 1 living, 3 fossil
Species: 12 known; 4 living, 12 fossil
Origin: possibly Siberian or North American;
though earliest fossil, *Eupterornis,* France

Order Podicipitiformes
(Family 20)

20 Grebes
Family Podicipitidae, Lower Miocene→
Genera: 3 living, 2 fossil
Species: 22 known; 17 living, 11 fossil
Origin: doubtless Holarctic; earliest fossil
Podiceps oligocaenus, Oregon

Order Procellariiformes
(Families 21–24)

21 Albatrosses
Family Diomedeidae, Middle Eocene→
Genera: 1 living, 2 fossil
Species: 16 known; 12 living, 8 fossil
Origin: probably southern or even
Subantarctic; earliest fossil, *Gigantornis,* Nigeria

Family 21

22 Petrels and shearwaters
Family Procellariidae, Middle Eocene→
Genera: 9 living, 2 fossil
Species: 63 known; 47 living, 40 fossil
Origin: probably southern; though earliest
fossil, *Puffinus raemdoncki,* Belgium

23 Storm petrels
Family Oceanitidae, Upper Miocene→
Genera: 7 living
Species: 20 known; 18 living, 1 lately
extinct, 6 fossil
Origin: probably southern; earliest fossil,
Oceanodroma hubbsi, California

24 Diving petrels
Family Pelecanoididae, Upper Pleistocene→
Genus: 1 living
Species: 4 known; 4 living, 2 fossil
Origin: probably Subantarctic; fossils, New
Zealand, Amsterdam Island and Perú

Order Pelecaniformes
(Families 25–34)

25 Tropic birds
Family Phaëthontidae, Lower Eocene→
Genera: 1 living, 1 fossil
Species: 4 known; 3 living, 3 fossil
Origin: probably tropical; earliest fossil,
Prophaeton, England

---

26 Pelicans
Family Pelecanidae, Lower Miocene→
Genera: 1 living, 1 fossil
Species: 17 known; 6 living, 16 fossil
Origin: probably tropical; earliest fossil,
Pelecanus gracilis, France

27 Cyphornis, Palaeochenoides and Tympanonesiotes
Family † Cyphornithidae, Lower Miocene
Genera: 3 fossil
Species: 3 fossil
Have been also placed in suborder
Cladornithes, before family 34

28 Pelagornis
Family † Pelagornithidae, Middle Miocene
Genus and species: 1 fossil
Has been also placed in order
Odontopterygiformes, after family 36

29 Gannets and boobies
Family Sulidae, Lower Oligocene→
Genera: 2 living, 2 fossil
Species: 27 known; 9 living, 22 fossil
Origin: probably tropical; earliest fossil,
Sula ronzoni, France

30 Elopteryx and allies
Family † Elopterygidae, Upper Cretaceous-
Middle Eocene
Genera: 3 fossil
Species: 3 fossil
Earliest fossil, *Elopteryx,* Romania

Cormorants

[Fam]ily Phalacrocoracidae, Upper
[Cret]aceous→
[Gen]era: 2 living, 3 fossil
[Spec]ies: 51 known; 26 living, 1 lately
[exti]nct, 36 fossil
[Ori]gin: probably tropical, possibly Indian
[Oce]an; earliest fossils, *Graculavus*, New
[Jers]ey

Snake birds

[Fam]ily Anhingidae, Middle (?) Eocene→
[Gen]era: 1 living, 1 fossil
[Spec]ies: 5 known; 1 living, 5 fossil
[Ori]gin: probably tropical; earliest fossil
[An]*plotus*, Sumatra

Frigate birds

[Fam]ily Fregatidae, Holocene→
[Gen]us: 1 living
[Spec]ies: 5 known; 5 living, 3 fossil
[Ori]gin: doubtless tropical

Cladornis

[Fam]ily † Cladornithidae, Lower Oligocene
[Gen]us and species: 1 fossil
[bas]ed on poorly preserved tarsometatarsus;
[has] been placed by several authorities in
[pen]guin order, near family 7

[Or]der † Odontopterygiformes

[(Fa]milies 35 and 36)

Odontopteryx

[Fam]ily † Odontopterygidae, Lower Eocene
[Gen]us and species: 1 fossil, England

36 Osteodontornis and Pseudodontornis

Family † Pseudodontornithidae, Miocene
Genera: 2 fossil
Species: 2 fossil
Osteodontornis from Upper Miocene,
California; *Pseudodontornis* from Lower
Miocene, South Carolina

Order Ciconiiformes

(Families 37–41)

37 Herons

Family Ardeidae, Lower Eocene→
Genera: 15 living, 8 fossil
Species: 78 known; 63 living, 1 lately extinct,
36 fossil
Origin: probably tropical or subtropical;
earliest fossil, *Proherodius*, England

38 Hammerhead

Family Scopidae, no fossil known
Genus and species: 1 living
Origin: doubtless Ethiopian

39 Storks

Family Ciconiidae, Lower Oligocene→
Genera: 10 living, 10 fossil
Species: 40 known; 17 living, 30 fossil
Origin: probably tropical or subtropical;
earliest fossils France and Patagonia

40 Shoebill

Family Balaenicipitidae, no fossil known
Genus and species: 1 living
Origin: doubtless African

40A Plegadornis

Family † Plegadornithidae, Upper Cretaceous
Genus and species: 1 fossil, Alabama

41 Ibises and spoonbills

Family Plataleidae, Upper Eocene→
Genera: 20 living, 3 fossil
Species: 38 known; 30 living, 19 fossil
Origin: probably tropical or subtropical;
earliest fossil, *Ibidopsis*, England

Order Phoenicopteriformes

(Families 41A–46)

41A Gallornis, Parascaniornis and Torotix

Family † Torotigidae, Lower to Upper
Cretaceous
Genera: 3 fossil
Species: 3 fossil
Earliest fossil, *Gallornis straeleni*, France;
latest, *Torotix clemensi*, Wyoming

42 Scaniornis

Family † Scaniornithidae, Lower Paleocene
Genus and species: 1 fossil, Sweden

43 Telmabates

Family † Telmabatidae, Lower Eocene
Genus and species: 1 fossil, Argentina

44 Agnopterus

Family † Agnopteridae, Upper Eocene—
Upper Oligocene
Genus: 1 fossil
Species: 3 fossil
Earliest fossil, *Agnopterus hantoniensis*, England

45 Palaelodus and Megapaloelodus

Family † Palaelodidae, Lower Miocene—
Lower Pliocene
Genera: 2 fossil
Species: 8 fossil
Earliest fossils, France and Germany

*Families 41A–45 are all doubtless primitive
flamingo-like birds*

46 Flamingos

Family Phoenicopteridae, Upper Eocene→
Genera: 3 living, 3 fossil
Species: 17 known; 5 living, 14 fossil
Origin: possibly subtropical; earliest fossil,
Elornis, England

171

Order Anseriformes
(Families 47–49)

47 Screamers
Family Anhimidae, Pleistocene→
Genera: 2 living
Species: 3 known; 3 living, 2 fossil
Origin: doubtless South American

48 Paranyroca
Family † Paranyrocidae, Lower Miocene
Genus and species: 1 fossil
Family status has been questioned; may be
tribe in family 49, between pochards etc.
(tribe Aythyini) and eiders, sawbills etc.
(Mergini)

49 Waterfowl
Family Anatidae, Upper Eocene→
Genera: 41 living, 2 lately extinct, 22 fossil
Species: 246 known; 147 living, 4 lately
extinct, 172 fossil
Origin: ancient and geographically uncertain
Earliest fossil, *Eonessa,* Utah

Order Falconiformes
(Families 50–56)

50 Neocathartes
Family † Neocathartidae, Upper Eocene
Genus and species: 1 fossil

51 New World vultures
Family Cathartidae, Lower Eocene→
Genera: 5 living, 10 fossil
Species: 21 known; 6 living, 20 fossil
Origin: possibly North American; though
earliest fossil, *Lithornis,* England; earliest New
World fossils Lower Oligocene, Colorado

Family 51

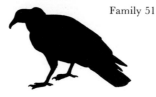

52 Teratorns
Family † Teratornithidae, Upper Pleistocene
Genera: 2 fossil
Species: 3 fossil
Should probably rate as subfamily of 51;
U.S.A. and México

53 Secretary birds
Family Sagittariidae, Upper Eocene or Lower
Oligocene→
Genera: 1 living, 1 fossil
Species: 3 known; 1 living, 2 fossil
Origin: probably Ethiopian; earliest fossil,
Amphiserpentarius schlosseri, France. May be
close to the S. American seriemas, family 80

54 Hawks and eagles
Family Accipitridae, Upper Eocene→
Genera: 58 living, 23 fossil
Species: 271 known; 208 living, 114 fossil
Origin: possibly Old World; earliest fossil,
Palaeocircus, England and France

55 Osprey
Family Pandionidae, Upper Pleistocene→
Genus and species: 1 living and fossil
Origin: uncertain; is cosmopolitan

56 Falcons
Family Falconidae, Middle Miocene→
Genera: 12 living, 3 fossil
Species: 70 known; 58 living, 1 lately
extinct, 29 fossil
Origin: uncertain; earliest fossil, *Badiostes,*
Patagonia

Family 56

Order Galliformes
(Families 57–64)

57 Hoatzins
Family Opisthocomidae, Middle Miocene
Genera: 1 living, 1 fossil
Species: 2 known; 1 living, 1 fossil
Origin: earliest fossil, *Hoazinoides,* Colomb
and family is doubtless South American

58 Gallinuloides
Family † Gallinuloididae, Middle Eocene
Lower Miocene
Genera: 8 fossil
Species: 15 fossil
A precursor of family 59; earliest is
Gallinuloides wyomingensis from Wyoming,
latest *Taoperdix* from France

59 Guans and curassows
Family Cracidae, Lower Oligocene→
Genera: 11 living, 4 fossil
Species: 48 known; 39 living, 17 fossil
Origin: probably North or Central Americ
earliest fossil, *Paracrax antiqua,* Colorado

60 Megapodes
Family Megapodiidae, Pleistocene→
Genera: 7 living, 1 fossil
Species: 12 known; 10 living, 1 lately exti
2 fossil
Origin: doubtless Australasian; earliest
fossil, *Chosornis,* Queensland

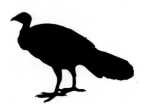

61 Grouse
Family Tetraonidae, Lower Miocene→
Genera: 11 living, 2 fossil
Species: 27 known; 17 living, 20 fossil
Origin: highly probably Nearctic; earliest
fossil, *Palaealectoris,* Nebraska

Family 61

Quails, pheasants, etc.

...ily Phasianidae, Lower Oligocene→
...era: 48 living, 1 lately extinct, 12 fossil
...cies: 218 known; 174 living, 1 lately
...nct, 70 fossil
...gin: possibly Palearctic; though earliest
... may be *Nanortyx*, Saskatchewan

Guineafowl

...nily Numididae, Upper Pleistocene or
...historic→
...era: 5 living
...cies: 7 known; 7 living, 1 fossil
...gin: doubtless Ethiopian; earliest fossil,
...meted guineafowl, *Numida meleagris*,
...choslovakia; reintroduced into Europe
...th century B.C.

Turkeys

...nily Meleagrididae, Lower Pleistocene→
...era: 2 living, 1 fossil
...cies: 9 known; 2 living, 9 fossil
...gin: doubtless North American; earliest
...il, *Agriocharis progenes*, Arizona

der Gruiformes

...milies 65–85A)

Roatelos or mesites

...nily Mesitornithidae, no fossils known
...era: 2 living
...cies: 3 living
...gin: doubtless Madagascan

Bustard quails

...nily Turnicidae, Pleistocene→
...nera: 2 living
...cies: 15 known; 15 living, 1 fossil
...gin: tropical Old World; only fossil, Asia

Family 66

67 Plains wanderer

Family Pedionomidae, no fossil known
Genus and species: 1 living
Origin: doubtless Australian; could perhaps
be relegated to subfamily of 66

68 Geranoides

Family † Geranoididae, Lower Eocene
Genus and species: 1 fossil, Wyoming

69 Eogrus

Family † Eogruidae, Upper Eocene—Upper
Miocene
Genus: 1 fossil
Species: 2 fossil (so far named), Mongolia

70 Cranes

Family Gruidae, Lower Eocene→
Genera: 4 living, 8 fossil
Species: 34 known; 14 living, 27 fossil
Origin: probably Palearctic, though earliest
fossil, *Paragrus*, Wyoming

71 Limpkins

Family Aramidae, Lower Eocene→
Genera: 1 living, 6 fossil
Species: 7 known; 1 living, 7 fossil
Origin: possibly North American; earliest
fossil, *Palaeophasianus*, Wyoming

72 Trumpeters

Family Psophiidae, no fossils known
Genus: 1 living
Species: 3 living
Origin: doubtless South American

73 Ergilornis, Proergilornis and Urmiornis

Family † Ergilornithidae, Lower or Middle
Oligocene to Upper Miocene
Genera: 3 fossil
Species: 3 fossil
May possibly be descended from family 69

74 Idiornis and ally

Family † Idiornithidae, Upper Eocene to
Lower Oligocene
Genera: 2 fossil
Species: 8 fossil, Wyoming and France

75 Rails

Family Rallidae, Upper Cretaceous→
Genera: 46 living, 5 lately extinct, 27 fossil
Species: 186 known; 119 living, 12 lately
extinct, 1 extinct before dodo, 84 fossil
Origin: uncertain; earliest fossils, *Telmatornis*,
New Jersey

76 Finfoots

Family Heliornithidae, no fossils known
Genera: 3 living
Species: 3 living
Origin: doubtless tropical

173

77 Kagu
Family Rhynochetidae, no fossil known
Genus and species: 1 living
Confined to New Caledonia

78 Sun bittern
Family Eurypygidae, no fossil known
Genus and species: 1 living
Origin: doubtless South American

79 Bathornis
Family † Bathornithidae, Lower Oligocene—
Upper Oligocene
Genus: 1 fossil
Species: 3 fossil
Earliest fossil, *Bathornis veredus*, Colorado,
Nebraska, and South Dakota. May possibly
be descended from family 68

80 Seriemas
Family Cariamidae, Lower Oligocene→
Genera: 2 living
Species: 2 known; 2 living, 1 fossil
Origin: unless directly descended from
Bathornithids, probably South American

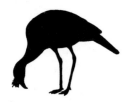

81 Psilopterus and allies
Family † Psilopteridae, Lower Oligocene—
Lower Pleistocene
Genera: 7 fossil
Species: 12 fossil
Earliest fossil, *Riacama*, Patagonia

174

82 Phorusrhacos and allies
Family † Phorusrhacidae, Lower Miocene—
Upper Pleistocene
Genera: 3 fossil
Species: 4 fossil
Earliest fossil, *Phorusrhacos*, Patagonia

82A Palaeociconia and allies
Family † Palaeociconiidae, Lower Oligocene
—Middle Pliocene
Genera: 3 fossil
Species: 4 fossil
Earliest fossil, *Andrewsornis*, Patagonia

83 Brontornis and allies
Family † Brontornithidae, Lower Oligocene
—Middle Miocene
Genera and species: 2 fossil
Earliest fossil, *Physornis*, Patagonia

*N.B. Families 79–83 can be held subfamilies of
one family, the Phorusrhacidae*

84 Cunampaia
Family † Cunampaiidae, Lower Oligocene
Genus and species: 1 fossil, Patagonia

85 Bustards
Family Otididae, Middle Eocene→
Genera: 11 living, 1 fossil
Species: 25 known; 22 living, 5 fossil
Origin: probably Ethiopian, though earliest
fossil, *Palaeotis*, Germany

85A Gryzaja
Family † Gryzajidae, Upper Miocene
Genus and species: 1 fossil, Odessa

Order † Diatrymiformes
(Families 86 and 87)

86 Gastornis and allies
Family † Gastornithidae, Upper Paleocene—
Upper Eocene
Genera: 4 fossil
Species: 6 fossil
Earliest fossils, *Gastornis* and *Remiornis*,
France and England

Family 86

87 Diatryma
Family † Diatrymidae, Middle Paleocene—
Middle Eocene
Genera: 1 fossil
Species: 4 fossil
Origin: uncertain; earliest fossils France;
recorded also from Germany, New Jersey,
New Mexico and Wyoming

Order Charadriiformes
(Families 87A–106)

87A Cimolopteryx and Ceramornis
Family † Cimolopterygidae, Upper
Cretaceous
Genera: 2 fossil
Species: 4 fossil, Wyoming

88 Jaçanas
Family Jacanidae, Upper Pleistocene→
Genera: 6 living
Species: 7 known; 7 living, 1 fossil
Origin: Tropical, possibly Old World; one
fossil, wattled jaçana *Jacana spinosa*, Brazil

89 Rhegminornis
Family † Rhegminornithidae, Lower Mioc[ene]
Genus and species: 1 fossil, Florida

90 Painted snipe
Family Rostratulidae, Middle Eocene→
Genera: 2 living, 1 fossil
Species: 3 known; 2 living, 1 fossil
Origin: probably Old World; only fossil,
Rhynchaeites, Germany

91 Oystercatchers
Family Haematopodidae, Lower Miocene→
Genera: 1 living, 2 fossil
Species: 6 known; 4 living, 3 fossil
Origin: possibly New World, earliest fossil
Paractiornis, Nebraska

Family 91

Plovers and turnstones

mily Charadriidae, Lower Oligocene→
era: 9 living, 2 fossil
cies: 65 known; 60 living, 17 fossil
gin: uncertain; earliest fossil,
achopterus, France

Snipe, sandpipers, and allies

nily Scolopacidae, Upper Cretaceous→
era: 21 living, 1 lately extinct, 4 fossil
cies: 107 known; 75 living, 2 lately
nct, 69 fossil
bably of Holarctic origin; earliest fossils,
aeotringa, New Jersey

Avocets and allies

nily Recurvirostridae, ? Lower Miocene→
era: 3 living
cies: 7 known; 7 living, 2 fossil
graphical origin uncertain; early fossil,
sibly France, needs reinvestigation;
liest otherwise are modern stilt and
cet from Middle Pleistocene Oregon and
rida

Presbyornis and Coltonia

mily † Presbyornithidae, Lower Eocene
nera and species: 2 fossil, Utah

96 Phalaropes

Family Phalaropodidae, Middle
Pleistocene→
Genus: 1 living
Species: 3 known; 3 living, 2 fossil
Origin: North American; earliest fossil,
northern or red-necked phalarope
Phalaropus lobatus, Oregon

97 Crab plover

Family Dromadidae, no fossil known
Genus and species: 1 living
Origin: probably Indian Ocean

98 Thick-knees

Family Burhinidae, Lower Miocene→
Genera: 3 living, 1 fossil
Species: 11 known; 9 living, 3 fossil
Origin: probably Old World; earliest fossil,
Milnea, France

99 Coursers and pratincoles

Family Glareolidae, no fossils known
Genera: 5 living
Species: 16 known; 15 living, 1 lately
extinct
Origin: probably Ethiopian

100 Seed snipe

Family Thinocoridae, no fossils known
Genera: 2 living
Species: 4 living
Origin: doubtless South American

101 Sheathbills

Family Chionididae, no fossils known
Genus: 1 living
Species: 2 living
Origin: probably Subantarctic

Family 101

102 Skuas

Family Stercorariidae, Middle Pleistocene→
Genera: 2 living
Species: 5 known; 4 living, 3 fossil
Origin: doubtless Holarctic; earliest fossil,
Stercorarius shufeldti, Oregon

103 Gulls and terns

Family Laridae, Lower Eocene→
Genera: 4 living, 5 fossil
Species: 92 known; 78 living, 48 fossil
Origin: doubtless Holarctic; earliest fossil,
Halcyornis, England

104 Skimmers

Family Rynchopidae, no fossils known
Genus: 1 living
Species: 3 living
Geographical origin uncertain, probably
tropical

105 Auks

Family Alcidae, Lower Eocene→
Genera: 11 living, 1 lately extinct, 4 fossil
Species: 32 known; 19 living, 1 lately
extinct, 29 fossil
Probably of North Pacific (?Bering Sea)
origin; earliest fossil, *Nautilornis,* Utah

175

106 Lucas auks

Family † Mancallidae, Upper Miocene—
Middle Pliocene
Genera: 3 fossil
Species: 4 fossil
Known only from California; could perhaps
be relegated to subfamily of 105

Order Columbiformes
(Families 107–109)

107 Sand grouse

Family Pteroclidae, Upper Eocene or Lower
Oligocene →
Genera: 2 living
Species: 19 known; 16 living, 5 fossil
Origin: doubtless Ethiopian; earliest fossils,
Pterocles validus and *P. larvatus,* France

108 Pigeons

Family Columbidae, Lower Miocene→
Genera: 48 living, 2 lately extinct, 4 fossil
Species: 299 known; 285 living, 6 lately
extinct, 1 extinct before dodo, 37 fossil
Origin: possibly Australasian; earliest fossil,
Gerandia, France

109 Dodo and solitaires

Family Raphidae, Recent
Genera: 2 lately extinct
Species: 3 lately extinct, 2 fossil
Origin: doubtless Mascarene; probably
descended from pigeons (108), possibly from
rails (75)

Order Psittaciformes
(Family 110)

110 Parrots

Family Psittacidae, Lower Miocene→
Genera: 69 living, 3 lately extinct, 2 fossil
Species: 340 known; 317 living, 15 lately
extinct, 3 extinct before dodo, 26 fossil
Origin: probably Australasian, though
earliest fossil, *Archaeopsittacus,* France

Family 110

Order Musophagiformes
(Family 111)

111 Touracos

Family Musophagidae, no fossils known
Genera: 5 living
Species: 18 living
Origin: doubtless Ethiopian

Order Cuculiformes
(Family 112)

112 Cuckoos

Family Cuculidae, Upper Eocene or Lower
Oligocene→
Genera: 34 living, 3 fossil
Species: 131 known; 125 living, 1 lately
extinct, 12 fossil
Origin: probably Old World; earliest fossil,
Dynamopterus France

Order Strigiformes
(Families 113–115)

113 Barn owls

Family Tytonidae, Lower Miocene→
Genera: 2 living, 1 fossil
Species: 18 known; 11 living, 8 fossil
Origin: probably Palearctic; earliest fossils,
2 species of modern genus *Tyto,* France

114 Protostrix

Family † Protostrigidae, Lower Eocene—
Middle Eocene
Genus: 1 fossil
Species: 5 fossil
Origin: probably North American; earliest
fossil, *Protostrix mimica,* Wyoming

Family 114

115 Typical owls

Family Strigidae, Upper Eocene or Lower
Oligocene→
Genera: 22 living, 3 fossil
Species: 148 known; 120 living, 3 lately
extinct, 56 fossil
Origin: probably Palearctic; earliest fossils,
4 genera (including modern *Bubo* and *Asio*)
France

Order Caprimulgiformes
(Families 116–120)

116 Oilbird

Family Steatornithidae, no fossil known
Genus and species: 1 living
Origin: doubtless South American

117 Owlet frogmouths

Family Aegothelidae, Holocene→
Genus: 1 living, 1 fossil
Species: 6 known; 4 living, 1 lately extinct,
1 fossil
Origin: probably Australasian; only fossil,
Megaegotheles, New Zealand

118 Frogmouths

Family Podargidae, no fossils known
Genera: 2 living
Species: 12 living
Origin: probably Oriental

Nightjars

mily Caprimulgidae, Lower Pleistocene→
era: 18 living
cies: 69 known; 69 living, 8 fossil
gin: probably New World, though earliest
il, living nightjar *Caprimulgus europaeus*,
mania

Potoos

nily Nyctibiidae, Upper Pleistocene→
nus: 1 living
cies: 5 known; 5 living, 1 fossil
gin: doubtless South American; only
il, Brazil

der Apodiformes

milies 121–124)

Aegialornis

nily † Aegialornithidae, Upper Eocene or
ver Oligocene
nus: 1 fossil
cies: 2 fossil
gin: probably Old World; only fossils,
nce

Swifts

nily Apodidae, Upper Eocene or Lower
gocene→
nera: 8 living, 1 fossil
cies: 69 known; 65 living, 11 fossil
gin: possibly Old World; earliest fossil,
selavus gallicus, France

Crested swifts

mily Hemiprocnidae, no fossils known
nus: 1 living
cies: 3 living
gin: probably Oriental

Family 123

124 Hummingbirds

Family Trochilidae, Upper Pleistocene→
Genera: 123 living
Species: 320 known; 320 living, 1 fossil
Origin: probably South American: only
fossil, Brazil

Order Coliiformes
(Family 125)

125 Colies

Family Coliidae, ? Lower Miocene→
Genus: 1 living
Species: 6 living
Origin: doubtless Ethiopian; German early
fossils await publication

Order Trogoniformes
(Family 126)

126 Trogons

Family Trogonidae, Upper Eocene or Lower
Oligocene→
Genera: 8 living, 2 fossil
Species: 39 known; 35 living, 6 fossil
Origin: possibly New World, though earliest
fossils, *Archaeotrogon*, France

Order Coraciiformes
(Families 127–136)

127 Kingfishers

Family Alcedinidae, Upper Eocene→
Genera: 12 living, 1 fossil
Species: 89 known; 86 living, 1 lately extinct,
7 fossil
Origin: doubtless Old World; earliest fossils,
Protornis, Switzerland

Family 127

128 Todies

Family Todidae, no fossils known
Genus: 1 living
Species: 5 living
Origin: probably North American

129 Motmots

Family Momotidae, Upper Pleistocene→
Genera: 6 living
Species: 8 known; 8 living, 1 fossil
Origin: probably North American; earliest
fossil, modern species, Brazil

130 Bee eaters

Family Meropidae, Pleistocene→
Genera: 6 living
Species: 25 known; 25 living, 1 fossil
Origin: doubtless Ethiopian; only fossil,
living common bee eater *Merops apiaster*,
Don Valley, USSR

131 Rollers

Family Coraciidae, Upper Eocene or Lower
Oligocene→
Genera: 2 living, 1 fossil
Species: 12 known; 11 living, 3 fossil
Origin: doubtless Old World; earliest fossil
Geranopterus, France

177

132 Ground rollers
Family Brachypteraciidae, no fossils known
Genera: 3 living
Species: 5 living
Origin: doubtless Madagascan

133 Cuckoo roller
Family Leptosomatidae, no fossil known
Genus and species: 1 living
Origin: doubtless Madagascan

134 Hoopoe
Family Upupidae, Middle Pleistocene→
Genus and species: 1 living and fossil
Origin: doubtless Ethiopian; earliest fossil
Palestine

135 Wood hoopoes
Family Phoeniculidae, Lower Miocene→
Genera: 2 living, 1 fossil
Species: 7 known; 6 living, 1 fossil
Origin: probably Ethiopian; only fossil,
Limnatornis, France

136 Hornbills
Family Bucerotidae, Middle Eocene→
Genera: 12 living, 2 fossil
Species: 46 known; 44 living, 3 fossil
Origin: probably Ethiopian; earliest fossil,
Geisleroceros, Germany

178

Order Piciformes
(Families 137–142)

137 Jacamars
Family Galbulidae, no fossils known
Genera: 5 living
Species: 15 living
Origin: doubtless South American

138 Puffbirds
Family Bucconidae, Middle Eocene→
Genera: 10 living, 1 fossil
Species: 31 known; 30 living, 3 fossil
Origin: only early fossil is *Uintornis*, Wyoming

139 Barbets
Family Capitonidae, Upper Pleistocene→
Genera: 13 living
Species: 72 known; 72 living, 1 fossil
Origin: probably Old World, though only
fossil Brazil

140 Honeyguides
Family Indicatoridae, no fossils known
Genera: 4 living
Species: 14 living
Origin: doubtless Ethiopian

141 Toucans
Family Ramphastidae, Upper Pleistocene→
Genera: 5 living
Species: 37 known; 37 living, 2 fossil
Origin: doubtless South American; only
fossils Brazil

142 Woodpeckers
Family Picidae, Lower Miocene→
Genera: 36 living, 3 fossil
Species: 214 known; 209 living, 31 fossil
Origin: possibly New World, though earl
fossil, *Palaeopicus*, France

Order Passeriformes
(Families 143–199)

143 Broadbills
Family Eurylaimidae, Lower Miocene→
Genera: 8 living, 1 fossil
Species: 14 living, 1 fossil
Origin: probably Oriental; but only early
fossil Germany

144 Furnariids
Family Furnariidae, 2 subfamilies raised
some authorities to family rank

144a Woodhewers
Subfamily Dendrocolaptinae, Upper
Pleistocene→
Genera: 13 living
Species: 47 known; 47 living, 2 fossil
Origin: doubtless South American; only
fossils Brazil

144b Ovenbirds
Subfamily Furnariinae, Upper Pleistocene
Genera: 58 living
Species: 215 known; 215 living, 2 fossil
Origin: doubtless South American; only
fossils Brazil

145 Ant thrushes
Family Formicariidae, Upper Pleistocene-
Genera: 53 living
Species: 224 known; 224 living, 1 fossil
Origin: doubtless South American; only
fossil Brazil

146 Ant pipits

Family Conopophagidae, no fossils known
Genera: 2 living
Species: 11 living
Origin: doubtless South American

147 Tapaculos

Family Rhinocryptidae, Lower or Middle
Eocene→
Genera: 12 living, 1 fossil
Species: 30 known; 29 living, 1 fossil
Origin: probably South American; only
fossil, *Neanis,* Wyoming, is but provisionally
assigned to this family

148 Pittas

Family Pittidae, no fossils known
Genus: 1 living
Species: 25 living
Origin: probably Oriental

149 Asities

Family Philepittidae, no fossils known
Genera: 2 living
Species: 4 living
Origin: doubtless Madagascan

150 New Zealand wrens

Family Acanthisittidae, no fossils known
Genera: 2 living
Species: 4 known; 3 living, 1 lately extinct
Origin: doubtless New Zealand

151 Tyrant flycatchers

Family Tyrannidae, Upper Pleistocene→
Genera: 116 living
Species: 364 known; 364 living, 9 fossil
Origin: probably South American; only
fossils Brazil, California, Virginia, Florida,
and W. Indies

152 Manakins

Family Pipridae, no fossils known
Genera: 21 living
Species: 61 living
Origin: doubtless South American

153 Cotingas

Family Cotingidae, no fossils known
Genera: 33 living
Species: 91 living
Origin: doubtless South American

154 Plantcutters

Family Phytotomidae, no fossils known
Genus: 1 living
Species: 3 living
Origin: doubtless South American

155 Lyrebirds

Family Menuridae, no fossils known
Genus: 1 living
Species: 2 living
Origin: doubtless Australian

156 Scrub birds

Family Atrichornithidae, no fossils known
Genus: 1 living
Species: 2 living
Origin: doubtless Australian

157 Larks

Family Alaudidae, Lower Pliocene→
Genera: 15 living
Species: 78 known; 75 living, 11 fossil
Origin: possibly Ethiopian; earliest fossils,
Alauda gypsorum and *A. major,* Italy

158 Palaeospiza

Family † Palaeospizidae, Middle or Upper
Oligocene
Genus and species: 1 fossil
Colorado only

159 Swallows

Family Hirundinidae, Lower Pleistocene→
Genera: 20 living
Species: 81 known; 79 living, 10 fossil
Origin: probably Oriental; earliest fossil,
extinct *Hirundo aprica,* Kansas

179

160 Wagtails and pipits
Family Motacillidae, Lower Miocene→
Genera: 5 living
Species: 56 known; 53 living, 10 fossil
Origin: probably Ethiopian, though earliest fossils, *Motacilla humata* and *M. major*, France

161 Cuckoo shrikes
Family Campephagidae, no fossils known
Genera: 9 living
Species: 70 living
Origin: probably Australasian, possibly Oriental

162 Bulbuls
Family Pycnonotidae, Middle Pleistocene→
Genera: 15 living
Species: 119 known; 119 living, 1 fossil
Origin: probably Ethiopian; only fossil, common bulbul *Pycnonotus barbatus*, Palestine

163 Leaf birds
Family Irenidae, no fossils known
Genera: 3 living
Species: 14 living
Origin: doubtless Oriental

164 Shrikes
Family Laniidae, Lower Miocene→
Genera: 12 living
Species: 75 known; 74 living, 7 fossil
Origin: probably Palearctic; earliest fossil, modern genus *Lanius*, France

180

165 Vanga shrikes
Family Vangidae, no fossils known
Genera: 9 living
Species: 13 living
Origin: doubtless Madagascan

166 Waxwings and allies
Family Bombycillidae, Upper Pleistocene→
Genera: 5 living
Species: 8 known; 8 living, 2 fossil
Origin: probably North American; earliest fossil, waxwing *Bombycilla garrulus*, Monaco

167 Palm chat
Family Dulidae, no fossil known
Genus and species: 1 living
Origin: doubtless West Indian

168 Dippers
Family Cinclidae, Upper Pleistocene→
Genus: 1 living
Species: 4 known; 4 living, 1 fossil
Origin: probably North American; earliest fossil, dipper *Cinclus cinclus*, Austria

169 Palaeoscinis
Family † Palaeoscinidae, Middle Miocene
Genus and species: 1 fossil
California only; some would place not here, but near families 162 and 163

170 Wrens
Family Troglodytidae, Middle Pleistocene→
Genera: 14 living
Species: 60 known; 59 living, 5 fossil
Origin: probably North American; earliest fossil, extinct *Cistothorus brevis*, Florida

Family 170

171 Thrashers and mockers
Family Mimidae, Upper Pleistocene (?Middle Pliocene)→
Genera: 13 living
Species: 31 known; 31 living, 8 fossil
Origin: probably North American; fossils Brazil, California, Virginia, and Puerto Rico; unnamed Méxican material of the Middle Pliocene may belong to this family

172 Accentors
Family Prunellidae, Pleistocene→
Genus: 1 living
Species: 12 known; 12 living, 2 fossil
Origin: doubtless Palearctic; fossils Italy, Monaco, England, Wales

173 Muscicapids
Family Muscicapidae; this is so large that we break it down into subfamilies (which some authorities rate as full families) as follows:

173a Thrushes
Subfamily Turdinae, Upper Pliocene→
Genera: 41 living, 1 fossil
Species: 304 known; 300 living, 3 lately extinct, 23 fossil
Origin: probably Old World; earliest fossil, blue rock thrush *Monticola solitarius*, France

173b Babblers
Subfamily Timaliinae, Middle Pleistocene→
Genera: 57 living
Species: 258 known; 258 living, 2 fossil
Origin: Old World, possibly Palearctic; earliest fossil, brown babbler *Turdoides squamiceps*, Palestine

73c Bearded tit and parrotbills

Subfamily Panurinae, no fossils known
Genera: 3 living
Species: 19 living
Origin: probably Palearctic

73d Gnatcatchers

Subfamily Polioptilinae, no fossils known
Genus: 1 living
Species: 11 living
Origin: doubtless North American

73e Old World warblers and gnatwrens

Subfamily Sylviinae, Lower Miocene→
Genera: 61 living
Species: 323 known; 320 living, 2 lately extinct, 10 fossil
Origin: Old World (only 7 species in New); earliest fossil, *Sylvia* species, France. Includes goldcrests, sometimes separated as subfamily Regulinae

73f Australian warblers

Subfamily Malurinae, no fossils known.
Genera: 25 living
Species: 83 living
Origin: doubtless Australasian

173g Old World flycatchers and fantails

Subfamily Muscicapinae, Middle Pleistocene→
Genera: 35 living
Species: 286 known; 286 living, 2 fossil
Origin: Old World, but zone uncertain; earliest fossil, spotted flycatcher *Muscicapa striata*, Palestine

173h Monarchs

Subfamily Monarchinae, no fossils known
Genera: 9 living
Species: 63 living
Origin: doubtless Australasian

173i Whistlers and piopio

Subfamily Pachycephalinae, Holocene→
Genera: 13 living
Species: 49 known; 49 living, 1 fossil
Origin: doubtless Australasian; only fossil, piopio *Turnagra capensis*, New Zealand

173j Bald crows

Subfamily Picathartinae, no fossils known
Genus: 1 living
Species: 2 living
Origin: doubtless Ethiopian

174 Titmice

Family Paridae, Upper Eocene→
Genera: 9 living, 1 fossil
Species: 63 known; 62 living, 9 fossil
Origin: probably Palearctic; earliest fossil, *Palaegithalus*, France

175 Nuthatches

Family Sittidae, Lower Pliocene→
Genera: 6 living
Species: 32 known; 31 living, 5 fossil
Origin: probably Palearctic; earliest fossil, *Sitta senogalliensis*, Italy. 6 species of *Climacteris*, Australian tree creepers, no fossils known, have been separated by one authority as family Climacteridae

176 Creepers

Family Certhiidae, Lower Pleistocene→
Genera: 2 living
Species: 6 known; 6 living, 1 fossil
Origin: doubtless Old World, possibly Palearctic; only fossil, tree creeper *Certhia familiaris*, earliest Romania

177 Flowerpeckers

Family Dicaeidae, no fossils known
Genera: 7 living
Species: 53 living, 1 lately extinct
Origin: probably Oriental

178 Sunbirds

Family Nectariniidae, no fossils known
Genera: 4 living
Species: 105 living
Origin: probably Ethiopian

179 Whiteyes

Family Zosteropidae, no fossils known
Genera: 10 living
Species: 79 known; 78 living, 1 lately extinct
Origin: probably Oriental

180 Honeyeaters
Family Meliphagidae, Holocene→
Genera: 65 living, 1 lately extinct
Species: 162 known; 158 living, 4 lately
extinct, 1 fossil
Origin: doubtless Australasian; only fossil,
tui *Prosthemadera novaeseelandiae*, New Zealand

181 Emberizids *Family Emberizidae; this is so large that we break it down into subfamilies and tribes as follows*

181a Emberizinae
(i) Buntings and American sparrows
Tribe Emberizini, Lower Pliocene→
Genera: 56 living, 1 fossil
Species: 201 known; 197 living, 1 lately
extinct, 26 fossil
Origin: probably North American, earliest
fossils, *Palaeostruthus*, Kansas and Florida

(ii) Darwin's finches
Tribe Geospizini, no fossils known
Genera: 4 living
Species: 14 living
Origin: doubtless Galápagos Is., probably
from C. or S. American Emberizine
ancestor

181b Cardinals and allies
Subfamily Cardinalinae, Upper Pleistocene→
Genera: 31 living
Species: 110 known; 110 living, 5 fossil
Origin: doubtless American, possibly South
American; fossils Brazil, Florida, California
and Puerto Rico

181c Plush-capped finch
Subfamily Catamblyrhynchinae, no fossil
known
Genus and species: 1 living
Origin: doubtless South American

182

181d Tanagers
Subfamily Tanagrinae, Holocene→
Genera: 61 living
Species: 191 known; 191 living, 2 fossil
Origin: doubtless American, possibly South
American, only fossils Puerto Rico

181e Swallow tanager
Subfamily Tersininae, Upper Pleistocene→
Genus and species: 1 living and fossil
Origin: doubtless South American; only
fossil Brazil

181f Honeycreepers
Subfamily Coerebinae
(i) Tanager-like honeycreepers
Tribe Dacnini, no fossils known
Genera: 9 living
Species: 26 living
Origin: doubtless South American; may be
in subfamily 181d

(ii) Wood warbler-like honeycreepers
Tribe Coerebini, Holocene→
Genera: 3 living
Species: 10 known; 10 living, 1 subfossil
Origin: doubtless South American, fossil
Puerto Rico, may be in family 182

182 Wood warblers
Family Parulidae, Middle Pleistocene→
Genera: 18 living
Species: 113 known; 113 living, 4 fossil or
subfossil
Origin: probably North American; earliest
fossil, yellowthroat *Geothlypis trichas*, Florida

183 Hawaiian honeycreepers
Family Drepanididae, no fossils known
Genera: 7 living, 2 lately extinct
Species: 22 known; 14 living, 8 lately
extinct
Origin· doubtless Hawaiian, from Emberizid
or more probably Fringillid ancestor from
the Americas

184 Vireos and allies
Family Vireonidae, Upper Pleistocene→
Genera: 8 living
Species: 42 known; 42 living, 2 fossil
Origin: probably North American, though
only fossils Brazil and Puerto Rico

185 Icterids
Family Icteridae, Middle Pleistocene→
Genera: 35 living, 3 fossil
Species: 93 known; 88 living, 19 fossil
Origin: doubtless New World, possibly
South American; earliest fossil, Florida

186 Finches
Family Fringillidae, Lower Pleistocene→
Genera: 29 living, 1 lately extinct
Species: 124 known; 123 living, 1 lately
extinct, 19 fossil
Origin: probably Old World, possibly
Palearctic; earliest fossils, chaffinch
Fringilla coelebs and hawfinch *Coccothraustes
coccothraustes*, Romania. Bones from the
Upper Miocene of Spain have been referred
to the genus *Fringilla*

187 Waxbills and allies
Family Estrildidae, no fossils known
Genera: 17 living
Species: 107 living
Origin: doubtless Old World, possibly
Ethiopian

188 Widow birds
Family Viduidae, no fossils known
Genera: 2 living
Species: 8 living
Origin: doubtless Ethiopian

Family 188

9 Weavers and true sparrows

nily Ploceidae, Lower Miocene→
nera: 17 living, 1 lately extinct
cies: 136 known; 132 living, 2 lately
inct, 8 fossil
gin: doubtless Old World, probably
iopian; earliest fossil, sparrow, *Passer*
cies, France

0 Starlings

mily Sturnidae, Upper Eocene→
nera: 24 living, 1 lately extinct, 1 fossil
cies: 114 known; 107 living, 4 lately
nct, 9 fossil
gin: doubtless Old World, possibly
iopian; earliest fossils, *Laurillardia,* France

1 Old World orioles

mily Oriolidae, Pleistocene→
nera: 2 living
cies: 28 known; 28 living, 2 fossil
gin: doubtless Old World, possibly
stralasian; earliest fossils, golden oriole
olus oriolus, Europe and Palestine

2 Drongos

mily Dicruridae, Pleistocene→
nera: 2 living
cies: 19 known; 19 living, 1 fossil
gin: doubtless Old World, possibly
iental; may be close to Old World
catchers, family 173; only fossil, *Dicrurus*
cies, China

193 Wattled crows

Family Callaeidae, Holocene→
Genera: 2 living, 1 lately extinct
Species: 3 known; 2 living, 1 lately extinct,
3 fossil
Origin: doubtless New Zealand, where all
found

194 Magpie larks

Family Grallinidae, no fossils known
Genera: 3 living
Species: 4 living
Origin: doubtless Australian

195 Wood swallows

Family Artamidae, no fossils known
Genus: 1 living
Species: 10 living
Origin: probably Australasian, possibly
Oriental

196 Bell magpies

Family Cracticidae, no fossils known
Genera: 3 living
Species: 10 living
Origin: doubtless Australian

197 Bower birds

Family Ptilononorhynchidae, no fossils known
Genera: 8 living
Species: 17 living
Origin: doubtless New Guinea or tropical
Australia

198 Birds of paradise

Family Paradisaeidae, no fossils known
Genera: 20 living
Species: 40 living
Origin: doubtless New Guinea

199 Crows

Family Corvidae, Middle Miocene→
Genera: 20 living, 4 fossil
Species: 113 known; 102 living, 37 fossil
Origin: probably Palearctic; earliest fossil,
Miocorvus, France

Identification of the feathers on page 27.
Numbers in brackets refer to the birds'
families or subfamilies, as listed in The
Regiment of Birds (pp. 168-183).

1. Quetzal (126)
2. Pennant-wing nightjar (119)
3. Sun bittern (78)
4. American kestrel (56)
5. Ostrich (9)
6. Peacock (62)
7. Superb lyrebird (155)
8. Common touraco (111)
9. King of Saxony bird of paradise (198)
10. Golden cock-of-the-rock (153)
11. Quetzal (126)
12. Mallard (49)
13. Scott's oriole (185)
14. Jaçana (88)
15. Vulturine guineafowl (63)
16. Rufous-sided towhee (181a)
17. Turkey (64)
18. Common pheasant (62)
19. Bohemian waxwing (166)
20. Snake bird or darter (32)
21. Blue-and-yellow macaw (110)
22. Dufresne's parrot (110)
23. Turquoise-browed motmot (129)
24. Roseate spoonbill (41)
25. James's flamingo (46)
26 and 27. Harlequin quail (62)
28. Red-shafted flicker (142)
29. Blue jay (199)
30. Emu (11)
31. Ruffed grouse (61)
32. King bird of paradise (198)

BIBLIOGRAPHY

This guide to further reading, intended for the general non-academic reader, is limited and arbitrarily selective. Many excellent works are omitted. A more extensive though less up-to-date list is available in THE WORLD OF BIRDS, Fisher and Peterson, 1964.

Fossil Birds

BRODKORB, Pierce (1963-67), *Catalog of Fossil Birds*. Gainesville, *Bull. Fla. State Mus.* Vol. 7: 179-293; vol. 8: 195-335; vol. 11: 99-220.
SWINTON, W. E. (1958), *Fossil Birds*, London, British Museum (Nat. Hist.), 63 pp.
WETMORE, Alexander (1956), *A Check-List of the Fossil and Prehistoric Birds of North America and the West Indies*, Smithson Misc. Coll. 131: no. 5; 105 pp.

General World

AUSTIN, Oliver L. Jr. and SINGER, Arthur (1961), *Birds of the World*, New York, Golden Press, 317 pp.
DARLING, Lois and DARLING, Louis (1962), *Bird*, Boston, Houghton Mifflin, 261 pp.
FISHER, James and PETERSON, Roger Tory (1964), *The World of Birds*, London, Macdonald & Co. 287 pp.
FITTER, R. S. R. (1963), *Collins Guide to Bird Watching*, London, Collins, 254 pp.
GILLIARD, E. Thomas (1958), *Living Birds of the World*, New York, Doubleday, 400 pp.
WETMORE, Alexander (1960), *A Classification for the Birds of the World*, Smithson. Misc. Coll. 139: no. 11; 37 pp.
WELTY, Joel Carl (1962), *The Life of Birds*, Philadelphia etc., Saunders, 546 pp.
VAN TYNE, Josselyn and BERGER, Andrew J. (1959), *Fundamentals of Ornithology*, New York, Wiley, 624 pp.
PETTINGILL, Olin Sewall Jr. (1956), *A Laboratory and Field Manual of Ornithology*, Minneapolis, Burgess, 379 pp.
PETERSON, Roger Tory (1963), *The Birds*, New York, Time, 192 pp.
PETERS, James Lee and others (1931-70), *Check-List of the Birds of the World*, Cambridge, Mass., Harvard University Press. 15 vols.
MAYR, E. and AMADON, D. (1951), *A Classification of Recent Birds*, Amer. Mus. Novit. no. 1496; 42 pp.
LANYON, Wesley E. (1963), *Biology of Birds*, Garden City, N.Y. The Natural History Press, 175 pp.
LANDSBOROUGH-THOMSON, A. (1964), *A New Dictionary of Birds*, New York, McGraw-Hill, 928 pp.
GOODERS, J. and others (1969-1970), *Birds of the World*, London, IPC Magazines Ltd. 6 vols.

Special Aspects

DORST, Jean (1962), *The Migrations of Birds*, Boston, Houghton Mifflin Co., 476 pp.
FISHER, James (1966), *The Shell Bird Book*, (historical), London, Ebury Press, Michael Joseph, 344 pp.
FISHER, J., SIMON, N. and VINCENT, J. (1969), *The Red Book: Wildlife in Danger*, London, Collins, 368 pp.
LOCKLEY, R. M. and RUSSELL, Rosemary (1953), *Bird-Ringing*, London, Crosby Lockwood, 119 pp.
MATTHEWS, G. V. T. (1968), *Bird Navigation*, London, Cambridge University Press, 197 pp.
STORER, J. H. (1948), *The Flight of Birds . . .*, Cranbrook Inst. Sci. Bull., no. 28; 94 pp.
THORPE, W. H. (1960), *Bird Song*, Cambridge, University Press, 143 pp.

North and South America, etc.

AMERICAN ORNITHOLOGISTS' UNION (1957), *Check-List of North American Birds*, Baltimore, A.O.U., 691 pp.
BLAKE, Emmett Reid (1953), *Birds of México*, Chicago, University of Chicago Press, 644 pp.
BOND, James (1961), *Birds of the West Indies*, Boston, Houghton Mifflin, 256 pp.
De SCHAUENSEE, R. Meyer (1970), *A Guide to the Birds of South America*, Wynnewood, Pa., Livingston Publishing Co., 470 pp.
EISENMANN, Eugene (1955), *The Species of Middle American Birds*, Trans. Linn. Soc. N.Y. 7; 128 pp.
GABRIELSON, Ira N. and LINCOLN, F. C. (1959), *Birds of Alaska*, Washington, D.C., Wildlife Management Institute, 922 pp.
GODFREY, W. E. (1966), *The Birds of Canada*, Ottawa, Queens Publisher, 428 pp.
HAVERSCHMIDT, F. (1968), *The Birds of Surinam*, London and Edinburgh, Oliver & Boyd, 445 pp.
LAND, H. C. (1970), *Birds of Guatemala*, Wynnewood, Pa., Livingston Publishing Co., 300 pp.
PALMER, Ralph S. ed. (1962), *Handbook of North American Birds*, New Haven and London, Yale University Press, vol. I; 567 pp.
PETERSON, Roger Tory (1947), *A Field Guide to the Birds*, Boston, Houghton Mifflin, 290 pp.
PETERSON, Roger Tory (1961), *A Field Guide to Western Birds*, Boston, Houghton Mifflin, 366 pp.
PETTINGILL, Olin Sewall Jr. (1951), *A Guide to Bird-Finding East of the Mississippi*, New York, Oxford University Press, 659 pp.
PETTINGILL, Olin Sewall Jr. (1957), *A Guide to Bird-Finding West of the Mississippi*, New York, Oxford University Press, 704 pp.
POUGH, Richard H. (1946), *Audubon Bird Guide: Small Land Birds of Eastern and Central North America . . .*, Garden City, Doubleday, 312 pp.
POUGH, Richard H. (1951), *Audubon Bird Guide: Water Birds*, Garden City, Doubleday, 352 pp.
POUGH, Richard H. (1957), *Audubon Western Bird Guide*, Garden City, Doubleday, 316 pp.
REED, Chester A. (1965), *North American Birds' Eggs*, New York, Dover Publications, Inc., 372 pp.
REILLEY, E. M., Jr. (1968), *The Audubon Illustrated Handbook of American Birds*, New York, McGraw-Hill, 524 pp.
RIDGWAY, R. and FRIEDMANN, H. (1901-50), *Birds of North and Middle America*, Bull. U.S. Nat. Mus., 11 vols.
ROBBINS, Chandler and SINGER, Arthur (1966), *Birds of North America*, New York, Golden Press, 340 pp.
WETMORE, Alexander and others (1964), *Song and Garden Birds of North America*, Washington, D.C. National Geographic Society, 400 pp.
WETMORE, Alexander and others (1965), *Water and Game Birds of North America*, Washington, D.C. National Geographic Society, 464 pp.

Eurasia (Palearctic)

BANNERMAN, D. A. and LODGE, G. E. (1953-63), *The Birds of the British Isles*, Edinburgh etc., Oliver & Boyd, 12 vols.
BRITISH ORNITHOLOGISTS' UNION (1952), *Checklist of the Birds of Great Britain and Ireland*, London, B.O.U., 106 pp.
BRUUN, B. and SINGER, A. (1969), *British and European Birds in Color*, London, Hamlyn.
BRUUN, B. and SINGER, A. (1970), *Hamlyn Guide to the Birds of Britain and Europe*, London, Hamlyn.
DELACOUR, J. and MAYR, E. (1946), *Birds of the Philippines*, New York, Macmillan, 309 pp.
DEMENTIEV, G. P. and GLADKOV, N. A. (1966-69), *Birds of the Soviet Union*, Vols. 1-4 and 6. Jerusalem, *Israel Prog. Sci. . . .* Translations.
FISHER, James (1947-64), *Bird Recognition*, Harmondsworth, Penguin, 4 vol.
FISHER, James (1967), *Thorburn's Birds*, London, Ebury Press, Michael Joseph, 184 pp.
FITTER, R. S. R. and RICHARDSON, R. A. (1952), *The Pocket Guide to British Birds*, London, Collins, 240 pp.
FITTER, R. S. R. and others (1955), *The Pocket Guide to Nests and Eggs*, London, Collins, 172 pp.
FITTER, R. S. R. and others (1969), *Book of British Birds*, London, Reader's Digest, Drive Publications, 472 pp.
GOODERS, J. (1970), *Where to Watch Birds in Britain and Europe*, London, Andre Deutsch.
HOLLOM, P. A. D. ed. (1952), *The Popular Handbook of British Birds*, London, Witherby, 424 pp.
HOLLOM, P. A. D. (1960), *The Popular Handbook of Rarer British Birds*, London, Witherby, 133 pp.
PETERSON, Roger Tory, MOUNTFORT Guy, and HOLLOM, P. A. D. (1954), *A Field Guide to the Birds of Britain and Europe*, London, Collins, 318 pp.
VAURIE, Charles (1959), *The Birds of the Palearctic Fauna*, Vol. 1. Passeriformes; Vol. 2. Non-passeriformes. London, Witherby, 762 pp. each vol.
VOOUS, K. H. (1960), *Atlas of European Birds*, London, Nelson, 284 pp.
WITHERBY, H. F. and others (1938-41), *The Handbook of British Birds*, London, Witherby, 5 vols.
YAMASHINA, Yoshimaro (1961), *Birds in Japan, a Field Guide*, Tokyo, Tokyo News Service, 233 pp.

Africa

BANNERMAN, David A. (1953), *The Birds of West and Equatorial Africa*, Edinburgh, Oliver & Boyd, 2 vols., 1526 pp.
ETCHECOPAR, R. D. and HÜE, F. (1967), *The Birds of North Africa*, English translation, London, Oliver & Boyd, 612 p
MACKWORTH-PRAED, C. W. and GRANT, C. H. B. (1952-1970), *African Handbook of Birds*.
Series 1, Eastern and Northeastern Africa (1952)
Series 2 Southern third of Africa (1962-63)

ies 3 West Central and Western Africa
70). London, Longmans Green.
LACHLAN, G. P. and LIVERSIDGE,
(1957), *Birds of South Africa*, Cape Town,
e Times, Ltd., 504 pp.
OREAU, R. E. (1966), *The Bird Faunas*
Africa and its Islands, New York, London,
ademic Press, 424 pp.
OZENSKY, O. M. (1970), *Field Guide to*
Birds of South Africa, London, Collins,
 pp.
LLIAMS, John G. (1963), *A Field Guide*
he Birds of East and Central Africa,
ndon, Collins, 288 pp.

lia, Australasia, etc.

I, Salim and RIPLEY, S. Dillon
68-1970), *Handbook of the Birds of India*
Pakistan, Vols. I-IV, London, Oxford
iversity Press,
YLEY, Neville W. (1931), *What Bird is*
at? A Guide to the Birds of Australia, Sydney,
gus & Robertson, 319 pp.
LACOUR, J. (1947), *Birds of Malaysia*,
w York, Macmillan, 382 pp.
LL, Robin (1967), *Australian Birds*,
lbourne, Thomas Nelson, 281 pp.
AYR, Ernst (1945), *Birds of the Southwest*
ific, New York, Macmillan, 316 pp.
ND, A. L. and GILLIARD, E. T.
67), *Handbook of New Guinea Birds*,
ndon, Weidenfeld & Nicholson, 622 pp.

SMYTHIES, Bertram E. (1953), *The Birds*
of Burma, Edinburgh, etc., Oliver & Boyd,
668 pp.
SMYTHIES, Bertram E. (1960), *The Birds*
of Borneo, Edinburgh, etc., Oliver & Boyd,
562 pp.

**Major Groups of Birds, Life Histories,
etc.**

ALEXANDER, W. B. (1954), *Birds of the*
Ocean, New York, Putnam, 428 pp.
BENT, Arthur Cleveland and others
(1919-), *Life Histories of North American*
Birds, Bull. U.S. Nat. Mus., 20 vols. to 1958.
BROWN, L. and AMADON, D. (1968),
Eagles, Hawks, and Falcons of the World.
London, Country Life, 2 vols.
DELACOUR, J. (1954-64), *The Waterfowl*
of the World, London, Country Life, ill.
Peter Scott, 4 vols.
DELACOUR, J. (1951), *The Pheasants of the*
World, London, Country Life, 347 pp.
FISHER, James and LOCKLEY, R. M.
(1954), *Sea-Birds*, London, Collins, *New*
Naturalist, 320 pp.
FORSHAW, J. M. (1969), *Australian*
Parrots, Melbourne, Lansdowne Press,
306 pp.
GOODWIN, D. (1967), *Pigeons and Doves of*
the World, London, British Museum,
446 pp.
GREENEWALT, Crawford H. (1960),

Hummingbirds, Garden City, N.Y.,
Doubleday, 250 pp.
GRISCOM, Ludlow and others (1957),
The Warblers of America, New York,
Devin-Adair, 356 pp.
GROSSMAN, M. L. and HAMLET, J.
(1964), *Birds of Prey of the World*, New York,
Clarkson N. Potter, 496 pp.
JOHNSGAARD, P. A. (1965), *Handbook of*
Waterfowl Behavior, London, Constable &
Co., 378 pp.
JOHNSGAARD, P. A. (1968), *Waterfowl:*
Their Biology and Natural History, Lincoln,
University of Nebraska Press, 138 pp.
MURPHY, R. C. (1936), *Oceanic Birds of*
South America, New York, Macmillan, 2 vols.,
1245 pp.
SCOTT, Peter (1968), *Key to the Wildfowl of*
the World, Slimbridge, Wildfowl Trust, 91 pp.
SPARKS, J. and SOPER, T. (1967),
Penguins, Newton Abbot, David & Charles,
263 pp.
STOKES, T. and SHACKLETON, K.
(1968), *Birds of the Atlantic Ocean*, Feltham,
Country Life Books, 156 pp.
STONEHOUSE, B. (1968), *Penguins*,
London, Arthur Baker, Ltd., 96 pp.
STOUT, G. D. and MATTHEISSEN, P.
(1967), *The Shorebirds of North America*,
New York, Viking, 270 pp.
WAYRE, P. (1969), *A Guide to the Pheasants*
of the World, London, Country Life, 176 pp.

OURCES OF
LLUSTRATIONS

ge by page, credits for picture sources. Key
picture position is (T) top, (M) middle,
 bottom, (L) left, (C) center, (R) right.
ge 8. (L) photo Eric Hosking; (R) photo
orge Porter
photo J. Fisher
 photo John Tarlton
 after Allan Brooks, courtesy *The Auk*
-23. after preparation in American Mus-
m of Natural History
 (L) after van Tyne and Berger, courtesy
n Wilsey & Sons Inc.; (R) after Fisher
 (R) after A. R. Akester, courtesy *Journal*
Anatomy (L) eye after Stuart Smith, courtesy
n. Collins Sons & Co., brain after van Tyne
 Berger
 (T) after van Tyne and Berger
 after Fisher and others
 (R) after R. P. Allen, courtesy National
dubon Society
 photos Los Angeles County Museum
 (L) after William C. Dilger
 (L) after Dr. and Mrs. N. Collias
 (T) information derived from D. Amadon
. information derived from J. P. Chapin

121. (MR) after G. Kramer, courtesy International Ornithological Congress; (BL) after
E. G. F. Sauer, courtesy *Scientific American*;
(BR) after D. R. Griffin, courtesy *Proceedings*
of the National Academy of Sciences
123. after E. Merikallio, courtesy *Fauna*
Fennica
125. information derived from J. M. D.
MacKenzie and G. R. Williams
129. (L) after F. Salomonsen, courtesy Int.
Orn. Congr.
140–141. Robin postures, some information
from D. Lack
143. (L) after preparation in The American
Museum of Natural History; (TR) information
derived from H. J. Frith
144. (BR) after photo by Geoffrey Allen
147. photo by Shelley Grossman, in The
American Museum of Natural History
148. (L) after preparation in The American
Museum of Natural History; (R) information
derived from D. Lack
149. (R) information derived from A. Skutch
150. (T) information derived from H. Friedmann; (B) after Stuart Baker, courtesy H. F.
and G. Witherby Ltd
152. (TL) after C. F. M. Swynnerton, courtesy
The Ibis
154. information derived from J. Dorst

155. (T) after Bailey and Sorenson, courtesy
Denver Museum of Natural History
157–158' after O. Köhler, courtesy Carl
Winter, Heidelberg
159. (B) after film by T. H. Work
160. from RTP's *Field Guide to Western Birds*,
2nd ed. (1961) courtesy Houghton Mifflin Co.
162. photo Nature Conservancy (U.K.)
163. from the Clubs and Societies cited in the
caption
164. photo R. T. Peterson
166. photo Eric Hosking
167. Nos. 1, 3, 7 after Huxley, courtesy
Zoological Society of London; no. 2 after Berg

Artists who have contributed illustrations
(apart from RTP) are: Sidney W. Woods:
pages 22, 23, 24, 25 (except MR), 84, 86 (L),
88, 89, 91 (R), 121 (MR BL BC), 154
Crispin J. Fisher: page 25 (R)
Brian Lee: page 62 (L)
Susan Tibbles: pages 20 (R), 125

INDEX

Every bird mentioned or figured in this book (with the exception of its introduction and bibliography) is indexed here under a common name that we believe to be jointly acceptable to English-speaking ornithologists on both sides of the Atlantic. Names used in practice alone are here often accompanied by a qualifier in brackets, *e.g.* sparrow (American) and sparrow (true), to make their meaning fully clear. This index is also a nomenclator: each species is given here what we believe to be its most acceptable scientific name. It can thus be used as a systematic glossary.

A typical entry consists of the English vernacular name of the bird in Roman type, followed by its Linnean name in italics. This scientific name is preceded by the conventional dagger when it refers to a fossil form. A generic name appearing for a second or further time under a heading is abbreviated as much as is prudent, often being represented by its initial letter. The figure in brackets after a bird name is that of the family (or subfamily) to which the bird or group of birds belongs (see The Regiment of Birds, pp. 168–83). The figures that then follow are page references; those in bold type denote the presence of at least one picture.

Accentor, *Prunella* (172), 90, 180
  Alpine, *P. collaris*, **108**
Aegialornis, †*Aegialornis* (121), 177
Aepyornis, *see* Elephant bird
Agnopterus, †*Agnopterus hantoniensis* (44), 171
Akepa, *Loxops coccinea* (183), **97**
Akiapolaau, *Hemignathus wilsoni* (183), **97**
Alauwahio, *Loxops maculata* (183), **97**
Albatross (21), 18, 37, 50, 106, 117, 154, 155, 156, 170
  Black-browed, *Diomedea melanophris*, **49, 155**
  Buller's (mollymawk), *D. bulleri*, 154
  Gray-headed, *D. chrysostoma*, **115**
  Laysan, *D. immutabilis*, **18**
  Royal, *D. epomophora*, 39, 148, 155
  Short-tailed, *D. albatrus*, **100**
  Wandering, *D. exulans*, **36,** 39, 148, **155**
Amakihi, Common, *Loxops virens* (183), **97**
American warbler, *see* Wood warbler
Andrewsornis, *Andrewsornis* sp. (82A), 174
Anhinga, *see* Snake bird
Ani, Smooth-billed, *Crotophaga ani* (112), 67
Anianiau, *Loxops parva* (183), **97**
Anomalopteryx, †*Anomalopteryx antiquus* (14), 169
Ant chat, Fire-crested, *Alethe castanea* (173a), 112, **113**
Ant pipit (146), 66, 112, 179
  Chestnut-belted, *Conopophaga aurita*, **66**
  Cinnamon-crested, *C. lineata*, **104**
Ant pitta, White-bellied, *Grallaria hypoleuca* (145), **104**
Ant thrush (New World) (145), 66, 112, 178
  Black-faced, *Formicarius analis*, **66**
Ant thrush (Old World) (173a)
  White-tailed, *Neocossyphus poensis*, 112, **113**
Anthropornis, †*Anthropornis nordenskjöldi* (7), 38, **39**

Antpecker, Jameson's, *Parmoptila jamesoni* (187), 112, **113**
Apapane, *Himatione sanguinea* (183), **97**
Apatornis, †*Apatornis celer* (6), 76, 169
Aracari, Chestnut-eared, *Pteroglossus castanotis* (141), **54,** endpapers
Archaeopsittacus, †*Archaeopsittacus verreauxi* (110), 176
Archaeopteryx, †*Archaeopteryx lithographica* (1), 18, 30, **72,** 73, 168
Archaeotrogon, †*Archaeotrogon cayluxensis* (126), **79,** 177
Asity (149), 179
Auk (105), 15, 21, 50, 78, 90, 108, 133, 148, 153, 165, 175
  Australca, †*Australca grandis*, **81**
  Great, *Pinguinus impennis*, **40,** 42, **98**
  Little, *Plautus alle*, **87**
  Razor-billed, *see* Razorbill
  see also Lucas auk
Australian tree creeper, *Climacteris* (175), 181
Australian warbler (173f), 181
Avocet (94), 29, 47, 175
  Common, *Recurvirostra avosetta*, **31**

Babbler (173b), 61, 180
  Brown, *Turdoides squamiceps*, 180
Bald crow, *Picathartes* (173j), 181
Bananaquit, *Coereba flaveola* (181f), 70, **71**
Baptornis, †*Baptornis advenus* (3), **75,** 76, 168
Barbet (139), 61, 149, 178
  Double-toothed, *Lybius bidentatus*, **55**
  Red-and-yellow, *Trachyphonus erythrocephalus*, **144,** 145
  Red-fronted, *Tricholaema diadematum*, **59**
Barn owl, *Tyto* (113), **53,** 80, 108, 126, 154, 176
  †*Tyto* sp., 176
Bateleur, *Terathopius ecaudatus* (54), **51, 156**
Bathornis, †*Bathornis veredus* (79), 174
Bearded tit, *Panurus biarmicus* (173c), 181
Becard, Rose-throated, *Platypsaris aglaiae* (153), **60**
Bee eater (130), 64, 105, **144,** 145, 153, 177
  Carmine, *Merops nubicus*, **67**
  Common, *Merops apiaster*, 177
  White-fronted, *Melittophagus bullockoides*, **64**
Bell magpie (196), 183
  White-backed, *Gymnorhina hypoleuca*, **106**
Bellbird, Three-wattled, *Procnias tricarunculata* (153), **102**
Bird of paradise (198), 138, 183
  Great, *Paradisaea apoda*, endpapers
  King, *Cicinnurus regius*, **59**
  Orange-wattled, *Macgregoria pulchra*, **54**
  Wilson's, *Diphyllodes respublica*, **106**
Bittern (37), 29, 153
  American, *Botaurus lentiginosus*, **28**
  see also Sun bittern
Blackbird
  Brea, †*Euphagus magnirostris* (185), **82**
  European, *Turdus merula* (173a), 59, **62,** 124, 129, 156
  Red-winged, *Agelaius phoeniceus* (185), 56, **119**
Blackcap, *Sylvia atricapilla* (173e), 66
Blackgame, *see* Grouse, Black
Bluebird
  Fairy, *Irena puella* (163), **108**
  Western, *Sialia mexicana* (173a), **111**
Bluethroat, *Erithacus (Luscinia) svecicus* (173a), endpapers
Bobolink, *Dolichonyx oryzivorus* (185), 56, **115**
Booby, *Sula* (29), 29, 50, 170
  Blue-footed, *S. nebouxii*, **28**
  Brown, *S. leucogaster*, **147**
  Guano, †*S. guano*, **81**
  Red-footed, *S. sula*, **49**
  †*S. ronzoni*, 170
Bower bird (197), 183
  Satin, *Ptilonorhynchus violaceus*, 141, **142**
  Spotted, *Chlamydera maculata*, **60**

Bower bird, *contd.*
  Stagemaker, *Scenopoeetes dentirostris*, 68
Brambling, *Fringilla montifringilla* (186), 12[?] **150,** 151
Bristlebill, Green-tailed, *Bleda eximia* (16[?] **112**
Broadbill (143), 80, 178
  Long-tailed, *Psarisomus dalhousiae*, endpape[rs]
Brontornis, †*Brontornis burmeisteri* (83), 80, 1[?]
  †*Physornis* sp., 174
Brush turkey, *Alectura lathami* (60), **106**
Budgerigar, *Melopsittacus undulatus* (110), 1[?] 158
Bulbul (162), 105, 112, 180
  Common, *Pycnonotus barbatus*, 180
Bullfinch, European, *Pyrrhula pyrrhula* (18[6] **58,** 129
Bunting (181a), 58, 81, 88, 97, 182
  Cirl, *Emberiza cirlus*, 129
  Lapland, *Calcarius lapponicus*, **57**
  Meadow, *E. cioides*, **150,** 151
  Snow, *Plectrophenax nivalis*, **60**
  Townsend's, *Spiza townsendi* (186), 99
  see also Painted bunting
Bustard, (85) 29, 32, 78, 105, 153, 174
  Arabian, *Choriotis arabs*, 39
  Great, *Otis tarda*, 39, **147**
  Kori (giant), *C. kori*, 39
  Little, *Tetrax tetrax*, 147
  Senegal, *Eupodotis senegalensis*, **44**
  Stanley, *Neotis denhami*, 39
Bustard quail (66), 44, 173
Buzzard, *Buteo* (54), 51, 116
  Honey, *Pernis apivoris*, 51

Cacique, *Cassiculus* (185), 70, **71**
Cahow, *Pterodroma cahow* (22), **100**
Cape pigeon, *Fulmarus capensis* (22), endpape[rs]
Capercaillie, *Tetrao urogallus* (61), **44**
Caracara, *Caracara* (56), **51,** 149, 154
  Brea, †*C. prelutosa*, **82, 83**
Cardinal (181b), **17,** 88, 182
  Red-crested, *Paroaria coronata*, endpapers
Cariama, 80, 81, 83
  see also Seriema
Cassowary, *Casuarius* (13), **38,** 41, 148, 169
  Australian, *C. casuarius*, **28, 39, 106**
Catbird
  American, *Dumetella carolinensis* (171), **147**
  Green, *Ailuroedus crassirostris* (197), **106**
Ceramornis, †*Ceramornis* sp. (87A), 174
Chachalaca, *Ortalis* (59), **80**
Chaffinch, *Fringilla* (186), 62, 157
  Blue, *F. teydea*, **96**
  Common, *F. coelebs*, 124, 129, 182
Chat, Yellow-breasted, *Icteria virens* (182), 1[?]
  see also Ant chat; Palm chat; Stonecha[t]; Whinchat
Chickadee, *Parus* (174), 20
  Black-capped, *P. atricapillus*, **17,** 66, 91
  Boreal, *P. hudsonicus*, 126
  Méxican, *P. sclateri*, **111**
Chosornis, †*Chosornis praeteritus* (60), 172
Chough, *Pyrrhocorax* (199), 110
Cimolopteryx, †*Cimolopteryx* sp. (87A), 174
Cisticola, Croaking, *Cisticola natalensis* (173[c] **152**
Cladornis, †*Cladornis pachypus* (34), 79, 171
Cock-of-the-Rock, Golden, *Rupicola rupic[ola]* (153), endpapers
Cockatoo (110)
  Greater sulfur-crested, *Kakatoe galerita*, **156**
  Roseate, *K. roseicapilla*, **107**
Coltonia, †*Coltonia recurvirostra* (95), **77,** 78, 1[?]
Coly (or Mousebird), *Colius* (125), 30, 177
  Blue-naped, *C. macrourus*, **105**
  Speckled, *C. striatus*, **29, 152**
Condor (51), 51, 78, 154, 155
  Andean, *Vultur gryphus*, 23, **36,** 39, 148, 15[?] **156**

or, contd.
  fornia, *Gymnogyps californianus*, 39, **100,**
  1, 154, 155
  at, †*G. amplus*, **82, 83**
 rnis, †*Coniornis altus* (4), 76, 168
 , *Fulica* (75), 29, 46, 149
rican, *F. americana*, **28**
ow-billed, *F. leucoptera*, **150**
orant (31), 21, 29, 50, 78, 148, 153, 156,
 , 171
htless, *Nannopterum harrisi*, **40,** 42
ctacled, *Phalacrocorax perspicillatus*, 42, 101
more's, †*P. wetmorei*, **81**
crake, *Crex crex* (75), **19,** 21
roba, *Coscoroba coscoroba* (49), 48, 149
 ga (153), 103, 104, 179
ser (99), 175
ird (185), **17,** 67, 149, 150
-winged, *Agelaioides badius,* 150
t, *Scaphidura oryzivora,* **149,** 150
aming, *Molothrus rufoaxillaris,* 150
plover, *Dromas ardeola* (97), 47, 69, 175
e, Ascension Island flightless, *Crecopsis* sp.
 ), 99
lso Corncrake
e (70), 46, 78, 79, 108, 117, 139, 148, 154,

n (or Siberian) white, *Grus leucogeranus,*
 ), **156**
mon, *G. grus,* **114**
wned, *Balearica pavonina*, endpapers
nchurian, *G. japonensis,* 39
dhill, *G. canadensis,* 81, **122**
ooping, *G. americana,* **100**
per (176), 59, 108, 181
wn, *Certhia americana,* 66, 91
e, *C. familiaris,* 66, 91, 181
lso Australian tree creeper; Honeycreeper
ed (or Tree) swift, *Hemiprocne* (123), 107,
 3, 177
tern, *H. mystacea,* **143**
bill, *Loxia* (186), 31
, *L. curvirostra,* **30, 111,** 125
te-winged, *L. leucoptera,* 125, **127**
 (corvid) (199), 56, 80, 90, 108, 139, 146,
 3, 183
, *Corvus ossifragus,* 29
lso Bald crow; King crow; Wattled crow
oo (112), 20, 30, 79, 149, 151
mon, *Cuculus canorus,* **114, 150,** 151, 176
erald, *Chrysococcyx cupreus,* 112, **113**
ra, *Guira guira,* **147**
ning, *Chalcites lucidus,* 118
ped, *Tapera naevia,* 151
low-billed, *Coccyzus americanus,* 59
oo roller, *Leptosomus discolor* (133), **105,**
 3
oo shrike (161), 61, 180
nion, *Coracina newtoni,* 101
mpaia, †*Cunampaia simplex* (84), 174
ssow (59), 44, 172
at, *Crax rubra,* **102**
ew, *Numenius* (93), 47, 156
tle-thighed, *N. tahitiensis,* 118
gypsorum, 116
ornis, †*Cyphornis magnus* (27), 80, 170
elavus, †*Cypselavus gallicus* (122), **79,** 177

er, *see* Snake bird
drochen, *see* Whistling duck
ryma, †*Diatryma steini* (87), 38, **39, 77,** 78.
 4
rnis, *see* Moa, Great
er, *Cinclus* (168), 68, 87, 108, 180
opean, *C. cinclus,* **69,** 180
r, *see* Loon
ng petrel, *Pelecanoides* (24), 21, 170
gellan, *P. magellani,* **87**
uvian, *P. garnotii,* **21**
o, *Raphus* (109), 83, 106, 176

Dodo, contd.
  Mauritius, *R. cucullatus,* **98,** 101
Dolichopterus, †*Dolichopterus viator* (92), 114
Dove (108)
  Blue-headed wood, *Turtur brehmeri,* 112, **113**
  Collared, *Streptopelia decaocto,* 126, **131**
  Senegal, *S. senegalensis,* **147**
  Tanna ground, *Gallicolumba ferruginea,* 99
  White-tipped, *Leptotila verreauxi,* **17**
  White-winged (*Zenaida asiatica*), **110**
Dromornis, †*Dromornis australis* (12), 83, 169
Drongo (192), 32, 66, 183
  †*Dicrurus* sp., 183
  Great racket-tailed, *D. paradiseus,* **64**
  Shining, *D. atripennis,* 112, **113**
Duck (49), 21, 29, 34, 42, 45, 47, 57, 90, 116,
  139, 148, 149, 153
  †*Anas integra,* **80**
  Black-headed, *Heteronetta atricapilla,* 149
  Domestic, *see* Mallard
  Freckled, *Stictonetta naevosa,* 48
  Labrador, *Camptorhynchus labradorius,* **98,** 101
  Mandarin, *Aix galericulata,* **35, 48,** 130
  Ruddy, *Oxyura jamaicensis,* **46,** 48, 130, 149
  White-headed, *O. leucocephala,* 149
  Wood, *Aix sponsa,* **48,** endpapers
Dunnock, *Prunella modularis* (172), **60,** 129,
  148, 167
Dynamopterus, †*Dynamopterus velox* (112), 176

Eagle (54), 20, 51, 52, 86, 90, 133, 148, 154,
  172
  Crowned hawk, *Spizaëtus coronatus,* 112, **113**
  Fish, *Haliaeetus vocifer,* **51**
  Golden, *Aquila chrysaëtos,* **84**
  Harpy, *Harpia harpyja,* 29
  Long-crested hawk, *A. occipitalis,* **51**
  Monkey-eating, *Pithecophaga jefferyi,* 38
Eclectus parrot, *Lorius roratus* (110), 34, **35**
Egret (37)
  Cattle, *Ardeola ibis,* **67, 129,** 131
  Little, *Egretta garzetta,* **45**
Eider (49), 48, 50, 69
  Common, *Somateria mollissima,* **152**
  King, *S. spectabilis,* **16**
  Steller's, *Polysticta stelleri,* **147**
Elephant bird (10), 36, 38, 41, 83, 106
  †*Eremopizus* sp., 78
  Great, *Aepyornis maximus,* **39,** 101, 146, 169
Eleutherornis, †*Eleutherornis helveticus* (8), 78,
  169
Elopteryx, †*Eloptreyx nopcsai* (30), **76,** 170
Elornis, †*Elornis* sp. (46), 78, 171
Enaliornis, †*Enaliornis* sp. (2), 75, **76,** 168
Eocathartes, †*Eocathartes robustus* (51), **78**
Eogrus, †*Eogrus aeola* (69), 173
Eonessa, †*Eonessa anaticula* (49), 172
Ergilornis, †*Ergilornis rapidus* (73), 173
Eupterornis, †*Eupterornis remensis* (19), 170

Falcon (56), 51, 52, 80, 86, 90, 133, 148, 153,
  172
  Collared forest, *Micrastur semitorquatus,* end-
  papers
Falconet, *Microhierax* (56), **51**
  Red-thighed, *M. caerulescens,* 51
False sunbird, *Neodrepanis* (149), **105**
Fantail (173g), 181
Fieldfare, *Turdus pilaris* (173a), 114, **129,** 131
Fig bird, Yellow-breasted, *Sphecotheres flavi-*
  ventris (191), **54**
Finch, 20, 57, 58, 80, 90, 97, 108, 139
  Chestnut-breasted negro, *Nigrita bicolor*
  (187), 112, **113**
  Crimson, *Zonaeginthus phaeton* (187), **59**
  Cuckoo, *Anomalospiza imberbis* (189), 150
  Darwin's (181a), 182

Finch, contd.
  Gray-crowned rosy, *Leucosticte tephrocotis*
  (186), **111**
  Kona, *Psittirostra kona* (183), **97**
  Laysan, *Ps. cantans* (183), **97**
  Locust, *Estrilda locustella* (187), **37**
  Melba, *Pytilia melba* (187), **149**
  Plush-capped, *Catamblyrhynchus diadema*
  (181c), 182
  Snow, *Montifringilla nivalis* (189), 110
  Woodpecker, *Camarhynchus (Cactospiza) palli-*
  dus (181a), 159
  see also Bullfinch; Chaffinch; Goldfinch;
  Hawfinch
Finfoot (76), 47, 173
Fire-crown, Chilean, *Sephanoides sephanoides*
  (124), 70
Flamingo (46), 20, 30, 31, 46, 67, 77, 90, 148,
  171
  Andean, *Phoenicoparrus andinus,* **31, 45**
  Florida, †*Phoenicopterus ruber,* **81**
  Greater, *Phoenicopterus ruber,* **68**
  James's, *Phoenicoparrus jamesi,* **45**
  Lesser, *Phoeniconaias minor,* **68**
Flicker (142)
  Gilded, *Colaptes chrysoides,* **96**
  Red-shafted, *C. cafer,* **96**
  Yellow-shafted, *C. auratus,* **96**
Flowerpecker (177), 70, 107, 181
  Four-colored, *Dicaeum quadricolor,* 101
  Pigmy, *D. pygmaeum,* **37**
Flowerpiercer, *see* Honeycreeper
Flycatcher, 19
  see Flycatcher (Old World), Monarch fly-
  catcher, Tyrant flycatcher
Flycatcher (Old World) (173g), 66, 88, 90,
  108, 181
  Pied, *Ficedula hypoleuca,* **64, 156**
  Spotted, *Muscicapa striata,* **115,** 181
  see also Paradise flycatcher
Fody, *Foudia* (189), 101
Fowl, *Gallus* (62), 30, 57
  Domestic, *G. gallus,* **124,** 139, 153
  LaFayette's jungle, *G. lafayetii,* **28**
  see also Mallee fowl; Peafowl
Francolin, *Francolinus* (62)
  Forest, *F. lathami,* 112, **113**
Frigate bird, *Fregata* (33), 19, 29, 155, 170
  Great, *F. minor,* **28, 136,** 137
  Magnificent, *F. magnificens,* **49**
Frogmouth (118), 107, 176
  see also Owlet frogmouth
Fulmar (22), 154, 155
  Common, *Fulmarus glacialis,* **128-9,** 165
  Giant, *Macronectes giganteus,* **30**

Gallinuloides, †*Gallinuloides wyomingensis* (58),
  77, 78, 172
Gallito, *Rhinocrypta lanceolata* (147), **103**
Gallornis, †*Gallornis straeleni* (41A), 73, 75, **76,**
  124, 171
Gannet (29), 50, 79, 134, 148, 154, 155, 170
  Australasian, *Morus serrator,* 123
  Cape, *M. capensis,* 123
  Northern, *M. bassanus,* **49, 122,** 123, **132,** 165
Gastornis, †*Gastornis* sp. (86), 77, 78, 174
Geisleroceros, †*Geisleroceros robustus* (136), 178
Genyornis, †*Genyornis newtoni* (12), 79, 169
Gerandia, †*Gerandia calcarea* (108), 176
Geranoides, †*Geranoides jepseni* (68), 78, 173
Geranopterus, †*Geranopterus alatus* (131), 177
Gigantornis, †*Gigantornis eaglesomei* (21), **36,**
  37, 78, 170
Gnatcatcher, *Polioptila* (173d), 181
Gnatwren (173e), 181
Godwit, *Limosa* (93), 47
  Limosa gypsorum, 78
  †*Limosa* sp., **81**
  Marbled, *L. fedoa,* **134**
Goldcrest, *Regulus regulus* (173e), 66, 126, 146

Goldeneye, *Bucephala* (49), 48
  Bone Valley, †*B. ossivallis*, **81**
Goldfinch, *Carduelis* (186)
  American, *C. tristis*, **119**
  European, *C. carduelis*, **57**, 129, **145**
Goosander, *Mergus merganser* (49), **46**
Goose (49), 47, 48,•57, 90, 116, 139, 148, 153, 155, 156
  African pigmy, *Nettapus auritus*, **46**
  Barnacle, *Branta leucopsis*, **122**
  Canada, *B. canadensis*, 130
  Flightless, †*Cnemiornis calcitrans*, **40**
  Magpie, *Anseranas semipalmata*, 47
  Néné (Hawaiian), *B. sandvicensis*, **100**
  Pigmy, *Nettapus* sp., 48
  Redbreasted, *B. ruficollis*, **46**
  Ross's, *Anser rossii*, **122**
  White-fronted, *Anser albifrons*, **18,** 21
Goshawk (54), 51, 52, 130
  Gabar, *Meliërax gabar*, 51, **52**
Grackle (185)
  Common, *Quiscalus quiscula*, **147**
  Great-tailed, *Cassidix mexicanus*, **147**
Graculavus, †*Graculavus* sp. (31), 76, 171
Grassquit, Yellow-faced, *Tiaris olivacea* (181b), **57**, 58
Grebe (20), 20, 45, 50, 76, 80, 148, 170
  Black-necked, *Podiceps caspicus*, **47**
  Bright-cheeked, *P. occipitalis*, 42
  Great crested, *P. cristatus*, **167**
  †*P. oligocaenus*, 170
  Titicaca, *P. micropterus*, **42**
  see also Sun grebe
Grosbeak
  Blue-black, *Cyanocompsa cyanoides* (181b), **57,** 58
  Evening, *Hesperiphona vespertina* (186), **111**
Ground roller (132), 178
  Pitta-like, *Atelornis pittoides*, **105**
Grouse (61), 20, 30, 32, 44, 108, 125, 172
  Black, *Lyrurus tetrix*, 125, **138**
  Blue, *Dendragapus obscurus*, 61
  †*Palaealectoris* sp., 172
  Red, *Lagopus lagopus scoticus*, 125
  Ruffed, *Bonasa umbellus*, **19**
  Sharp-tailed, *Pedioecetes phasianellus*, **147**
  Spruce, *Canachites canadensis*, **108**
  Willow, *see* Ptarmigan, Willow
  see also Prairie chicken; Sand grouse
Gryzaja, †*Gryzaja* sp. (85A), 174
Guan (59), 44, 103, 104, 172
Guanay, *Phalacrocorax bougainvillii* (31), **122,** 134
Guillemot (including murre, *Uria*) (105), 133
  Arctic (murre), *Uria lomvia*, **108, 147,** 153
  Black, *Cepphus grylle*, **21,** 114
  Common (murre), *U. aalge*, **9**
Guineafowl (63), 44, 173
  Helmeted, *Numida meleagris*, **105,** 173
  Vulturine, *Acryllium vulturinum*, **44**
Gull (103), 29, 50, 78, 90, 108, 116, 148, 149, 153, 155, 156, 165, 175
  Black-headed, *Larus ridibundus*, 156
  Elmore's, †*L. elmorei*, **81**
  Franklin's, *L. pipixcan*, **115**
  Glaucous-winged, *L. glaucescens*, 94, **95**
  Herring, *L. argentatus*, **49, 93,** 94, **95,** 137, 155
  Iceland, *L. glaucoides*, 94, **95**
  Laughing, *L. atricilla*, **148**
  Lesser black-backed, *L. fuscus*, **93,** 94, **95**
  Ross's, *L. (Rhodostethia) roseus*, endpapers
  Thayer's, *L. thayeri*, 94, **95**
  Western, *L. occidentalis*, **49**
  Yellow-legged, *L. argentatus* or *L. fuscus*, 94, **95**
Gyrfalcon, *Falco rusticolus* (56), **51**

Halcyornis, †*Halcyornis toliapicus* (103), 175
Hammerhead, *Scopus umbretta* (38), **105,** 171
Harrier (54), 51

Harrier, *contd.*
  Hen (Marsh hawk), *Circus cyaneus*, 156
  Montagu's, *C. pygargus*, **51**
Hawaiian honeycreeper (183), **97,** 182
  Crested, *Palmeria dolei*, **97**
Hawfinch, *Coccothraustes coccothraustes* (186), **30,** 31, 182
Hawk (54), 20, 52, 78, 86, 87, 133, 148, 155, 172
  Bat, *Machaerhamphus alcinus*, 52
  Broad-winged, *Buteo platypterus*, **19**
  Marsh, *see* Harrier, Hen
  †*Palaeocircus* sp., 78, 172
  Red-tailed, *B. jamaicensis*, **51**
  Sparrow, *see* Sparrow hawk
  Swainson's, *B. swainsoni*, **114**
Hedge sparrow, *see* Dunnock
Helmet-crest, *Oxypogon guerinii* (124), **71**
Hemipode, Collared, *see* Plains wanderer
Heron (37), 20, 29, 46, 78, 79, 90, 126, 139, 148, 153, 156, 171
  Great blue, *Ardea herodias*, **147**
  Night (Black-crowned night), *Nycticorax nycticorax*, 156
Hesperornis, †*Hesperornis* (4), 76, 168
  †*H. gracilis*, **75**
  †*H. regalis*, **75**
Heterorhea, †*Heterorhea dabbeni* (17), 169
Hillstar, Estella, *Oreotrochilus estella* (124), 154
Hoatzin, *Opisthocomus hoazin* (57), 80, **103,** 172
Hoazinoides, †*Hoazinoides magdalenae* (57), 172
Hobby, *Falco subbuteo* (56), 52
Honeycreeper (181f), 70, 90, 104, 107, 109, 182
  Coerebine, 182
  Dacnine, 182
  Red-legged, *Cyanerpes cyaneus*, **17**
  see also Hawaiian honeycreeper
Honeyeater (180), 32, 106, 109, 182
  Scarlet, *Myzomela dibapha*, **71**
Honeyguide (140), 63, 69, 105, 149, 178
  Scaly-throated, *Indicator variegatus*, **151**
Hoopoe, *Upupa epops* (134), 178
  see also Wood hoopoe
Hornbill (136), 30, 63, 78, 105, 154, 178
  Long-crested, *Berenicornis comatus*, endpapers
  Silvery-cheeked, *Bycanistes brevis*, **29, 143,** 145
Huia, *Heteralocha acutirostris* (193), 43, **98**
Hummingbird (124), 19, 26, 58, 70, 103, 140, 146, 153, 177
  Amethystine, *Calliphlox amethystina*, 20
  Bee, *Mellisuga helenae*, 36, **38,** 146
  Black-chinned, *Archilochus alexandri*, **111**
  Broad-tailed, *Selasphorus platycercus*, **111**
  Emerald, *Chlorostilbon* sp., 20
  Giant, *Patagona gigas*, 20
  Hermit, *Phaethornis* sp., 20
  Racket-tailed, *Loddigesia mirabilis*, 138, endpapers
  Ruby-throated, *Archilochus colubris*, **19,** 20, 21, **142**
  Rufous, *Selasphorus rufus*, 70, **115,** 143, **144**
  Sword-billed, *Ensifera ensifera*, 70
  see also Firecrown; Hillstar; Topaz

Ibidopsis, †*Ibidopsis hordwelliensis* (41), 78, 171
Ibis (41), 19, 46, 149, 171
  Nippon (Japanese crested), *Nipponia nippon*, **100,** 101
  Scarlet, *Eudocimus ruber*, **45**
  White, *E. albus*, **18, 31**
  White-faced, *Plegadis chihi*, endpapers
  see also Wood ibis
Ibisbill, *Ibidorhyncha struthersii* (94), 29
Ichthyornis, †*Ichthyornis* (5), 76, 169
  †*I.* sp., 75
  †*I. victor*, 75
Icterids (185), 15, 70, 103, 150, 153, 182
Idiornis, †*Idiornis* sp. (74), 173
Iiwi, *Vestiaria coccinea* (183), **71, 97**

Incubator bird, *Megapodius freycinet* (60),

Jacamar (137), 64, 178
  Great, *Jacamerops aurea*, **102**
Jaçana (88), 28, 47, 174
  Pheasant-tailed, *Hydrophasianus chirurgus*,
  Wattled, *Jacana spinosa*, **147,** 174
Jackdaw, *Corvus monedula* (199), 67, **157,** 167
Jay (199), 62, 157
  Black-headed, *Cyanocorax cyanomelas*, **147**
  Blue, *Cyanocitta cristata*, **17, 119,** 156
  Common (Old World), *Garrulus glandariu*
  Gray, *Perisoreus canadensis*, **60,** 61
  Mexican, *Cyanocitta ultramarina*, **111**
Junco, Slate-colored, *Junco hyemalis* (181a

Kagu, *Rhynochetos jubatus* (77), 43, 47, **106**
Kakapo, *Strigops habroptilus* (110), **42,** 43
Kakariki, Raiatea, *Cyanoramphus ulie* (110), 99
Kea, *Nestor notabilis* (110), 67
Kestrel, *Falco* (56)
  Mauritian, *F. punctatus*, 101
King crow, *Dicrurus macrocercus* (192), 67
Kingbird, *Tyrannus* (151)
  Cassin's, *T. vociferans*, **111**
  Eastern, *T. tyrannus*, 33, **147**
  Gray, *T. dominicensis*, **147**
Kingfisher (127), 30, 32, 63, 68, 78, 126, 153, 177
  Blue-breasted, *Halcyon malimbica*, 112, **11**
  Common, *Alcedo atthis*, **69**
  Riu Kiu Island, *H. miyakoensis*, **98**
  Ruddy, *H. coromanda*, 68
Kinglet, Golden-crowned, *Regulus sa* (173e), 66, **111**
Kite (54), 51, 52, 68, 69, 116
  Everglade, *Rostrhamus sociabilis*, **70**
  Swallow-tailed, *Elanoides forficatus*, **51**
Kittiwake, Red-legged, *Larus (Rissa) brea tris* (103), **49,** 165
Kiwi (16), 31, 41, 146, 148
  Common, *Apteryx australis*, **30, 40, 106**
Korhaan (85)
  Black, *Afrotis atra*, **32**
  Rüppell's, *Eupodotis rüppellii*, **32**

Lammergei , *Gypaëtus barbatus* (54), 21
Lapwing, *Vanellus* (92), 156, endpapers
  Red-wattled, *V. indicus*, **45**
Lark (157), 81, 105, 179
  †*Alauda gypsorum*, 179
  †*Al. major*, 179
  Horned, *Eremophila alpestris*, 21
  Sand, *Ammomanes deserti*, **33**
  see also Magpie lark; Meadowlark; Skyla
Laughing thrush, streaked, *Garrulax line* (173b), **150,** 151
Laurillardia, †*Laurillardia* sp. (190), 183
Leaf bird (163), 107, 180
Limnatornis, †*Limnatornis paludicola* (135),
Limpkin, *Aramus guarauna* (71), 46, 68, **70,** 149, 173
Lithornis, †*Lithornis vulturinus* (54), 53, 172
Lonchodytes, †*Lonchodytes* sp. (18A), 76, 1
Longclaw, Yellow-throated, *Macronyx crc* (160), **87, 152**
Loon (or Diver), *Gavia* (19), 20, 21, 45, 50, 77, 78, 108, 148, 170
  Black-throated, *G. arctica*, **47**
  Red-throated, *G. stellata*, **147**
Lorikeet (110), 70, **71**
  Rainbow, *Trichoglossus haematodus*, **71**
Lovebird, Black-collared, *Agapornis swir niana* (110), 112, **113**
Lucas auk, †*Mancalla* (106), 176
Lyrebird, *Menura* (155), 106, 179
  Superb, *M. novaehollandiae*, **106**

...aw (110), 31, 58
...an red, *Ara tricolor,* **98**
...ninican green-and-yellow, *Ara atwoodi,*
)1
...cinthine, *Anodorhynchus hyacinthinus,* **31**
...pie, Common or Black-billed, *Pica pica*
)9), 61
lso Bell magpie
...pie lark, Common, *Grallina cyanoleuca*
...4), **106,** 183
...mbe, *Malimbus* (189), 90, 112
...sin's, *M. cassini,* **92**
...sted, *M. malimbicus,* 112, **113**
...-bellied, *M. erythrogaster,* 112, **113**
...ard (and domestic duck), *Anas platy-*
nchos (49), **28,** 48, 156
...ee fowl, *Leipoa ocellata* (60), **143,** 145
...o, *Drepanis* (183)
...:k, *D. funerea,* **97**
...waii), *D. pacifica,* **98**
...akin (152), 66, 179
...-capped, *Pipra mentalis,* **102**
...bou, *Leptotilos crumeniferus* (39), **36,** 105
...in (159), 52
...se, *Delichon urbica,* 21
...inetta, *see* Tinamou
...lowlark, Eastern, *Sturnella magna* (185),
...apaloelodus, †*Megapaloelodus* sp. (45), **80,**
1
...apode (60), 145, 153, 172
...anser, *Mergus* (49), 30, 31, 48
...-breasted, *M. serrator,* **30**
...te, *see* Roatelo
...r bird, *Acrocephalus familiaris* (173c), 101
...ea, †*Milnea gracilis* (98), 175
..., Great, †*Dinornis* (15), 38, **40,** 41, 68, 80,
..., 87, 106, 108, 126, 169, 180
...*maximus,* **39**
...*novaezealandiae,* 169
..., Lesser (14), 169
...king bird, *Mimus polyglottos* (171), 20, 61,
..., 180
...ymawk, *see under* Albatross
...arch flycatcher (173h), 66, 181
...rhen, *Gallinula chloropus* (75), 29
...not (129), 30, 64, 78, 104, 153, 177
...sebird, *see* Coly
...re, *see* Guillemot (*Uria*)
...ton bird, *see under* Shearwater

...ortyx, †*Nanortyx* sp. (62), 173
...ilornis, †*Nautilornis* sp. (105), 78, 175
..., *see under* Goose
...athartes, †*Neocathartes grallator* (50), **78,**
...2
...aeornis, †*Neogaeornis wetzeli* (3), 168
... Zealand wren, *Xenicus* (150), 179
...k, *X. gilviventris,* **106**
...phen Island, *X. lyalli,* 43, 101
...tor, West African, *Nicator chloris* (162),
...2, **113**
...thawk, Common, *Chordeiles minor* (119),
..., **64, 115,** 121, **147**
...tjar (119), 29, 32, 63, 64, 69, 87, 101, 121,
...6, 153, 177
...nmon, *Caprimulgus europaeus,* 177
...l-necked, *C. ruficollis,* **33**
...ndard-wing, *Macrodipteryx longipennis,* end-
...apers
...va, Rufous-bellied, *Niltava sundara* (173g),
...0, 151
...puu, *Hemignathus lucidus* (183), **97**
...racker, *Nucifraga* (199), 56, 57
...rk's, *N. columbiana,* **111**
...ropean, *N. caryocatactes,* **56**
...atch, *Sitta* (175), 59, 66, 81, 108, 181
...nmon (or European), *S. europaea,* 66
...my, *S. pygmaea,* **111**
...l-breasted, *S. canadensis,* 126, **127**

Nuthatch, *contd.*
†*S. senegalliensis,* 181
White-breasted, *S. carolinensis,* **17,** 66, **147**

Odontopteryx, †*Odontopteryx toliapica* (35), 78,
80, 171
Oilbird, *Steatornis caripensis* (116), 69, **102,** 121,
176
Oo, *Moho* (180)
Hawaii, *M. nobilis,* **98**
Kauai, *M. braccatus,* **100,** 101
Open-bill, *Anastomus* (39), 46, 68
Opisthodactylus, †*Opisthodactylus patagonicus*
(17), 77, 169
Oriole (New World: Icterid) (185)
Scott's, *Icterus parisorum,* **111**
Oriole (Old World) (191), 56, 183
Black-naped, *Oriolus chinensis,* 56
Golden, *O. oriolus,* 56, **60,** 183
Oropéndola (185), 70
Montezuma, *Gymnostinops montezuma,* **149**
Osprey, *Pandion haliaetus* (55), **29,** 30, 31, 51,
52, **53,** 86, **144,** 154, 172
Osteodontornis, †*Osteodontornis orri* (36), **36,**
37, 171
Ostrich, *Struthio camelus* (9), **28,** 29, 36, 38, **39,**
41, 42, 57, 81, **105,** 145, 148, 155, 169
Ou, *Psittirostra psittacea* (183), **97**
Ovenbird (144b), 87, 88, **103,** 178
Ovenbird (a wood warbler), *Seiurus aurocapillus*
(182), **147**
Owl (typical) (115), 25, 30, 32, 52, 53, 69, 78,
79, 87, 108, 133, 148, 153, 154, 155, 156, 176
American pigmy, *Glaucidium gnoma,* **33,** 145
†*Asio* sp., 176
†*Bubo* sp., 176
Eagle, *B. bubo,* **156**
Elf, *Micrathene whitneyi,* **144**
Great horned, *B. virginianus,* **19,** 21, 53, **147**
Little, *Athene noctua,* 13
Long-eared, *Asio otus,* **53**
New Zealand laughing, *Sceloglaux albifacies,*
100
Screech, *Otus asio,* **29**
Seychelles Island, *O. insularis,* **98,** 101
Short-eared, *Asio flammeus,* **53**
Snowy, *Nyctea scandiaca,* 114, 125, **126**
Spectacled, *Pulsatrix perspicillata,* **53**
†*Strix dakota,* **80**
see also Barn owl
Owlet frogmouth (or nightjar), *Aegotheles*
(117), 64, 176
Little, *A. cristatus,* **106**
†*Megaegotheles* sp., 176
Oxpecker, Red-billed, *Buphagus erythrorhynchus*
(190), **67**
Oystercatcher (91), 80, 145, 174
Common, *Haematopus ostralegus,* **47**

Painted bunting, *Passerina ciris* (181b), **147**
Painted snipe, *Rostratula benghalensis* (90), **45,**
47, 78, 174
Palaegithalus, †*Palaegithalus cuvieri* (174), 78,
181
Palaelodus, †*Palaelodus* sp. (45), 79, 80, 171
Palaeoborus, †*Palaeoborus rosatus* (54), **80**
Palaeochenoïdes, †*Palaeochenoïdes miocaenus*
(27), 170
Palaeociconia, †*Palaeociconia* sp. (82A), 174
Palaeophasianus, †*Palaeophasianus meleagroides*
(71), 78, 173
Palaeopicus, †*Palaeopicus* sp. (142), 178
Palaeorallus, †*Palaeorallus troxelli* (75), **77**
Palaeoscinis, †*Palaeoscinis turdirostris* (169), **80,**
180
Palaeospiza, †*Palaeospiza bella* (158), 79, 179
Palaeostruthus, †*Palaeostruthus* sp. (181a), 182
Palaeotis, †*Palaeotis weigelti* (85), **78,** 174
Palaeotringa, †*Palaeotringa* sp. (93), **76,** 78, 175
Palila, *Psittirostra bailleui* (183), **97**

Palm chat, *Dulus dominicus* (167), **102,** 180
Paracrax, †*Paracrax antiqua* (59), 172
Paractiornis, †*Paractiornis perpusillus* (91), 174
Paradise flycatcher, Gray-breasted, *Terpsi-
phone rufocinerea* (173h), 111, **112**
Paragrus, †*Paragrus prentici* (70), **77,** 78, 173
Parakeet (110)
Blossom-headed, *Psittacula cyanocephala,* **55**
Carolina, *Conuropsis carolinensis,* **98,** 101
Crimson-winged, *Aprosmictus erythropterus,*
endpapers
Splendid, *Neophema splendida,* **100**
Paranyroca, †*Paranyroca magna* (48), 172
Parascaniornis, †*Parascaniornis stensiöi* (41A),
76, 171
Parrot (110), 30, 58, 70, 80, 104, 107, 145, **156,**
176
Broad-billed (Mauritian), *Lophopsittacus
mauritanus,* 101
Least pigmy, *Micropsitta keiensis,* **37**
Owl, *see* Kakapo
see also Eclectus parrot
Parrotbill (173c), 181
Parrotbill, Maui, *Pseudonestor xanthophrys*
(183), **97**
Partridge (62), 44
Common, *Perdix perdix,* 146
Peafowl (62)
Common, *Pavo cristatus,* 34, **35**
Congo, *Afropavo congensis,* 112, **113**
Pelagornis, †*Pelagornis miocaenus* (28), 80, 170
Pelican (26), 20, 29, 50, 79, 90, 154, 155, 170
Brown (Alcatráz), *Pelecanus occidentalis,* **49**
Gray (Dalmatian), *P. roseus,* **36,** 39
Old World white, *P. onocrotalus,* **36,** 39
†*P. gracilis,* 170
Pink-backed, *P. rufescens,* 39
Penguin (7), 15, 41, 50, 77, 80, 90, 106, 133,
148, 154, 155, 169
Adélie, *Pygoscelis adeliae,* 134, **137,** 155
Blue, *Eudyptula minor,* **43**
Chinstrap, *Pygoscelis antarctica,* **43**
Emperor, *Aptenodytes forsteri,* 38, **39,** 145, 146,
154
Gentoo, *Pygoscelis papua,* **42,** 134
Jackass, *Spheniscus demersus,* **43,** 134
King, *Aptenodytes patagonica,* 20, **43,** 145, 155
Magellan, *Spheniscus magellanicus,* **50**
Rockhopper, *Eudyptes crestatus,* **43, 116**
Royal, *Eudyptes schlegeli,* 134
Yellow-eyed, *Megadyptes antipodes,* **43**
Peregrine, *Falco peregrinus* (56), 19, 21, **147**
Petrel (22), 15, 18, 31, 41, 50, 79, 90, 106,
148, 154, 155, 170
Snow, *Pagodroma nivea,* **49**
see also Diving Petrel; Storm petrel
Phalarope, *Phalaropus* (96), 45, 47, 50, 108, 175
Red (gray), *P. fulicarius,* **115**
Red-necked (northern), *P. lobatus,* **108,** 175
Wilson's, *P. tricolor,* **47**
Pheasant (62), 20, 30, 32, 34, 44, 80, 108, 159,
173
Common, *Phasianus colchicus,* **146**
Lady Amherst, *Chrysolophus amherstiae,* end-
papers
Mikado, *Syrmaticus mikado,* **100**
Phoebe, Black, *Sayornis nigricans* (151), **111**
Phorusrhacos, †*Phorusrhacos* sp. (82), 174
Piapiac, *Ptilostomus afer* (199), **67**
Piculet, White-browed rufous, *Sasia ochracea*
(142), **37**
Pigeon (108), 15, **26,** 80, 107, 119, 146, 148,
153, 176
Crested Choiseul, *Microgoura meeki,* **98,** 99
Green, *Treron australis,* **112**
Passenger, *Ectopistes migratorius,* **98,** 101, 124,
135
(Pretty) fruit, *Ptilinopus pulchellus,* **54**
Queen Victoria crowned, *Goüra victoria,* end-
papers

Pigeon, *contd.*
  Racing, *Columba livia*, **19,** 21
  see also Cape pigeon
Pintail, *Anas acuta* (49), **115**
Piopio, *Turnagra capensis* (173i), 181
Pipit, *Anthus* (160), 180
  Meadow, *A. pratensis*, 107, **150, 151**
  Water, *A. spinoletta*, **147**
  see also Ant pipit
Piquero, *Sula variegata* (29), **122**
Pitta, *Pitta* (148), 32, 107, 179
  Black-backed, *P. superba*, **35**
  Fairy, *P. brachyura*, **65**
  see also Ant pitta
Plains wanderer (or Collared hemipode), *Pedionomus torquatus* (67), 44, **106,** 173
Plantain eater, Giant, *Corythaeola cristata* (111), 112, **113**
Plantcutter, *Phytotoma* (154), 179
  Chilean, *P. rara*, **102**
Plegadornis, †*Plegadornis antecessor* (40A), 76, 171
Plesiocathartes, †*Plesiocathartes europaeus* (51), **79**
Plover (92), 47, 67, 79, 90, 145, 175
  American (lesser) golden, *Pluvialis dominica* **115,** 118
  Banded, *Charadrius bicinctus*, 118
  Black-bellied (gray), *P. squatarola*, **147**
  Ringed, *C. hiaticula*, 32, **33, 144**
  see also Crab plover
Pochard (49), 48
  Red-crested, *Netta rufina*, **46**
Poor-will, *Phalaenoptilus nuttallii* (119), 114
Potoo, *Nyctibius* (120), 64, 104, 177
  Common, *N. griseus*, **102**
Prairie chicken, *Tympanuchus* (61)
  †*T. stirtoni*, **80**
Pratincole (99), 105, 175
Presbyornis, †*Presbyornis pervetus* (95), 78, 175
Proergilornis, †*Proergilornis minor* (73), 173
Proherodius, †*Proherodius oweni* (37), 171
Propelargus, †*Propelargus cayluxensis* (39), **79**
Prophaethon, †*Prophaethon shrubsolei* (25), 170
Protoplotus, †*Protoplotus beauforti* (32), 171
Protornis, †*Protornis* sp. (127), 177
Protostrix, †*Protostrix mimica* (114), **77,** 176
Pseudodontornis, †*Pseudodontornis longirostris* (36), 80, 171
Psilopterus, †*Psilopterus sp.* (81), 174
Ptarmigan, *Lagopus* (61), **28, 32,** 33, 114, **147,** 153
  Willow (or Willow grouse), *L. lagopus*, 125
Puaiohi, *Phaeornis palmeri* (173a), **100,** 101
Puffbird (138), 64, 178
  Swallow-winged, *Chelidoptera tenebrosa*, **103**
Puffin, *Fratercula* (105), 21, 31, 38, 133
  Atlantic, *F. arctica*, **50, 122**
  Horned, *F. corniculata*, **30**
  Tufted, *F. cirrhata*, **50**

Quail (62), 44, 79, 173
  Mountain, *Oreortyx picta*, **44**
  see also Bustard quail
Quelea, *Quelea* (189)
  Red-billed, *Q. quelea*, **57,** 134
Quetzal, *Pharomachrus mocino* (126), 33, **35**

Rail (75), 20, 43, 46, 77, 79, 146, 149, 173
  Bensch's, *see* Roatelo
  Clapper, *Rallus longirostris*, **147**
  Flightless blue, *Aphanapteryx leguati*, 101
  King, *R. elegans*, **45**
  Laysan Island, *Porzanula palmeri*. **98,** 101
  New Caledonian wood, *Tricholimnas layfresnayanus*, 100
  Samoan wood, *Pareudiastes pacificus*, 99
  Wake Island, *R. wakensis*, 101
  Zapata, *Cyanolimnas cerverai*, **42, 43**

Raven, *Corvus corax* (199), 114, **158,** 159, 167
Razorbill, *Alca torda* (105), 42, **152,** 153
Redstart
  Common, *Phoenicurus phoenicurus* (173a), 156
  Painted, *Setophaga picta* (182), endpapers
Remiornis, †*Remiornis minor* (86,) 77, 78, 174
Rhea (17), 38, 41, 44, 57, 77, 81, 148, 169
  Common, *Rhea americana*, **39**
  Darwin's, *Pterocnemia pennata*, **103**
Rhegminornis, †*Rhegminornis calobates* (89), 80, 174
Rhynchaeites, †*Rhynchaeites messelensis* (90), 174
Riacama, †*Riacama caliginea* (80), 174
Roadrunner, *Geococcyx californiana* (112), **29,** 30, 69
Roatelo (65), 43, 173
  Bensch's "rail," *Monias benschi*, **105**
Robin (173a)
  American, *Turdus migratorius*, 59, **62, 91, 119,** 156
  European, *Erithacus rubecula*, 124, 137, **140, 141, 148,** 156
  Japanese, *E. akahige*, **65**
  Seychelles magpie, *Copsychus seychellarum*, 101
Roller (131), 30, 64, 79, 177
  see also Cuckoo roller; Ground roller
Rook, *Corvus frugilegus* (199), **61,** 129, 134, **135**
Ruff, *Philomachus pugnax* (93), 138, **139**

Saddleback, *Creadion carunculatus* (193), **106**
Saddlebill, *Ephippiorhynchus senegalensis* (39), **45**
Sand grouse (107), 79, 87, 105, **127,** 176
  Pallas's, *Syrrhaptes paradoxus*, 125
  †*Pterocles larvatus*, 116, 176
  †*P.* sp., **79**
  †*P. validus*, 176
  Yellow-throated, *P. gutturalis*, **153**
Sandpiper (93), 33, 47, 108, 175
  Cooper's, *Calidris cooperi*, 99
  Pectoral, *Erolia melanotos*, **19,** 21
  Tahitian, *Prosobonia leucoptera*, **98,** 99
Sapsucker, *Sphyrapicus* (142), 61
Scaniornis, †*Scaniornis lundgreni* (42), 171
Scoter, *Melanitta* (49), 48
  Velvet (White-winged), *M. fusca*, 21
Screamer (47), 149, 172
  Crested, *Chauna torquata*, **103**
Scrub bird, *Atrichornis* (156), 43, 101, 106, 179
  Noisy, *A. clamosus*, **100**
  Rufous, *A. rufescens*, **43, 106**
Secretary bird, *Sagittarius serpentarius* (53), 51, 69, 79, 80, 86, **105,** 154, 172
  †*Amphiserpentarius schlosseri*, 79, 172
Seed snipe (100), 87, 175
Seriema (80), 79, 86, 174
  †*Andalgalornis* sp., 81
  Crested, *Cariama cristata*, **103**
  †*Onactornis* sp., 81
Shag, Blue-eyed (King), *Phalacrocorax atriceps* (31), **49,** 165
Shearwater (22), 50, 116, 170
  Manx, *Puffinus puffinus*, 117, 119
  †*P. raemdonckii*, 170
  Short-tailed (Tasmanian mutton bird), *P. tenuirostris*, 155
  Sooty (New Zealand mutton bird), *P. griseus*, 111, **115**
  Tristan great, *P. gravis*, **49,** 117, **122**
Sheathbill, *Chionis* (101), 106, **108,** 175
Sheldgoose (49), 48
Shelduck, *Tadorna* (49)
  Common, *T. tadorna*, **46,** 48
  Crested, *T. cristata*, **98**
Shoebill, *Balaeniceps rex* (40), **105,** 171
Shoveler, *Anas (Spatula)* sp. (49), 48
Shrike (164), 80, 90, 108, 180
  †*Lanius miocaenus*, 180
  see also Cuckoo shrike; Vanga shrike
Silvereye (179), 61
  see also Whiteye

Siskin, Pine, *Carduelis pinus* (186), 126, 12
Skimmer, *Rynchops* (104), 31, 68, 175
  Black, *R. nigra*, **30**
Skua (102), 15, 19, 50, 108, 153, 175
  Arctic, *Stercorarius parasiticus*, **115**
  Great, *Catharacta skua*, **49**
  Long-tailed, *S. longicaudus*, **18**
  †*S. shufeldti*, 175
Skylark, *Alauda arvensis* (157), **29, 61,** 129
Snake bird (Darter), *Anhinga anhinga* (32) 153, 171
Snipe (93), 31, 32, 47, 126, 175
  Common, *Gallinago gallinago*, 140, **141**
  see also Painted snipe; Seed snipe
Solitaire (109), 42, 106, 176
Sparrow (American) (181a), 88, 182
  Fox, *Passerella iliaca*, **65**
  White-throated, *Zonotrichia albicollis*, **17**
Sparrow (true), *Passer* (189), 20, 58, 62, 8
  House, *P. domesticus*, **58, 92, 124,** 129, 130, 183
  †*P.* sp., 183
Sparrow hawk, Madagascar, *Accipiter mad* *cariensis* (54), **147**
Spoonbill (41), 31, 171
  Roseate, *Ajaia ajaia*, **31**
Standard wing, Wallace's, *Semioptera wa* (198), **136,** 138
Starling (190)
  Bourbon crested, *Fregilupus varius*, **23**
  European or Common, *Sturnus vulgaris*, **1** 56, 58, **61,** 62, 67, 78, **124,** 126, 129, 134, 136, 149, 156, 183
  Leguat's, *F. rodericanus*, **98**
  Rosy, *S. roseus*, 126, **127**
Steamer duck, *Tachyeres* (49), 42, 48
  Falkland flightless, *T. brachypterus*, **42**
Stifftail (tribe Oxyurini) (49), 48
Stilt, Black-winged, *Himantopus himantopus* 29, **45,** 47
Stonechat, *Saxicola torquata* (173a), 126
Stork (39), 20, 46, 79, 90, 137, 139, 148, 171
  Asphalt, †*Ciconia maltha*, **82, 83,** 85
  White, *C. ciconia*, 101, **116, 137**
  see also Open-bill
Storm petrel (23), 80, 133, 153, 155, 170
  Leach's, *Oceanodroma leucorrhoa*, **49**
  †*Oceanodroma hubbsi*, 170
  Wilson's, *Oceanites oceanicus*, 15, **115,** 117, 133
Sun bittern, *Eurypyga helias* (78), 47, **103**
Sun grebe, *Heliornis fulica* (76), **47**
Sunbird (178), 70, 181
  Gray-chinned, *Anthreptes rectirostris* (112
  see also False sunbird
Swallow (159), 52, 66, 67, 107, 117, 134, 157, 179
  Barn (Old World), *Hirundo rustica*, **114,** **119**
  Rufous-chested, *Cecropis semirufa*, **64**
  Wire-tailed, *H. smithi*, **67**
  see also Wood swallow
Swallow tanager, *Tersina viridis* (181e), 1
Swan, *Cygnus* (49), 20, 47, 48, 57, 139, 1
  Bewick's, *C. bewickii*, 34
  Black-necked, *C. melanocoryphus*, **46**
  Mute, *C. olor*, 37, 39
  Trumpeter, *C. buccinator*, 39
Swift (122), 20, 21, 28, 30, 64, 79, 116, 154, 155, 156, 177
  Brown-throated spine-tailed, *Chaetura g* *tea*, **19,** 21
  Chapin's spine-tailed, *C. melanopygia*, 112
  Chimney, *C. pelagica*, **114, 119**
  see also Crested swift
Swiftlet, *Collocalia* (122), 121

Tailor bird, Long-tailed, *Orthotomus su* (173e), 143, **145,** 159

kahé, *Notornis mantelli* (75), 43, **100**, 101
nager (181d), 56, 88, 182
rimson-backed, *Ramphocelus dimidiatus*, **55**
ed-crowned ant, *Habia rubica*, **66**
carlet, *Piranga olivacea*, **63**
carlet-rumped, *R. passerinii*, **60**
estern, *P. ludoviciana*, **147**
e also Swallow tanager
paculo (147), 78, 179
Veanis sp., 78
tler, Wandering, *Heteroscelus incanum* (93), 18
al (49), 48
aikal, *Anas formosa*, **46**
own, *A. aucklandica*, **42**
lmabates, †*Telmabates antiquus* (43), 77, 171
lmatornis, †*Telmatornis* sp. (75), 76, 173
ratorn, †*Teratornis* (52), **36**, 37, **53**, 83, 85, **6**, 172
erriam's, †*T. merriami*, **83**
rn (103), 50, 68, 91, 137, 155, 156, 165, 175
ntarctic, *Sterna vittata*, **90,** 91
rctic, *S. paradisaea*, **90,** 91, 117, **118**
ommon, *S. hirundo*, 91
legant, *see* Sandwich
ica, *Larosterna inca*, **50**
erguelen, *S. virgata*, 91
andwich (incl. Elegant), *S. sandvicensis*, **142**
ooty, *S. fuscata*, **49,** 134
outh American, *S. hirundinacea*, 91
ick-knee (98), 80, 175
rasher (171), 180
rissal, *Toxostoma dorsale*, **147**
hite-breasted, *Ramphocinclus brachyurus*, **100**
rush (173a), 56, 88, 180
ue rock, *Monticola saxatilis*, 81, 180
ray-cheeked, *Catharus minimus*, 90, **115**
ermit, *C. guttatus*, 90, **91**
aiatea, *Turdus ulietensis*, 99
ong, *T. philomelos*, 68, 129, 156
ood, *T. mustelinus*, 90, **91**
e also Ant thrush; Laughing thrush
namou (18), 15, 81, 104, 148, 170
hilean, *Nothoprocta perdicaria*, **147**
ommon (Martinetta), *Eudromia elegans*, **44,** **103,147**
ufescent, †*Crypturellus cinnamomeus*, **17**
(or Titmouse) (174), 58, 62, 108, 139, 181
zure, *Parus cyanus*, endpapers
lue, *Pa. caeruleus*, 66, 125, **159**
oal, *Pa. ater*, 66
reat, *Pa. major*, **62,** 66, 125
ong-tailed, *Aegithalos caudatus*, **58**, 126
larsh, *Pa. palustris*, 66
igmy, *Psaltria exilis*, **37**
/illow, *Pa. montanus*, 91
e also Bearded tit
anis, †*Titanis walleri* (80), **81,** 83
yra, Masked, *Tityra semifasciata* (153), **17**
dy, *Todus* (128), 30, 64, 177
uban, *T. multicolor*, **64**
uerto Rican, *T. mexicanus*, **102**
paz, Ruby, *Chrysolampis mosquitus* (124), **71**
rotix, †*Torotix clemensi* (41A), 76, 171
ucan (141), 30, 31, 104, 153, 178
ulfur-breasted, *Ramphastos sulfuratus*, **31**
oco, *R. toco*, **102**
ucanet, Emerald, *Aulacorhynchus prasinus* (141), **17**
uraco (111), 30, 176
ommon, *Tauraco corythaix*, **55, 105**
agopan (*Tragopan* (62)
atyr, *T. satyra*, **44**
ee duck, *see* Whistling duck
ee swift, *see* Crested swift

Trogon (126), 30, 79, 80, 104, 153, 177
Coppery-tailed, *Trogon elegans*, **29**
Cuban, *Priotelus temnurus*, **55**
Mountain, *T. mexicanus*, **17**
Narina, *Aphaloderma narina*, **60**
Tropic bird (25), 19, 50, 78, 154, 170
Red-billed, *Phaëthon aethereus*, **147**
Red-tailed, *P. rubricauda*, **18**, 19, **49**
Troupial, *see* Icterid
Trumpeter, *Psophia* (72), 44, 173
White-winged, *P. leucoptera*, **103**
Tui, *Prosthemadera novaeseelandiae* (180), 182
Turkey (64), 44, 108, 173
†*Agricharis* sp., 173
Brea, †*Parapavo californicus*, **82, 83**
Common, *Meleagris gallopavo*, 39
see also Brush turkey
Turnstone, *Arenaria* (92), 47, 68, 69, 175
Tympanonesiotes, †*Tympanonesiotes* sp. (27), 170
Tyrannulet, Yellow-bellied, *Phylloscartes ventralis* (151), **147**
Tyrant flycatchers (151), 66, 68, 103, 179
Coues's, *Contopus pertinax*, **111**
Fire-crowned, *Machetornis rixosa*, 67
Royal, *Onychorhynchus mexicanus*, 33
Short-tailed pigmy, *Myiornis ecaudatus*, **37**
Vermilion, *Pyrocephalus rubinus*, **64, 111**

Uintornis, †*Uintornis lucaris* (138), 178
Ula-ai-hawane, *Ciridops anna* (183), **97**
Umbrella bird, *Cephalopterus ornatus* (153), 34, **35**
Urmiornis, †*Urmiornis* sp. (73), 173

Vanga shrike (165), **105**, 180
Veery, *Catharus fuscescens* (173a), 90, **91, 147**
Vireo, *Vireo* (184), 182
Yellow-throated, *V. flavirrons*, **63**
Vulture, 20, 51, 52, 148, 156
Vulture (New World) (51), 30, 51, 78, 79, 85, 90, 108, 154
King, *Sarcorhamphus papa*, **13, 155**
New World (American) black, *Coragyps atratus*, **147**
Turkey, *Cathartes aura*, **29**, 51, **52**
Vulture (Old World) (54), 30, 51, 86, 90, 154
Egyptian, *Neophron percnopterus*, 51, **52**
Giant Maltese, *Gyps melitensis*, 52
Griffon, *G. fulvus*, **39**, 154
Lappet-eared, *Torgos tracheliotus*, 51, **52**
Old World black, *Aegypius monachus*, **39, 105**
Palm-nut, *Gypohierax angolensis*, 51
Pondicherry, *T. calvus*, endpapers

Wagtail, *Motacilla* (160), 80, 116, 180
Gray, *M. cinerea*, 126
†*M. humata*, 180
†*M. major*, 180
Pied, *M. alba*, **65,** 167
Yellow, *M. flava*, **67,** 117
Warbler, 61, 88, 139
see also Australian warbler; Warbler (Old World); Wood (American) warbler
Warbler (Old World) (173e), 80, 90, 116, 181
Arctic, *Phylloscopus borealis*, **115**, 117
Great reed, *Acrocephalus arundinaceus*, **150**
Long-legged, *Trichocichla rufa*, 99
Reed, *A. scirpaceus*, 151
Rodriguez, *Bebrornis rodericanus*, 101
Willow, *P. trochilus*, **123**, 124, 141
Wood, *P. sibilatrix*, 66
Waterfowl (swans, ducks, geese) (49), 21, 172
Wattled crow (193), 43, 183
Waxbill (187), 55, 61, 150, 182
Common, *Estrilda astrild*, **57**

Waxwing, *Bombycilla* (166), 51, 108, 126, 180
Bohemian, *B. garrulus*, **127,** 180
Cedar, *B. cedrorum*, **59**
Weaver (189), 20, 51, 90, 105, 150, 183
Baya, *Ploceus philippinus*, **159**
Black-capped social, *Pseudonigrita cabanisi*, **92**
Buffalo, *Bubalornis albirostris*, **92**
São Thomé grosbeak, *Neospiza concolor*, 101
Sociable, *Philetairus socius*, 90, **92**
Thick-billed, *Amblyospiza albifrons*, **92**
White-browed sparrow, *Plocepasser mahali*, **92**
Weka, *Gallirallus australis* (75), **42,** 43
Wheatear, Common, *Oenanthe oenanthe* (173a), 117, **118**
Whimbrel, Common, *Numenius phaeopus* (93), **45,** 47
Whinchat, *Saxicola rubetra* (173a), **166**
Whip-poor-will, Common, *Caprimulgus vociferus* (119), **29**
Whistler (173i), 66, 181
Whistling (or Tree) duck (49), 48
Red-billed, *Dendrocygna autumnalis*, **46**
Whiteye (179), 107, 181
Gray-breasted (Common silvereye), *Zosterops lateralis*, **97**
Slender-billed, *Z. tenuirostris*, **97**
White-breasted, *Z. albogularis*, **97**
Widow bird (188), 149, 182
Willet, *Catoptrophorus semipalmatus* (93), **34**
Wood hoopoe (135), 80, 178
Cuckoo-tailed, *Phoeniculus purpureus*, **105**
Wood ibis (39)
African, *Ibis ibis*, endpapers
Wood swallow, *Artamus* (195), 19, 64, 66, 107, 183
Wood (or American) warbler (182), 66, 182
Blackpoll, *Vermivora (Dendroica) striata*, **115**
Black-throated gray, *V. (D.) nigrescens*, **110**
Hooded, *Wilsonia citrina*, **63**
Kirtland's, *V. (D). kirtlandii*, 123
Lucy's, *V. luciae*, **110**
Myrtle, *V. (D.) coronata*, **60**
Red-faced, *Cardellina rubrifrons*, **111**
Virginia's, *V. virginiae*, **111**
Woodcock (93), 31, 32
European, *Scolopax rusticola*, 156
Woodcreeper (144a), 104
Barred, *Dendrocolaptes certhia*, **104**
Woodhen, Giant flightless, †*Aptornis defossor*, **40**
Woodhewer (144a), 88, 178
Woodpecker (142), 30, 31, 80, 149, 153, 159, 178
Acorn, *Melanerpes formicivorus*, **60,** 62, **111**
Buff-spotted, *Campethera nivosa*, **112**
Downy, *Dendrocopos pubescens*, 66
Golden-crowned, *Thripias xantholophus*, 112, **113**
Gray, *Mesopicos goertae*, **151**
Great spotted, *D. major*, 61, 66
Hairy, *D. villosus*, **17**
Ivory-billed, *Campephilus principalis*, **29**, **100**, 101
Magellanic, *Campephilus magellanicus*, **31**
Three-toed, *Picoides tridactylus*, **29**
Wren (170), 126, 180
Cactus, *Campylorhynchus brunneicapillum*, **111**
Carolina, *Thryothorus ludovicianus*, 66
†*Cistothorus brevis*, 180
House, *Troglodytes aëdon*, **147**
Winter (Old World), *Tr. troglodytes*, 66
see also New Zealand wren
Wydah (188), 149, 150
Paradise, *Steganura paradisaea*, **149**
Pin-tailed, *Vidua macroura*, **105**